THE SOCIOLOGICAL MOVEMENT IN LAW

THE SOCIOLOGICAL MOVEMENT IN LAW

ALAN HUNT

MACMILLAN PRESS
LONDON

First edition 1978
Reprinted 1983

Published by
THE MACMILLAN PRESS LTD
London and Basingstoke
Companies and representatives
throughout the world

British Library Cataloguing in Publication Data

Hunt, Alan
The sociological movement in law
1. Sociological jurisprudence
I. Title
340.1'15 [Law]

ISBN 0 333 22614 3 (hardcover)
ISBN 0 333 23421 9 (paperback)

Printed in Hong Kong

Contents

1   THE SOCIOLOGICAL MOVEMENT IN LAW   1

2   ROSCOE POUND: A SOCIOLOGICAL JURISPRUDENCE?   11
   Introduction   11
   The social background of Pound's thoughts   12
   The intellectual basis of sociological jurisprudence   15
   Pound's methodology   17
   Pound and sociology   18
   The theory of interests   22
   The valuation of interests   25
   The evolutionary theory of law   29
   The significance of sociological jurisprudence   33

3   AMERICAN LEGAL REALISM   37
   Introduction   37
   The social context of American realism   38
   The intellectual origins of American realism   40
   The theoretical framework of American realism   45
     Realism and the positivist tradition   46
     The Realist model of society   46
     Realism as functionalism   48
     Behaviouralism in American realism   53
   Methodology of American realism   55
   What price Realism?   58

4   EMILE DURKHEIM – TOWARDS A SOCIOLOGY OF LAW   60
   Introduction   60

Durkheim's sociology   61
Durkheim's sociological analysis of law   65
    Introduction   65
    Law and social solidarity   66
    The theory of crime   74
    The evolution of punishment   79
    Contract   85
    Property   88
    Durkheim: A systematic sociology of law?   90

5 MAX WEBER'S SOCIOLOGY OF LAW   93
    Max Weber lives   93
    The political and ideological location of Weber   94
        Biographical sketch   94
        Weber's ideological position   95
        Weber and German politics   97
    Weber's sociological enterprise   98
    The sociology of law   102
        Introduction   102
        A note on sources   103
        The definition of law   103
        The internal typology of law   104
        The rationalisation of law   107
        Law and domination   112
        Law and capitalism   118
        The 'England problem'   122
        Contract   128
    Conclusion   130

6 THE   SOCIOLOGICAL   MOVEMENT: RESULTS   AND
   PROSPECTS   135

   ABBREVIATIONS   152
   NOTES   153
   BIBLIOGRAPHY   172
   INDEX   181

1 The Sociological Movement in Law

The twentieth century has produced a movement towards the sociologically oriented study of law. The study of law can no longer be regarded as the exclusive preserve of legal professionals, whether practitioners or academics.[1] There has emerged a sociological movement in law which has had as its common and explicit goal the assault on legal exclusivism; it is a movement that has excited hope and commitment from its protagonists and considerable resistance from its opponents. It is this movement which is the object of inquiry upon which this book focuses.

The modern expression of the movement is the area of activity that is designated by the label 'the sociology of law'. Modern sociology of law is the indirect object to which this study relates. The sociological movement in law has provided the intellectual and theoretical roots for the sociology of law. An understanding of the intellectual origins that are embraced within the sociological movement are a crucial requirement for coming to grips with its current stage of development as expressed within the sociology of law. Underlying the present work is an orientation towards contemporary sociology of law which needs to be made explicit. The development of modern sociology of law, and the emergence of radical and Marxist kinds, will be dealt with more extensively in a book being prepared, *Law and the Social Order*, to be published by Macmillan in late 1978.

The sociology of law is now established, especially in the United States, as a distinct and recognised area of academic specialisation, and example of C. Wright Mills describes as 'the professionalisation of higher learning'.[2] It now has its own departments, courses and programmes but it is important to note that the location of sociology of law in institutions of higher education reproduces the dual origins of its intellectual genesis in that it is to be found within both law faculties and sociology faculties, and occasionally as an outpost of criminology. In Britain this process of academic institutionalisation is not so advanced; sociology of law leads a somewhat precarious existence predominantly located on the fringes of law departments and faculties. Its general institutionalisation is also marked by the existence of specialist journals.[3] This process has resulted in a very considerable quantitative expansion of work produced under its label. However I hold very considerable reservation about both the quality and direction of modern sociology of law. I have elsewhere developed the critique of modern sociology of law more fully;[4] I will therefore restrict my comments here to a brief and assertive characterisation of modern sociology of law.

The sociology of law has, to date, failed to develop a coherent theoretical framework within which to base its research activities. It has failed to achieve its explicit goal of overcoming the narrow and restrictive jurisprudential tradition within which discussion and analysis of law has been confined. Modern sociology of law exhibits very significant continuities not only with sociological jurisprudence, but more generally with the wider jurisprudential tradition.[5] It takes as its starting point the 'law-society' relation but the perspective has remained underdeveloped and unelaborated with the result that work carried out under its label has, in general, been characterised by an electic empiricism; anything that relates 'law' and 'society' is deemed to fall within the sociology of law.

This book then takes as its primary focus and examination of the intellectual precursors of modern sociology of law. It is the intellectual developments which have preceded modern sociology of law that constitute the sociological movement in law. This movement is studied from a dual perspective: firstly in its own right as containing a number of key figures who have a considerable importance and, on the other hand, with reference to the extent to which this movement has determined the orientation and characteristics of modern sociology of law and, at the same time, which account for the weaknesses in its current stage of development outlined above. The concept of a 'sociological movement in law' needs some explanation. To what extent can the different strands examined be regarded as constituting a 'movement'? In the narrowest and most literal sense of the term there was no 'movement' as a cohesive tendency working in conscious collaboration and with shared objectives. The differing intellectual spheres within which the major figures to be examined operated ensures that no movement in this narrow sense did or could exist. Nor can it be considered a movement in the sense of being able to demonstrate a direct set of 'influences' exercised by one individual over others in a chronological or developmental pattern. The key figures to be studied all produced their major works within a very narrow time band and there is no evidence that any of them had anything other than the most casual acquaintance with the work of the others.[6] The sense in which it is both possible, and indeed desirable, to speak of the existence of a movement is that of a movement which represents a generalised intellectual current which involves the emergence of a new orientation in the analysis of law. The general orientation has as its core the requirement that law be subjected to an analysis premised upon its identification as a social phenomenon. This minimum characteristic embodies a reaction against legal traditionalism which isolates law from other social phenomena and which holds, explicitly or implicitly, that law can be examined as an autonomous entity. This tendency is most pronounced in the Anglo-American tradition represented by he ascendancy of analytical jurisprudence.

The sociological movement in law can be identified as an intellectual trend which emerges at the end of the nineteenth century and which can be followed through to modern sociology of law. It takes as its specific orientation that which subjects the phenomenon of law to sociological analysis. It is the specific project of developing an analysis of law within the context provided by sociological theory and method that constitutes the essential characteristic of the sociological movement. It is also the characteristic which serves to distinguish it from earlier trends, especially within continental jurisprudence and in political theory which located the analysis of law in its social context. The most obvious example is the considerable importance and influence of what have come to be known as the sehools of historical jurisprudence, associated with such figures as Savigny and Maine. While the historical school undoubtedly had its impact upon some of the key figures of the sociological movement, in particular upon Pound and Weber, they will not be studied within this book for it is not intended to provide a chronological history of intellectual ideas.[7]

The sociological movement takes it characteristics, in contrast to the earlier historical schools, from the explicit orientation to sociology. The period spanned by the sociological movement is one marked by the increasing intellectual ascendancy of sociology. It is the explicit orientation to sociology, albeit in its different forms, that constitutes a communality in the work of the diverse authors who are treated here as the key expressions of the sociological movement. This can be seen most clearly in the case of sociological jurisprudence, embodied in the work of Roscoe Pound and the related Realist jurists, which set itself the explicit objective of harnessing the approach, resources and methods of sociology whereas in previous periods the dominant influences to which jurisprudence related had been provided by philosophy and political theory. The two key sociologists, Max Weber and Emile Durkheim, who are analysed as contributors to the sociological movement, share at least one major orientation, namely their concern to delimit the intellectual sphere or territory of sociology and within this to subject social phenomena, including law, to a specifically sociological mode of analysis and in the process to radically demarcate that treatment from other intellectual orientations. Hence, in the sense which I use it, the sociological movement in law constitutes a movement because it is characterised by a persistent and generalised enterprise to develop a 'sociological' analysis of law.

Developments and movements in the intellectual arena are never exclusive or self-contained. A particular intellectual trend or initiative may for a period provide a self-sustaining momentum and hence acquire a degree of autonomy. Yet intellectual activity cannot remain for ever self-generating and self-determining; it must stand in some relationship to social and economic conditions which with varying degree of directness will influence, and that sense determine, the developments that take place in the intellectual sphere. This is as true of jurisprudence and sociology as it is for all other fields of human inquiry. That this point needs to be made at all is a consequence of, and a reaction against, the exclusively internal account and analysis that is conventionally given of the history of jurisprudential thought. However it is also important to stress that the location of intellectual trends or ideas within the social and economic conditions that constitute the historical context of its existence is an extremely difficult problem. The introductory location of the sociological movement makes no claim to being more than a sketch. The task of establishing causal relationships is beyond the present work; the immediate concern is to establish the context or framework within the sociological movement in law developed and influenced the formation of modern sociology of law.

The period with which this study is concerned stretches from the last decade of the nineteenth century to the outbreak of the Second World War. It is a formidable, and possibly foolhardy, task to seek to encapsulate such a complex period in a few paragraphs. The theorists discussed in this work have in general presented only a very limited view of the social background and context within which they worked. The jurists in particular have suggested that the sociological movement is to be accounted for as a response to the rapidity of social change which resulted in a tendency for law to 'lag' behind social development. Such an analysis is superficial; while the rapidity of social change is undoubtedly significant, it does not offer a sufficient account.

The rise of the sociological movement in law must be seen in the context of certain key features of Western European, and in particular of American, society at the turn of the century. These societies were ones in which capitalist economic systems were well established; a new type of expansion was occurring from the 1890s foremost in the United States and Britain and more slowly in Germany and France; it was an expansion within consolidated economic systems. These systems and their social characteristics have come to appear as natural and largely self-evident; their expanded consolidation in the period leading up to 1914 was international in character. There existed a number of industrialised nations whose characteristic economic units were no longer the thrusting entrepreneurial concerns of the formative period of industrial capitalism, but were the corporate industrial and financial institutions that have dominated in the twentieth century.

The political structures of Western societies had also undergone significant changes, the major process being the extension of political democracy which had brought the mass of the working class more directly onto the political stage. This development was associated with the emergence of mass working class political parties in most countries, but significantly not so in the United States, and of mass labour and trade union movements in all countries. These pressed upon the established political order more strenuously and persistently a wide range of social and economic demands and either directly or potentially presented the spectre of radical or revolutionary social change. Many of the claims and demands advanced were ones which required their institutionalisation through the legislative process. Indeed it became an increasing characteristic of the period that political and social struggle took place around demands for the enactment or repeal of legislation.

This assertion of claims, by and on behalf of the newly enfranchised working classes, had another consequence. The predominant content of litigation had been profoundly *bourgeois* in the sense that it was concerned with the mutual regulation of the affairs of the propertied classes. The majority encountered law as the recipients of a criminal law which was a direct and none too sophisticated system of public order. It would be wrong to suggest that the pattern of work of the courts changed decisively during the period, but what was significant was the perception amongst jurists of the new claims, actual or potential, pressed upon the legal system as necessitating a re-evaluation of law and its institutions.

The nature and extent of the economic, political and social changes brought into even greater prominence the state and its institutions. Over the whole field of social and economic affairs the state came to play an increasingly interventionist and active role. So too did the legal system come to play a more prominent and a more direct role; no longer could the courts be backwaters within which the relations of the propertied classes could be leisurely, if expensively, adjusted.

It was these social and economic changes which resulted in a consciousness of impending change amongst a small but growing number of those concerned with the legal system, in particular amongst legal academics. Amongst those who welcomed, or at least accepted, the prospects of change within the legal system there emerged a tendency to look towards a socially, and increasingly sociologically, oriented perspective towards law. Such a stance was consistent with their concern about the social relevance and consequence of law. Nowhere was this tendency more apparent than in the United States; there the attempt to break with legal traditionalism was something more than simply an intellectual revolt; it had its roots in the momentous changes that were producing modern industrial capitalism and which brought in their train tensions and crises within the existing legal system.

A continuing role played by legal theory, varying in the extent to which it is explicit, is that of articulating a rationale for the existing social and political order. Social and economic changes, considered in conjunction with the political challenge of labour and socialist parties, rendered traditional accounts of the basis of the social and legal order inadequate. It will be argued that a major underlying theme within the sociological movement has been the articulation of a new ideological basis for the existing social order in an era of mass parliamentary democracy.

Both the proponents and the opponents of the sociological movement have regarded it as radical or progressive. So also has each of its stages been regarded as more radical than its predecessors. Thus, for example, the American Realists were to attack sociological jurisprudence for its failure to break decisively with certain key aspects of the jurisprudential tradition. Similarly American sociology of law has portrayed the failure of Realism as its inability to complete this stage. Sociologists of law throw at each other the accusation, with perjorative implications, that their writing is affected by jurisprudential overtones. A persistent theme of this work will be to attempt to elucidate how far these successive stages did make radical departures or innovations.

The significant characteristic of the sociological movement in law is the interrelationship between the jurisprudential and sociological strands. A schematic preliminary view suggests a model in which sociological jurisprudence is seen as arising from the jurisprudential tradition, while the sociology of law has its roots in the sociological tradition; these two strands would then be seen as interacting in such a way that the sociological element becomes dominant. A cursory view of the personnel selected for systematic attention lends some support to such an analysis. Pound and Llewellyn were both first and foremost jurists, while Durkheim and Weber were both sociologists. But such an approach is misleadingly simple. It will be part of the argument advanced to suggest that the two facets of the sociological movement have not had an autonomous development. It is erroneous to give the jurisprudential and the sociological strands equal weight; in the main the developments have taken place within the domain of jurisprudence into which sociological concepts and perspectives have been imported. This proposition can be defended despite the fact that individual contributions, paramountly those of Durkheim and Weber, were demonstrably located within the intellectual domain of sociology. Even where the sociological element has been pronounced it has never wholly replaced the persisting jurisprudential orientation within the movement as a whole. The primary thesis that the chapters which follow are concerned to elaborate and to substantiate is that the two phases of the sociological movement manifest a basic unity of perspective and direction in which the differences between them are largely with respect to form and emphasis.

This unity between the jurisprudential and sociological tendencies exists not because of any inherent or necessary linkage between the parent disciplines of jurisprudence and sociology; nor, in passing it may be observed, is there a basis for the view that the different intellectual traditions should necessarily give rise to markedly different substantive positions. The unity stems from the view of law and its relationship to the social system that is embodied within the substantive jurisprudential and sociological theories which have been incorporated in the sociological movement in law. It will be an objective of this work to seek to substantiate this hypothesis. That there are significant variations and even major conflicts present in the theories that are to be examined is not denied, nor indeed will they be ignored, but the work rests on the claim that if the hypothesis can be demonstrated then a new perspective on the sociological movement is necessary. It is a perspective that is significant both for historical interpretation of the movement and, in particular, for its future development.

The distinction between 'sociological jurisprudence' and 'sociology of law' is relied upon heavily. In general such a distinction gives rise to few difficulties and as a consequence a rigid definitional distinction is not necessary. Such a classification rests in the first instance upon the self-classification of the authors considered; but the proviso must be borne in mind that self-ascription can be as unreliable in intellectual matters as it is with respect to most other questions. Freedom must be consciously reserved to take issue with individual self-ascription. In general the distinction that is relied upon is based upon the intellectual roots and primary sources of influence upon the individual; thus for the key figures to be discussed there is little or no doubt as to the appropriate camp. However the distinction must be read in the context of an adherence to a point of view which denies any ultimate existence to such abstractions as 'jurisprudential approaches' or 'sociological orientation'. Such divisions do not mark objective boundaries in human knowledge; rather they indicate the way in which different intellectual traditions and concerns express themselves in distinctions between the kind of questions posed and in the mode of their formulation.

The strategy to be pursued should now be made clear. It will be to examine the work of a limited number of key figures: Roscoe Pound, Karl Llewellyn, Emile Durkheim and Max Weber. Such a strategy has a number of consequences. First, it does not constitute a 'history'; it is in no sense a chronological approach, indeed the very ordering of the chapters departs from a strictly chronological ordering. Thus, for example, Karl Llewellyn and the American Realists are chronologically 'later' than both Durkheim and Weber but are discussed before them. While there is a sequential relation between Pound and the American Realists this is not the case with respect to Durkheim and Weber, who pre-date much of sociological jurisprudence and constitute distinct and independent interventions as sociological theories of law. There is another sense in which I am not engaged in writing a history; I do not seek to present a series of intellectual biographies by tracing all the formative influences on the various manifestations of the sociological movement or to follow their mutual influences. The exhaustive encylopaedic method is much favoured in jurisprudence; this was true of Pound himself, and in more recent sociological jurisprudence in the voluminous texts of Julius Stone which provide an exhaustive account of the stages, formative influences and varieties of socially oriented juristic theory.[8] My present concern is not to repeat the intellectual history of the emergence of the movement but rather to focus attention upon the substantive content of the major expressions of that movement and, in particular, of those contributions that provide significant theoretical points of reference for modern sociology of law. Consideration of developmental influences will be restricted to a discussion of primary influences alone.

The second consequence of the strategy is that it does not seek to provide an intellectual biography of the central figures under discussion. The intention is to focus upon the sociological theory of law that is present in their work. This requires that it be situated in the context of the general orientation, theoretical position and methodology of the individuals concerned, but I have consciously tried to restrict that element of the treatment to that which is necessary to expound and explore the sociological theory of law contained within the writings of the selected individuals.

The third implication concerns the problem of the grounds for inclusion and exclusion. Pound, Llewellyn, Durkheim and Weber are by no means the only people who can be considered to be of importance within the context of the sociological movement in law. Any process of exclusion requires some form of justification. Rather than attempt to advance any general criteria for exclusion I will consider the grounds for exclusion with respect to a number of the most obvious omissions. First let us consider the case of Eugen Ehrlich; he was undoubtedly an important figure in the development of sociologically oriented jurisprudence and as such might be seen as deserving attention. The substantive content of Ehrlich is contained in his single oft-quoted dictum that 'the centre of gravity of legal development lies not in legislation, nor in juristic science, nor in judicial decision, *but in society itself.*'[9] While he was of very considerable significance as a polemicist for a sociologically defined 'living law' he has not been a major point of reference, save as a signpost, for subsequent work. To take a second example of exclusion from consideration, both Gurvitch and Timasheff produced substantial attempts to advance a systematic and general theoretical sociology of law.[10] However their work has received little attention and has not been taken up in any significant respect in subsequent developments.[11]

A further consequence of the strategy of selecting a limited number of key figures is that the work has a marked Anglo-American emphasis. This remains true despite, or perhaps because of, the inclusion of Durkheim and Weber who it must be recognised are both dealt with in terms of their reception in the English-speaking world. This ethnocentric bias is a manifestation of my own personal limitations; it is one which is in general shared especially in the field of jurisprudence, but is also present within the development of sociology, for there to be significant intellectual boundaries which are established in the first instance by language. Anglo-American jurisprudence has been characterised by an over-reverent emphasis upon the uniqueness of the common law system which has resulted in a tendency to minimise interest in work emanating from continental Europe. The Anglo-American emphasis is further underlined by my stated concern with the subsequent development of the sociology of law; this has in very important respects been a predominantly American development. While it is important to recognise that the sociology of law has had particular expressions in both France and Germany, it is in the United States that it has become most firmly established.[12]

The selection of Pound, Llewellyn, Durkheim and Weber for extented treatment is almost automatic; there is little or no need to justify their inclusion. Where this may perhaps be necessary is with respect to Llewellyn and the American Realists. The primary ground for inclusion is provided by their role as the immediate precursors for modern sociology of law. The restricted focus strategy has certain advantages. It allows for a detailed study of the individual contributions; for although there a number of general treatments of work of Pound and Llewellyn, they are by way of being general intellectual biographies which do not focus explicitly on their relationship to the sociological movement. Similarly with respect to Durkheim and Weber, while there is a massive general literature there has been very little work done on their substantive contributions to the sociology of law. The second advantage of selecting two key figures from both the jurisprudential and the sociological tradition provides a certain symmetry which facilitates the exploration of the relationship between jurisprudence and sociology in the formation of the sociological movement in law.

The intellectual standpoint from which I approach this study perhaps needs comment. I hold a strong commitment to Marxism but I do not claim that this work is 'Marxist'. This apparently contradictory formulation should perhaps be explained. I do not start out upon a critique of the sociological movement in law from the standpoint of a developed or an assumed Marxist theory of law. No such developed theory exists and to base a critique of the dominant intellectual tradition on the assumption that it does would be both misleading and dishonest. I have already had something to say elsewhere about the problem of Marxist theory of law and continue to work in this direction.[13] Elements of a Marxist approach enter into this study at a more general level and find their expression in the treatment of the epistemological, methodological and theoretical positions of the figures studied; yet this falls short of constituting in itself a Marxist study. The present task is more limited; it is premised on the view that it is necessary for both Marxists and non-Marxists concerned with the analysis of law to come to grips with the characteristics of the sociological movement in order to understand its impact upon the current stage of development and the debates within the field.

The espousal of Marxism, both theoretically and politically, does not for me require that Marxists should seek to operate as demolition contractors, knocking down and laying bare the lumber of *bourgeois* scholarship before starting afresh to erect a new and shining Marxist edifice. It is also important to stress that Marxist and non-Marxist positions cannot simply be conflated; there are fundamental differences of both theory and method which necessarily impede any attempt made to combine or to fuse Marxist and non-Marxist positions. This work can be said to have a Marxist emphasis but does not itself claim to be a fully Marxist approach. It is a study directed at establishing the consequences both in terms of direction and of theory that have emerged from the specific history and characteristics of the sociological movement in law.

2 Roscoe Pound:
A Sociological Jurisprudence?

INTRODUCTION

Roscoe Pound was the most prominent member of the school of jurisprudence that has been labelled 'sociological jurisprudence'. The intention is not to attempt to review all the aspects of Pound's work but rather to examine those elements that are most closely connected with the sociological aspects of his thought. Such a restriction is made necessary by the very breadth and quantity of his output.[1] The problem is not merely a quantitative one; in an academic career stretching over some seventy years Pound wrote on many topics from the most general philosophical issues, through legal history, to more conventional expositions of specific areas of positive law, to empirical studies of the operation of law. Yet he made little or no conscious effort to coordinate these diverse fields of study. This is most clearly demonstrated in his most comprehensive work *Jurisprudence*,[2] published in five volumes shortly before his death. In this massive work he gave himself the opportunity to draw together the threads of his life's work. Yet the overriding imperssion is that his work remains disjointed, with disparate elements of thought joined by mere physical proximity. It is significant that in this work Pound retains the same structure that had first been used in his lecture notes published in 1903.[3]

The difficulty in approaching Pound's writing is not simply its quantity but also his method. The methodology underlying Pound's thought will be dealt with more fully;[4] it is sufficient here to point to the eclectic nature of his thought. His own ideas are developed out of the detailed exposition of the thought of previous writers and with very considerable 'borrowing' from them on the way. This approach is not only Pound's; much jurisprudential writing has traditionally consisted of the chronological

11

exposition and refutation of earlier jurists. His method is essentially encylopaedic. He takes this method to extremes; the majority of his major jurisprudential writings take this form.[5] It is not merely that he examined the work of his predecessors, he is truly eclectic in that he borrowed widely and liberally from others. Grossman, not unfairly, credits him with '. . . possessing the happy faculty of finding a kernel of truth in every doctrine.'[6] Indeed a major criticism that has been levelled against Pound is that he contributed nothing new to jurisprudence;[7] that every major component of his thought is borrowed from others. While his dependence on others is established beyond doubt, indeed is freely admitted by Pound himself,[8] this is not in itself a sufficient ground for denying Pound's contribution to jurisprudence. It is a truism that nearly all great intellectual advances may be traced back to thoughts and insights already advanced. True intellectual genius is very often nothing more than the combination or recombination of already existing thought which in the process reveals fresh insight and opens up new perspectives. It is hoped to show that it is Pound's failure adequately to carry through this task of combination and recombination that is the true basis for a critique of his work and not merely that it is in origin unoriginal.

His review of trends in jurisprudence in the nineteenth century is presented in such a way that 'all trends lead to Pound'. He advances a picture of all stands of thought having their 'best' elements preserved under some unexplained centripetal force which culminates in sociological jurisprudence.[9]

The inherent difficulties imposed by his eclecticism are further exaggerated by his propensity for and delight in classifying all the material that he examines. Many commentators[10] have drawn attention to the fact that this predeliction may be traced to his early work as a botanist. Thus Simpson[11] speaks of him as having 'botanised' law. However it is hoped to show that it is not that Pound resorted to classification, but rather it is *the way* in which he classified from which the defects in this work arose.

The approach adopted here, conscious of these initial problems, is to treat Pound's thought at a general level and to examine its main components. It will then be possible to pose the question: can his sociological jurisprudence be reduced to a single consistent theory, or is it nothing more than a collection of inconsistent strands? Finally it should be possible to assess the general contribution of Pound's thought to the development of the sociological study of law.

THE SOCIAL BACKGROUND OF POUND'S THOUGHTS

Developments in jurisprudence, and for that matter in sociology, cannot be explained exclusively in terms of their own internal logic or progression. Jurisprudence is too often merely the history of juristic thought presented as a self-acting history with the occasional borrowing from other fields of thought and as such has a fundamentally idealist character. The development of jurisprudence cannot be comprehended without first situating it in the historical context in which it emerged. The rise of sociological jurisprudence is crucially interwoven with major changes that were taking place within American society.

Pound's major works appeared during the first quarter of the twentieth century. The United States had emerged from its pioneer background[12] into a period of very rapid social change. In particular it was a period of enormous economic growth which was rapidly turning the United States into a major world power. This very growth and power brought with it immense new problems. It was an era characterised by new and sharper tensions and conflicts. It is against this background that there emerges a strong and increasingly centralised state and administrative system. Indeed it is in part the very tempo of social change that ensures an increasingly interventionist role for the state. American law enters the twentieth century characterised by what Stone has called 'legal laissez-faire' enshrined in the dominance of analytical jurisprudence under which the intervention through law in social and economic matters was regarded as a necessary evil which was most effective when the intervention was smallest; this fitted in well with the still influential 'frontier' philosophy. The law was dominated by an abstentionist ideology. While this ideology was powerful it never described the reality of the role of the state or of the legislature. Such general attitudes to law and legal activity may usefully be characterised as 'legal traditionalism' of practitioners, judges and academics. Law was conceived as a self-contained system which through the logical elaboration of rules might be more systematically formulated, but the process would be one of adjustment rather than of transformation. On the bench there persisted an adherence to the declaratory theory of the judicial role. At the same time there existed a rather exaggerated view of the necessary excellence of the common law system, a corollary of which was a considerable aversion to legislation. It is this composite picture that I have labelled 'legal traditionalism'.

In a period of rapid social and economic change the American legal system, common law based on and dominated by legal traditionalism, was beset by wide-ranging criticisms. It was pressed by contending forces in social conflict in contradictory directions. It had neither time nor opportunity for a leisurely adjustment to the changed circumstances. The pressure from the rapidly emerging labour movement brought pressure on the legislators for intervention through 'social legislation'.[13]

It is against this background that Pound's academic career developed. He joined at an early age the revolt against legal traditionalism. His early training was dominated by English analytical jurisprudence. The review article which first brought Pound to prominence was significantly entitled *Causes of the Popular Dissatisfaction with the Administration of Justice*[14] and indicated his growing concern with the malfunctioning of the law. Pound's reaction against analytical jurisprudence is marked by a turning towards continental juristic thought. One of Pound's minor, but nevertheless significant, contributions has been to make more widely known, and to make available in English translation, a wide range of continental jurisprudential writing.

> More than any other man, he has made American jurisprudence international and not merely a colonial copy of English analytics.[15]

Pound himself, along with major figures such as Holmes and later Cardozo, played an important part in the attack on legal traditionalism.[16] Pound rejected much of the conventional legal wisdom but retained sufficient attachment to the common law tradition to make his parallel adoption of a sociological bent to a large degree palatable to a predominantly conservative profession. While advocating a new line of development he succeeded in staying very much within the main stream of American legal academic life. Throughout his work is filled with a marked adulation of the common law system, in particular of the judicial role reflected in his view that

> the trained intuition and disciplined judgment of the judge must be our assurance that causes will be decided on principles of reason and not according to the chance dictates of caprice.[17]

Pound manifests a very distinct 'reverence for law'. The virulence of his attacks on the Realists[18] embodies the fact that his critique of legal traditionalism stemmed from what he saw 'as a fundamentally more conservative'[19] orientation than that adopted by the Realists.

It needs to be emphasised that Pound's attack on traditionalism was not in itself original. It was part of a wider movement that was taking place. His attack on 'mechanical jurisprudence' merely elaborates the criticism made by von Jhering of the 'jurisprudence of conceptions'.

> Jurisprudence is the last in the march of the sciences away from the method of deduction from predetermined conceptions.[20]

It is von Jhering's influence that adds a new element to his critique of prevailing juristic thought, namely, the domination of individualistic interpretations, particularly that developed by Kant, viewing law as an expression of individual free will. This view penetrated deeply into jurisprudence and is exemplified in the analysis of legal relations in terms of rights and duties. It is in seeking to overcome this approach, necessary if Pound is to prove himself to be the apostle of the 'socialisation of law', that he again borrows from von Jhering and insists upon the analysis of legal relations in terms of the interests involved; an orientation which takes him much closer to the social sciences than previous legal theorists.

THE INTELLECTUAL BASIS OF SOCIOLOGICAL JURISPRUDENCE

Pound's explicit philosophical orientation is, as he continually reminds us, that of pragmatism. In particular Pound relies heavily upon William James. While he seeks to differentiate the two, there is little doubt that pragmatism is in its essentials a continuation of the utilitarian trend in philosophical and social thought.[21] However I shall suggest that there are other, and perhaps inconsistent, strands in the philosophical underpinning of his theory. But first it is necessary to explore some of the important consequences of Pound's pragmatism.

Pragmatism underlies a number of other elements in his thought. His approach is activist; he continually stresses the importance of 'practical' problems. Indeed he distinguishes between sociological jurisprudence and the sociology of law by stressing the concern of the former with 'practical problems', while the latter is concerned solely with 'theoretical problems'.[22] We find throughout a persistent ambivalence towards theory. At one level he is immersed in the philosophical themes of jurisprudence, at another the activist implications of his pragmatism assert themselves. In this tension may lie the explanation of his failure to complete a systematic exposition of a sociological theory of law. This activism is very closely associated with Pound's faith in the 'efficacy of human effort'. The sociological jurist, he argues, 'holds that legal institutions and doctrines are instruments of a specialised form of social control, capable of being improved with reference to their ends by conscious, intelligent effort.'[23] This concern with intelligent effort is central to his 'social engineering' analogy; he insists that sociological jurisprudence is an 'applied science'. A similar line of thought is contained in the insistence upon a 'functional' approach which leads to an explicit concern with the results or consequences of law. 'In the past century we studied law from within. The jurists of today are studying it from without.'[24] This practical orientation is expressed in one of his most influential phrases in which he distinguishes between 'law in books, and law in action.'[25]

He exhibits, consistent with his pragmatic philosophical view, a pronounced positivist tendency, 'In common with most Americans who had a scientific training in the eighties of the last century, I was brought up on Comtian positivism and turned thence to the Comtian sociology at the beginning of the present century.'[26]

This orientation leads him to reject philosophy constructed on the basis of *a priori* propositions explored solely through logical elaboration. Instead he insists upon basing all philosophical discussion firmly in existing observable reality. This manifests itself in his insistence that in constructing his classification of interests these must be extracted from positive law. Similarly when he seeks to derive the jural postulates of civilisation he states explicitly, '. . . schemes of necessary presuppositions of law and of legal institutions seem to me to be at bottom schemes of observed elements in actual legal systems'[27] and again, 'the first step in such an investigation is a mere survey of the legal order and an inventory of the social interests which have pressed upon lawmakers and judges and jurists for recognition.'[28]

I turn now to the other strand in his philosophical makeup which exists at a less clearly articulated level, but recognition of the existence of which is central to an understanding of the contradictions within his legal theory. A number of writers, in particular Friedmann[29] and Reuschlin,[30] have noted a trend in the later writings to retreat from the rigidly relativist position of his earlier writings in which he comes close to espousing a natural law doctrine. This trend is most marked in *Contemporary Juristic Theory*.

> The idea of natural law . . . shows many signs of reviving to meet the
> demand for a creative theory in a new period of legal development
> on which we appear to have entered.[31]

This apparent reversal of approach in his later life, while in part being a reaction to the upheavals of the time, was also inherent in his earlier writings. He was considerably influenced by the idealist tradition in philosophy. This element finds its immediate philosophical source in the neo-Hegelian writings of Kohler[32] from whom he derived the concept 'jural postulates'. But it is possible to detect a more general Hegelian element within his writing. It is to be found in particular in the emphasis placed upon the role of the 'ends of law'; that is the 'philosophical, political and ethical ideas as to the end of law'[33] which he regarded as central to the understanding of the legal process and especially for an understanding of the evolutionary stages through which law passes, '. . . the history of ideas as to the end of law is part of the very history of legal precepts and legal doctrines.'[34]

Pound contends that ideas interact with the 'actual legal situation' and that they mutually determine each other. He thus implies that 'ideas of law' and 'positive law' are to be differentiated as two autonomous spheres. While it is not intended to suggest that concepts of 'ends', 'values' and 'ideals' are not central to the analysis of law, it is to be emphasised that the autonomy that Pound posits for them places him in the camp of philosophical idealism and necessarily comes into conflict with his more overt pragmatism. This component of his thought may be explained by the considerable influence of the historical school of continental jurisprudence which was very substantially dependent upon the Hegelian philosophical tradition. Grossman[35] sees in Pound's 'stages of legal development' a decidedly Hegelian approach in which Pound implies that the history of law reflects the unfolding of the idea of justice through the changing 'ends of law'. Such an interpretation also explains a considerable congruence of his thought with Stammler's[36] notion of 'natural law with changing content'; his variant of this being what he describes as a 'practical natural law'.

It will be said that this formulation of the jural postulates gives us natural law once more. It does. But it is natural law drawn from observation of the concrete civilisation . . . it is practical natural law . . . a natural law with a changing or a growing content.[37]

In one important respect there is a strong parallel between the idealist and pragmatic strands in Pound's thought. They reinforce each other in their insistence upon law as a historically and culturally relative phenomenon.

POUND'S METHODOLOGY

It is central to an analysis of the weaknesses inherent in sociological jurisprudence to appreciate that they arise not only from a lack of consistency in his philosophical orientation. The deficiencies in his theory are closely related to his failure to deal adequately with the problem of *how* his theory was to be constructed. His method does not go much beyond 'botanising'; that is in essence he relies upon a classificatory approach. This is manifested both in his treatment of the central idea of 'interests' and also in his treatment of the development of juristic thought.

The consequence of his failure to articulate a more developed method is a major source of the lack of structure in his jurisprudence. He utilises many concepts but nowhere does he seek to relate his major concepts within the framework of a general theory. It may be argued that he argued that he never did this because the objective of each of his works was to deal with a particular area of concern. Yet when at the end of his career he presented the full range of his thought in the massive *Jurisprudence* it exhibits an amazing lack of integration. It is clear from a reading of any of his books that such concepts as 'jural postulates', 'interests', 'ends of law' and 'stages of legal development' have special importance. Yet nowhere does he do more than hint at their interrelations. This lack of theoretical perspective is one of the contributory factors underlying the rather narrowly empirical contributions which his work inspired.[38] While the difficulties in providing a general theory for a sociological study of law should not be minimised, experience over a wide range of disciplines seems to suggest that unless a clearly articulated theoretical framework is provided empirical studies are likely to be of purely limited utility.

The method of classification based on observation of existing data was central to botany which was his original discipline. What is to be stressed is that his approach gives rise to a *particular type* of classification. This may be illustrated with reference to a major element in his theory, namely, his 'stages of legal development'. Important and suggestive though his stages may be he nowhere indicated on what basis they are constructed. He does not tell us which elements of the legal system constitute the distinctive variables between one stage and the next. Are they purely descriptive of the content of legal rules? Are they differentiated on the basis of different forms of law? Or ary they an attempt to relate evolutionary stages of law to an evolutionary typology of the wider society? Pound does not give us the answer to these questions. The pervading impression is that he treats his material in a substantially descriptive manner. His stages are merely convenient descriptive categories. It is this failure to treat legal phenomena at more than a descriptive level that lays him open to the charge that he does nothing more than extract the general features of the Anglo-American legal system and turn them into universal categories.[39]

A further consequence of this method is that it leads towards fragmentation. He tends to deal with one of his concepts, for example 'interests', and then to move on to a treatment of the 'ends of law'. While he does give hints as to the relationship between them they are usually by way of *obiter dicta* and for this reason are often inconsistent. Thus in dealing with interests it is sometimes suggested that these are determined by the jural postulates of the civilisation, but at other times it appears that the jural postulates are determined by the interests. Nowhere does he deal with the more fundamental problem of seeking to relate either interests, ends or jural postulates to extra-legal factors, to some more general characteristic of social or economic reality. This deficiency arises to a large extent from his *a priori* rejection of monist or determinist theories.[40] He commits himself, as a matter of principle, to multi-causal explanation. In this respect he is very close to modern pluralism. The dilemma of pluralism tends to be not with respect to the existence of a plurality of variables, but arises from whether or not any causal primary of rank-ordering is to be attached to these variables. For the pluralist the contradiction encountered is that if he does so he runs the danger of tending towards monism which he has already rejected. If he refuses to discuss causal priority, his explanation tends to indeterminacy. The nearest Pound comes to a discussion of causal priority is when he produces a paradigm indicating in general terms and relationship between the stages of legal development and the ends of law, but even here he has little to say about the nature of the relationship.[41] One is forced to agree with the criticism levelled by Llewellyn that 'Critical reading of Pound's work, it may be noted in passing, and especially the phrasing of any concrete criticism, are embarrassed by the constant indeterminacy of the level of his discourse.'[42] His ideas may often be illuminating, but the 'constant indeterminacy' of the level of discourse makes it extremely difficult to treat his sociological jurisprudence as a consistent whole.

POUND AND SOCIOLOGY

Pound must be clearly recognised as having made a major contribution to breaking down the intellectual isolation of legal thought and in particular to the winning of recognition for the social sciences as valuable sources in the development of legal thought. Sociological jurisprudence has significantly promoted the recognition of law as a social phenomenon; but, having said this, it must be frankly stated that his contribution is at the most general level only. The advocacy of the sociological approach must be considered largely polemical in that it mainly consists in the assertion and reassertion of 'the social character of law'. It is to his credit that he made a considerable impact on the ideas of legal professionals to such an extent that the assertion of the social character of law is no longer contentious, but is often regarded merely as the painful elaboration of the obvious.

However he drew only to a limited extent upon sociology; for all his extensive reading over many disciplines it was perhaps narrowest in the field of sociology. He appears to have studied only a limited number of American sociologists writing around the turn of the century. They may be loosely characterised as belonging to the 'social control' school, a tendency that was influential primarily in American sociology.

The concern with social control arises fairly directly from the positivist tradition. It found its major exposition in the work of Edward Ross,[43] and it was Ross who was the primary sociological influence upon Pound. Ross argued that the stability of primitive societies was instinctive, resting upon 'primal moral feelings'. With the development of impersonal social relations characterised by the predominance of contractual relations in more advanced societies the social instincts weakened. Their role as the preservation of social stability was taken over by specific agencies of social control. Most of Ross's work consisted of the elaboration and differentiation of the forms of social control. Pound on a number of occasions quoted approvingly Ross's characterisation of law as 'the most specialised and highly finished engine of social control employed by society.'[44]

This approach was extended by Sumner[45] who is remembered in particular for introducing the concept 'mores', a general system of social values which operate not through the means of externally imposed sanctions but internally through their 'internalisation' by the individual. Pound referred to Sumner's work, but since Sumner was more concerned with the informal modes of social control than with the externally sanctioned forms, of which law is the prime example, he has rather less impact upon Pound's thought than Ross.

The concern with social control remained central in American sociology in the early part of the century and plays an important part in the work of both Cooley[46] and Small.[47] The concern with social control finds its way into the work of the functionalists before the Second World War and thence into the modern strands of American sociological thought. Pound appears not to have followed this trend through to its developments in the second quarter of the century. This is probably because, as suggested above, the sociologists were increasingly concerned not with the formal means of social control but rather with its informal forms. As a con sequence the sociologists of the 'social control' school gave very limited attention to the phenomenon of law. It may be observed in passing that this is a trend which, with a few exceptions, has persisted in recent sociological writing. The implication of this lack of attention to law was that sociology had a less direct relevance to Pound's primary interest in law. The concern with social control has had a continuing but indirect impact upon jurisprudence. For example when Hart seeks to refute some of the contentions of the imperative school he quite explicitly treats law as a generalised form of social control.[48]

The influence upon Pound of the early American sociologists had a contradictory effect upon the development of sociological jurisprudence. Rather than lead him towards an increasing recognition of the role of sociology it in fact resulted in his turning away from sociology. The social control theorists had concentrated on classifying the forms of social control, and in so doing had recognised law as one of these forms, but increasingly emphasised the distinction between it and other forms. Pound thereupon took over Ross's formulation and clearly basing himself upon it advanced his own 'social control' definition of law as 'a highly specialised form of social control, carried on in accordance with a body of authoritative precepts, applied in a judicial and administrative process.'[49] His concern became to elaborate the distinctive features and mode of operation of law. He ceases to pay any more than cursory attention to the interrelationship and interaction between law and other forms of social control. The overall impact of 'social control' theory was to provide Pound with a sociological starting point, but it was one which took him away from sociology and back into the well trodden paths of jurisprudence. It was Llewellyn who concluded sharply, but not without justification, that 'sociological jurisprudence remains bare of most that is significant in sociology.'[50]

Such a conclusion is supported by the fact that while he was familiar with the early developments in sociology, for example he stressed the importance of Montesquieu, Comte and Spencer and noted their impact on juristic thought,[51] yet he gave only very limited attention to developments in sociology outside the work of the social control theorists. He gives brief consideration to Durkheim[52] against whose strict positivist methodology he reacts sharply. His only other significant comment is to try, rather artificially, to force Durkheim's distinction between repressive and restitutive law into correspondence with his own distinction between individual and social interests.

Pound also shows some acquaintance with he work of Max Weber,[53] but his treatment betrays a misunderstanding of his general position; he is accused of evading the problem of values in social action. He fails to see that Weber's insistence on a sharp methodological distinction between the social role of values and the ethical process of valuation does not mean that the question of values is not central to Weber's sociology. It is significant that in fact a very considerable degree of overlap exists between Weberian sociology, and its later elaboration in the hands of Talcott Parsons, and Pound's own orientation.

The starting point of Pound's theory is with the individual advancing claims; it thus rests upon methodological individualism. Similarly the starting point for Weber is the individual 'actor' placed in the social context and seeking to realise ends with available means. This parallelism between his own approach and that of Weber was apparently not recognised by Pound. Weber sought to develop an exhaustive analysis of the role of values and ends in social action, again a theme very much germane to Pound's own concern with the operation of law. Instead Pound insists on trying to make Weber do service for pragmatic utilitarianism.[54]

Pound frequently insists upon the necessity of cooperation between jurisprudence and the social sciences. Indeed he himself warns against any mechanical separation.

> All the social sciences must be co-workers, and emphatically all must be co-workers with jurisprudence. When we set off a bit of social control and define its bounds by analytical criteria and essay to study it by its own light and with its own materials and its own methods exclusively, our results, however logical in appearance, are as arbitrary and futile for any but theoretical purposes.[55]

Yet it is exactly this 'setting off a bit of social control' of which Pound himself is guilty. For this reason it is contended that the self-ascribed label of 'sociological jurisprudence' is misleading. More accurate perhaps is the label which Pound uses less frequently, namely, 'functional jurisprudence'. His work is concerned primarily with the effect of law *upon* society, with the *results* of law, to a much greater extent than he is with the social determination of law. It is significant that when he set out his programme for sociological jurisprudence,[56] its six points do not include any injunction to study the social determinants of legal phenomena. Pound then is concerned with part of the field of study that a sociological approach would suggest, but it is only one half of that orientation. Although Pound applauds Ehrlich's insistence on the social production of law,[57] by himself retaining more traditional imperature definition of law,[58] Pound does not grapple with the wider problems posed by a sociological orientation.

Pound's reliance upon the social control approach has one further consequence. It leads him to adopt a number of implicit assumptions. One of the main reasons for the subsequent decline of 'social control' theory was that it tended to focus attention upon the factors leading to 'stability' or 'order' in society; it tended to presume an equilibrium model of society. Pound's whole social engineering approach rests upon an equilibrium model. Law is conceived of as operating to achieve a positive social function through 'eliminating friction nd waste'. It rests upon the assumption that the task of law is concerned with the 'balancing of interests'. Such an approach implies an over-simplified conception of the function of law based upon an equilibrium model of society in which law intervenes, when necessary, to restore some presumed natural balance or equilibrium within society. As Lepaulle comments 'to say that law is a mere balancing of interests involves the postulate that the legal system is an impartial, impassive receptacle in which more or less automatic reactions take place.'[59] Pound's concern with stability and order is consistent with the conservatism of his thought discussed earlier.

THE THEORY OF INTERESTS

The theory of interests lies at the very heart of sociological jurisprudence. The intention is to deal with it as the primary aspect of his substantive thought and it will therefore be discussed in some detail. This approach may be justified on a number of grounds. Firstly this aspect of his work embodies the main components of his thought which have been discussed in the preceding sections. Secondly it relates most closely to the more specifically sociological aspect of his writings with which this analysis is concerned.

Pound defines an interest as: 'A demand or desire which human beings, either individually or through groups or associations or in relations, seek to satisfy.'[60] Later this becomes 'the claims or demands or desires ...'[61] Finally he added 'expectations' to the list.[62] He regards these claims as primary social 'facts', in the positivist sense, for he speaks of them as 'manifestations of internal nature.'[63] The interest is for Pound, as for Jhering, secured by attributing to those interests that are protected, the status of legal rights. Thus the immediate impact is to shift the focus of analysis from the abstract consideration of rights and duties to the more empirical focus of interests.

Underlying his use of the concept interest is a 'scarce resources' theory. 'There has never been a society in which there has been a surplus of the means of satisfying these claims.'[64] This approach is derived from classical political economy and is an approach which has had a considerable impact upon both legal and sociological thought in both he nineteenth and twentieth centuries. But such an analysis carries with it certain dangerous and misleading implications. It exemplifies the impact that classical political economy of the nineteenth century had on social thought in general; it has resulted in a tendency uncritically to import narrowly economic concepts such as 'resources' or 'exchange' into social and legal theory. While *economic* resources are material, and as such are necessarily finite and hence subject to scarcity, *social* resources, since they are not necessarily physical, cannot be treated as 'scarce' in the same direct sense as economic resources may be. Hence any view of the law as a system for allocating scarce resources through a 'competition' model of society is an artificial and potentially misleading analogy.

The definition of interests as claims-demands-desires-expectations is not itself without weaknesses. The definition seems to imply that the concepts utilised are synonyms, but a closer examination shows that there are two distinct elements which have apparently been combined. He confuses objective and subjective elements. 'Claims' and 'demands' would appear to be objective in that they are interests *actually advanced*, while 'desires' and 'expectations' are subjective in that they are not necessarily externalised by individuals. It is this confusion which underlies the criticism made by Lepaulle that the theory of interests only takes account of 'conscious' interests. A similar criticism is made by Felix Cohen[65] who argues that Pound's view of interests rests upon the fallacy that society is 'vocal' in the sense that all demands that actually exist are in fact vocalised. Not only is it that some claims will never actually be articulated, and further that it would be erroneous to believe that all claims will be vocalised with the same intensity; some individuals and groups are more vocal than others, some are more powerful and better organised than others. Cohen concludes that such a view of interests results in '. . . a somewhat complacent acquiescence in the economic and political demands of dominant social groups.'[66] These criticisms suggest that the concepts claim and demand are not as simple as Pound implies and that it is necessary, in seeking to construct a theory around them, to give some consideration to exactly what constitutes them, and to indicate how they come to be recognised. This he fails to do and this to a very considerable extent detracts from what he claims to be the main virtue of the interest theory, namely that it is 'practical'.

A further consequence of the above criticism is that his theory may be seen as resting on a tautology and indeed a tautology that provides a very inadequate ethical theory, namely that the law ought to recognise those interests which in fact it does recognise. Such a conclusion appears to rest upon Pound's assumption that interests are 'self-legitimating' which will be discussed in more detail below. His approach lays itself open to the further criticism that it rests upon an undisclosed premise that the law and its institutions are 'value neutral', that the machinery of law stands above society weighing in its scales the conflicting interests of members of society.

A further undisclosed premise may be detected. Pound regards interests as being 'self-legitimating'. This is quite explicit in James: 'everything which is demanded is by that fact a good.'[67] In other words a sufficient criterion for the process of recognition of interests by the courts to occur requires simply that the interest is advanced. It carries with it the implication that all claims are equal. It is significant that Pound himself, having expressly adopted this formula in his earlier writings, in his later works appears to move away from it. For example he introduces the idea that the function of law is to protect 'reasonable interests'.[68] By the mere addition of one word he has moved a long way from the strict pragmatic dictat. However such an addition necessitates some intermediary evaluative criterion and he does not make very clear how the 'reasonable interest' is to be distinguished from other interests. It is now necessary to turn our attention to the way in which Pound utilised the interest theory. Again following closely upon von Jhering's work he proceeded to advance a *classification of interests*. He distinguished between individual, social and public interests. These he defines in the following uniform manner:

> Individual interests are claims or demands or desires involved in and looked at from the standpoint of the individual life immediately as such — asserted in title to the individual life.[69]

> Social interests are claims, or demands or desires involved in social life in civilised society and asserted in title to that life.[70]

> Public interests are claims or demands or desires asserted by individuals involved in and looked at from the standpoint of political life.[71]

Doubts have been expressed as to the precise implications of this classification; particularly active in this debate have been Patterson[72] and Stone.[73] In his later works Pound went some way actually to amending the content of his inventory, but did not seek to clarify the general problems to which the basic classification itself gives rise.

The central issue of debate is: do the three types constitute three distinct entities or are they merely three different ways of viewing the same reality? This leads on to the further question: are the three types equal in status? Most commentators agree that the category of public interests need not be advanced as a separate type and is best treated as a sub-type of social interests. Occasionally Pound suggests as much himself, 'ultimately these (public interests) come down to a social interest in the security of social institutions.'[74] But he appeared reluctant finally to abandon their independent status. It is intended to ignore any further discussion of the status of public interests on the grounds that the important debate concerns the relation between individual and social interests.

Stone and Patterson advance alternative analyses. Stone[75] argues that the different types of interests are merely different ways of referring to *de facto* claims; they are ways of looking at, or imposing order upon, the claims jostling for recognition. Thus if an individual asserts 'this is my pen' it is an individual interest of substance and at the same time a social interest in the security of acquisitions. This interpretation relies upon phrases which recur throughout Pound's writing and which also appear in the definitions quoted above, 'looked at from the standpoint of . . .'. According to this interpretation social and individual interests are merely different ways of looking at the same claim. This view is further supported by Pound's insistence that in comparing interests there is a need to 'compare them on the same plane'.[76] This implies that individual interests may be transposed into the form of social interests.

Patterson argues that the distinction between individual and social interests is more than that between different *types* of interests, but rather that they exist on different *levels*.[77] The social interests are seen as being a means of evaluating the individual interests advanced in society. Again he relies on certain textual authority. Pound speaks of jurisprudence needing to ask 'how far may those individual demands be put in terms of these social interest and . . . give the fullest effect to those social interests with the least sacrifice.'[78] Elsewhere he speaks of the task of law as being 'one of securing all social interests as far it may, of maintaining a balance or harmony among them that is compatible with the securing of all of them.'[79] For Patterson the concept of social interest is in fact Pound's criterion for the evaluation of interests rather than merely just another type of interest. He concludes that 'the social interests are a synthesis of values for all law'.[80]

While it must be admitted that a number of Pound's formulations lend support to Patterson's interpretation, the weight of argument lies with Stone's exposition. Pound himself explicitly rejects the 'social utilitarian' view that individual interests are to be recognised only in so far as they coincide with social interests.[81] Stone's interpretation is not only closest to the general direction of Pound's thought, but it is also more consistent with the whole framework of his theory. However it must be recognised that many of the difficulties are of Pound's own making. The interest theory is a very good illustration of the confusion of his thought. In particular the deficiencies of the interest theory stem from his threefold usage of the theory. It is used firstly as an inventory of 'observed elements in actual legal systems';[82] secondly as an historical typology in that he emphasises that different types of interests predominate at certain stages of legal development and thirdly as an analytical framework upon which he constructs his ethical theory. These three applications are in continual flux.

THE VALUATION OF INTERESTS

The theory of interests lies at the root of Pound's ethical theory. He seeks to provide an answer to the question: which claims advanced in society *should* be recognised and protected? It is pertinent to note in passing that, in marked contrast to the Realists, despite his positivistic leanings, Pound paid very little attention to the 'predictive' problem of seeking to determine the interests that the courts *will* recognise.

His solution to the ethical problem posed is given in what may be described as the 'pragmatic equation'. The goal is specified as aiming to give 'the most complete security and effect to the whole scheme of human demands and desires . . . with the least sacrifice to the scheme as a whole, the least friction, the least waste.'[83] This formulation, with the use of the notions of 'friction' and 'waste', is consistent with his use of the engineering analogy.

He however refuses to stake all upon he pragmatic ethical theory. He is insistent that it constitutes only a temporary 'practical' method of securing a 'rough compromise'. He argues that 'to the proposition that we can't arrive at a measure of values we may say that we have found one, and a very workable one, whether we can prove its philosophical validity or not.'[84] He contends that there is a need for philosophers to continue working towards a more universal theory of value while in the meantime he commends the utility of the pragmatic ethical theory. In so qualifying his position it may be considered that he is securing himself against the inevitable attacks that will be mounted on his pragmatic equation. It is also probable that his hesitancy is related to his later retreat from the pragmatic relativism of his early years. Such a consideration clearly underlines one of his later statements of his position.

> I have come to feel that instead of putting the task of law, as William James did, in terms of satisfying as much as we can of the total of human demands, we do better to speak of providing as much as we may of the total of men's reasonable expectations in life in civilised society with the minimum of friction and waste.[85]

This restatement, with the addition of the crucial word 'reasonable', seems to indicate a much higher level of concern with more absolute questions of value.

The most important criticism, which arises from the self-validating character of interests, is that it carries the implication that all interests advanced are equal and consequently are of equal value. To suggest that all claims and demands asserted in society are of equal worth, and explicitly to deny at the same time that individual interests should be assessed in terms of wider social interests, is not so much a theory of valuation, but a negation of evaluation itself. The aim of securing the maximum number of interests implies a purely quantitative approach; it reduces a qualitative problem to purely quantitative terms. Thus Pound argues that the end of law is 'to give effect to he greatest total of interests'.[86] It is because of this that the label 'pragmatic equation' has been used. Yet it is extraordinary that the sentence quoted above continues: 'or to the interests weighed most in our civilisation'. Pound is apparently unaware of the contradiction between these two formulations. In precisely the same way it is suggested that the same contradiction reappears when he adds to the pragmatic equation the addendum 'with the least sacrifice to the whole', since this necessitates the introduction of an additional evaluatory criterion. Yet he nowhere indicates what this further criterion is to be; nor does he appear aware of the philosophical difficulties to which it gives rise.

Pound thus implies that the process of ethical evaluation can be reduced to a process of quantification, but he fails to indicate how this quantification is to be carried out. He appears happy to rest upon the hope that, if all interests have equal value, the question is purely one of simple additions on the presupposition that interests may be compared on a one-to-one basis. Rather than providing a means of quantification he slips back to a much more indeterminate approach by seeking to secure a 'balancing' of contending interests. But as Llewellyn notes 'balancing of interests remains with no indication of how to tell an interest when you see one, much less any study of how they are or should be balanced.'[87]

Important though these defects in the theory of evaluation are, they are not sufficient for us to reject it in its entirety. This is because Pound has, in effect, another ethical theory running in parallel. This second ethical theory is the one that it is suggested he applies in practice when he is called upon to make, for example, an assessment of the development of the rules in a particular area of substantive law. This method is the evaluation of interests by reference to the 'jural postulates of civilisation' and the 'ends of law'. He attributes to them the function of being 'a measure of interests to be recognised and secured.'[88] As developed by Kohler jural postulates were ideal concepts, Pound adds a postivist content, as with interests, by seeking to extract them from the positive law. The jural postulates are conceived of as being the most universal forms of social presuppositions with respect to the reasonable expectations of what the legal order may be expected to secure. They are seen as 'not rules of law but ideas to be made effective by legal institutions and legal precepts.'[89] Pound suggests that valuation by reference to jural postulates and ends of law, which are merely more generalised expressions of the objectives which the legal system is conceived of pursuing, have in practice been widely used for evaluation; indeed he argues that it is this activity that underlies natural law theory.

There is some difficulty in assessing the exact importance and role that Pound attributes to valuation with reference to jural postulates. In *Social Control Through Law* he argues that there have been three main methods by which the process of evaluation has been undertaken: firstly by reference to jural postulates; secondly by reference to authoritative ideals of the social order, and thirdly by experience in the seeking of a rough compromise between competing interests. He argues that the first and second methods are of declining importance and that the method of experience has come to predominate; it is this method which in his hands becomes the pragmatic equation. But he does imply that this method is of a temporary character.

> The practical work of the courts in adjusting relations and ordering conduct must go on. The legal order . . . cannot stand still until the social order has settled down for a time in a condition of stability in which its jural postulates can be recognised and formulated . . . In

the meantime the courts must, as in the past, go on finding out by experience and developing by reason the modes of adjusting relations and ordering conduct.[90]
This presentation carries the implication, which fits well with the qualification, previously noted concerning the temporary character of the pragmatic theory. In a similar vein in *Jurisprudence* he suggests that there are two approaches to the valuation of interests, one with respect to jural postulates, the other by classifying interests. While acknowledging his debt to Kohler he goes on to say 'I have preferred to build on Jhering's idea of interest'.[91]

From the above considerations it would appear that he had discarded the valuation by reference to jural postulates. Yet if he is regarded as having abandoned their use it is rather surprising that he should devote as much effort as he does in elaborating the jural postulates of contemporary civilisation. His original scheme of jural postulates was advanced in 1919;[92] by 1942[93] he found it necessary to suggest the need to add two new postulates, namely the expectation of security of employment and the expectation that enterprise liability should bear the misfortunes of normal life befalling individuals. This classification of jural postulates is further amended in *Jurisprudence*. Julius Stone attempted to resolve the problems inherent in Pound's ethical theory.[94] He notes:

> At times he presents this scheme of interests as part (along with the jural postulates) of the apparatus of one method, the two elements then functioning together. . . . At other times, however, the scheme of interests is regarded as providing in itself a sufficient means to this adjustment, and the jural postulates are then relegated to the role of an alternative method of analysis and criterion of equal, but separate validity, on which the efficacy of the scheme of interests is in no way dependent.[95]

As noted previously Stone's general conclusion is that it is the interest theory of evaluation. Perhaps a rather less charitable view justifies the conclusion that Pound was unable to advance a consistent ethical theory. In recognising the deficiencies of both the pragmatic and the idealistic theory, he tried to resolve his dilemma by combining the two, and in so doing produces an inevitable and irresolvable contradiction. This contradiction is a manifestation of the deeper conflict between the two strands of thought, the utilitarian and the idealistic upon the unstable fusion of which he seeks to construct the edifice of sociological jurisprudence; as a consequence this very edifice itself is inherently unstable.

This fundamental weakness in his ethical theory is manifested in his most frequent formulation of the pragmatic equation which reproduces this same contradiction. He adds to the Jamesian version of pragmatism the requirement that interests should be evaluated with 'the least sacrifice to the whole of the scheme'. Such a formulation appears to supersede the image of the legal system as concerned solely with evaluating competing claims advanced by individuals by importing a more general requirement of weighing the unit claim against the totality. Plausible though this appears, its fundamental untenability is that he does not indicate by what means the individual claim is to be balanced against the totality. It implies some additional criterion which is not specified. Yet it provides a means of importing, without any recognition of the consequences, evaluation by means of the jural postulates into the pragmatic equation; it thereby manifests the attempt to combine the disparate ethical theories within the same framework.

THE EVOLUTIONARY THEORY OF LAW

One of the more consistent elements in Pound's thought is his insistence upon an evolutionary approach to legal phenomena. Such an orientation unites the diverse elements of his philosophical approach, that of the historical tradition, greatly influenced by Hegelian philosophy on the one hand and on the other the relativism implicit in the pragmatic philosophy.

Pound advances an explicit typology of 'stages of legal development'.[96] Throughout his work is suffused with a general evolutionary or developmental approach, even though it is not always couched in the precise form of 'stages'. This is particularly evident in what is perhaps his most prolific area of activity, namely the history of legal thought.[97]

He distinguishes five stages of legal development; primitive or ancient law, strict law, equity or natural law, maturity of law and the socialisation of law.[98] In *Jurisprudence* he suggests a possible sixth stage, 'the law of the world'. He seeks to give a characterisation of each stage and to indicate the form that each takes and the ends of law associated with them. This typology may be represented as in the table on p. 30.

Pound also regarded his other major categories, for example the jural postulates, as being similarly evolutionary, but he made no effort to relate them to the five main stages; he presents them as different set of stages which do not consistently correspond to his general five stage model.

He is insistent that these stages do not successively replace each other, but rather that aspects of previous stages persist. For example the end of law in he primitive stage is that of securing public peace; this is a continuing function of legal systems though it occupies successively a less central role. In this respect Pound's typology of legal development is similar to those advanced by Durkheim and Weber in that the stages are ideal-typical because they constitute both *forms* of law as well as being *stages* of law. However the variation and inconsistency in the articulation of these stages indicates that they are essentially categories in contrast to the more theoretically elaborated work of Durkheim and Weber.

Pound does not make it explicit how he constructs his typology. It is clear that it is not a construct in which legal evolution is related to other

	PRIMITIVE LAW	STRICT LAW	EQUITY/NATURAL LAW	MATURITY OF LAW	SOCIALISATION OF LAW
END	Public peace	Security	Ethical conduct, conformity to good morals	Equality of opportunity, security of acquisitions	Maximum satisfaction of wants
MEANS	Composition	Legal remedies	Enforcement of duties	Maintenance of rights	Recognition of interests
PERMANENT CONTRIBUTION	Peaceable ordering of society	Certainty and uniformity	Good faith and moral conduct, attained by reason	Thorough working out of idea of individual rights	Overcoming of individualism, wider securing of social interests

wider characteristics of society, whether it be levels of economic development or forms of social organisation in the same way, for example, that Durkheim seeks to relate legal evolution to stages in the social division of labour. Pound's typology emerges, rather than being constructed, by the same method that has previously been criticised, from an observation of positive systems of law. It is therefore an inductive method which produces a purely descriptive typology in terms of the internal development of law itself. There is no attempt to discuss, let alone formulate, the criteria upon which it is based. His typology therefore lacks any underlying theoretical clarity. This shortcoming accounts for the inconsistent use that he makes of his evolutionary model in that some aspects of his developmental consideration of law or juristic thought is presented in terms of the five stage model; other parts of the discussion are not.

A further major weakness that may be pointed to is that it is not based on any consistent comparative study of legal evolution. The typology is very narrowly related to the evolution of the common law system; its stages are most clearly those that are readily discernible in the more traditional interpretations of English legal history. Even his terminology sharply reflects his primary focus upon the common law.

It has been suggested above that Pound has no formal criteria for the construction and delination of the stages. Is it possible to detect any consistent theoretical underpinning of his system? Perhaps the most central concept that Pound utilises is the motion of 'ends of law'. This concern with the ends of law is part of his reaction against analytical jurisprudence which viewed law as a self-sufficient encapsulated system. It also reflects the deep impact of the neo-Hegelian tradition particularly through the writings of Kohler.[99] The application of the idea of 'ends of law' allows Pound to see a mediation between law and society in that the ends of law developed at the most general level, indeed often at an unconscious level and can be seen as having an impact upon the evolution of law. At a number of points he seeks to relate the predominant 'ends' to wider social factors. Thus, for example, in discussing the individualism that was dominant during the nineteenth century he suggests 'this is indeed a philosophy of law for discoverers and pioneers and traders and entrepreneurs and captains of industry.'[100] His concept of ends of law is decidedly Hegelian in that they are perceived as having an autonomous existence, as acting independently in the process of social causation. Pound indeed seems strangely confused about the process of social causation in general; he is reluctant to commit himself as to whether it is social factors that determine the 'ends' or whether it is the 'ends' which determine the social and economic reality. In seeking to steer a course between the Scylla and Charybdis of metaphysical philosophy and positivism Pound ends up without a theory of causation. Despite his ability to impose order and clarity upon the thinking of others, Pound is incapable of, or unwilling to, apply the same conditions to his own theories. Because of this the concept of the 'ends of law' remains a rather rarified notion. He clearly sees it as being detectable in legal rules and in legal theories. It is not clear whether rules and theories determine the ends or whether ends determine the rules and theories.

There is a further dimension to his evolutionary approach to law that merits consideration. Pound frequently refers to the dichotomy between 'certainty' or 'stability' on the one hand and 'change' on the other. 'Law must be stable and yet it cannot stand still.'[101] This dialectic of change-stability is seen as underlying the process and function of law and continually re-emerges during the course of his writings. Such an approach indicates yet again a very distinctive Hegelian influence although Pound himself never explicitly notes the connection. The process of legal evolution is seen as embodying a dialectical process determined by the interaction of the two forces of change and stability. Thus for example he sees legal philosophies as in some periods being forces for change (for example the rationalist natural law of seventeenth and eighteenth centuries), while others are seen as forces resulting in the predominance, for the period, of stability.[102] He frequently comes close to positing a cyclical theory. He implies the possibility that natural law may be associated with periods of growth and that this may account for the revival of natural law that he detects prior to the Second World War.[103]

An important consequence of his developmental view of legal evolution may be seen in his attacks upon individualism in legal thought that reached its peak during the nineteenth century and which conceived of the end of law as being the ideal of maximum individual self-assertion. The function of the legal order was seen as that of reconciling conflicting free wills. This view indelibly marked not only legal theory but also the content of the positive law itself; the most consistent manifestation of which was the elevation of contract. This tendency worshipped at the altar of Maine's famous thesis concerning the transition from status to contract.[104] The very discussion of legal rules in terms of rights and duties is stamped by this same orientation. The dogma of the maximisation of individual free will seeped into every facet of legal thought and activity. Its impact has lasted into the present century and to a marked extent it provides the ideological basis of much legal thought and judicial practice to the present day.

In Pound's view, despite the long period of its predominance, the free will theory was a temporary aberration and is not a permanent condition of legal thought and practice. In asserting the social character of law he attached considerable importance to combating legal individualism. It is this effort which constitutes the major element in his rejection of legal traditionalism. He saw the work of von Jhering as representing the turning point in juristic thought. Perhaps rather over-confidently Pound concluded 'the conception of law as a securing of interests . . . has all but universally superseded the individualist theory.'[105]

A rejection of individualism is a necessary condition for the development of a consistently sociological study of law. His attack was significant in that it helped to undermine the persistent individualism of the jurisprudential tradition, but it is important to stress that an anti-individualist position does not itself constitute a sufficient condition for a sociological theory of law. Yet at the same time it is true that he was not entirely able to free himself from some of the ramifications of individualistic modes of thought. As has already been shown his theory of interests is based upon methodological individualism. Such an orientation is consistent with Pound's wider social and political attitudes. For example, despite his advocacy of social legislation, he shows himself to be hostile to the ramifications of state activity that such legislation gives rise to.[106] Such a view is consistent with his life-long Republican sympathies.

His evolutionary view of law has been shown to have had a number of substantial deficiencies. Yet this criticism should not be allowed to obscure the fact that his historical and philosophical discussion of legal evolution provides a starting point for any criticism of other trends of juristic thought that are hostile to a sociological approach to law.

THE SIGNIFICANCE OF SOCIOLOGICAL JURISPRUDENCE

It is now possible to attempt an assessment of sociological jurisprudence. The concern is not so much to provide an overall assessment of Pound's jurisprudence, but rather to gauge its specific contribution to the sociological movement.

Pound was undoubtedly a major force, not necessarily because he succeeded in creating a sociological theory of law which future generations merely needed to apply as Pound himself, in laying down the programme of sociological jurisprudence, clearly envisaged.[107] His success lay in the fact that he laid a basis upon which the development of a sociological jurisprudence, more consistent and systematic than he himself was able to develop, might be constructed. This basis which he provided was the overcoming of traditional habits and modes of thought in jurisprudence which have been characterised as 'legal traditionalism'. Pound constantly reasserted, in many different ways, the social character of law. He was not alone in this endeavour, nor was he the first in he field, but he certainly kept at it for the longest and in so doing probably had a wider impact than any other upon legal thought. His approach, in this respect similar to that of Ehrlich, was the polemical task of undermining the credibility of previous modes of thought and thereby opening up a considerable potential for new theoretical perspectives. His efforts may therefore be regarded as a pre-condition of the sociological study of law. Pound was the propagandist for a sociological jurisprudence, but he cannot be regarded as having given it an adequate theoretical basis.

The numerous weaknesses and defects that have been pointed to in his work are in large measure a result of the very ambitious tasks that he set himself. In seeking to link neo-Hegelian idealist philosophy with positivistic pragmatism he was inevitably doomed to failure. His work does not constitute a 'theory' in that he is unable to provide a framework in which the disparate elements are tied together. Julius Stone attempted to do just this to Pound's work, but he has done so within the structure of Pound's own thought without seeking to make the necessary breaks that its internal contradictions require.

Without undue disservice to Pound's contribution it is possible to accept Patterson's characterisation of sociological jurisprudence as 'a loose theory created by an imaginative mind looking at legal phenomena with the aid of pragmatism, mid-western shrewdness, Hegelian and native American idealism and a touch of sociology.'[108]

Patterson points correctly to the subsidiary status of sociology in Pound's jurisprudence. He used sociology when he saw fit; he cannot be regarded as having developed a sociological theory of law.

The essential requirements of an autonomous sociological jurisprudence are a number of rather sharper breaks with the jurisprudential tradition. This inability to transcend previous jurisprudential thought arises from his basic philosophical orientation and from an excessive reverence for certain elements of the common law tradition. In particular this manifests itself in his faith in the efficacy of the judicial process within the common law system. Thus observations such as 'the trained intuition and disciplined judgment of the judge must be our assurance that causes will be decided on principles of reason and not according to the chance dictates of caprice'[109] would not seem to emanate from the same pen that had earlier been attacking the jurisprudence of concepts, nor to constitute a sufficiently critical spirit to provide the basis for a sociological approach.

The significance of sociological jurisprudence has remained at the polemical level of the assertion of the social character of law. Whilst such a function is still necessary, the objectives that Pound set himself went much beyond this limited function. It is therefore necessary to pose the question: why did sociological jurisprudence not succeed in establishing the basis for a sociological theory of law?

The preceding discussion of Pound's substantive theory has largely focused upon the internal analysis of the components of his jurisprudence and indicated a number of significant defects and weaknesses. These in themselves do not account for the limitations of the whole enterprise. The significance and root of the failure to break more fundamentally with the jurisprudential tradition may now be specified more closely.

The object of inquiry of any theory is given by the central feature or aspect of the phenomenon that is placed in the centre of the conceptualisation of that phenomenon. In sociological jurisprudence that object is a conception of law as an autonomous phenomenon whose distinctive character may be specified as 'law as rules'. The significance of the method of conceptualising law is not that it is in any sense 'wrong' or 'incorrect'; we are not therefore engaged in the time-honoured jurisprudential activity of debating rival definitions of law. Its importance is that, in choosing to highlight this aspect of the observed phenomenon, it reveals the stance from which the phenomenon of law is perceived and also has major and determining consequences for the theory that is elaborated around this conceptualisation.

'Law as rules' is a perception that perpetuates legal traditionalism in that it embodies the perception of law of the legal practitioner. It corresponds with the practitioner's self-declared role within the legal system. It is furthermore a position that is a direct continuation of the traditional imperative concept of law of analytical jurisprudence. The emphasis is upon the normative character of legal phenomena in which legal rules are conceived as 'purposive' in that they embody ends or objectives. Seen in this way the assertion of the social character of law serves only to obscure the fact that the persepctive adopted embodies a conception of law as an autonomous phenomenon which in turn perpetuates the assumption of the centrality of law that characterises the jurisprudential tradition against which sociological jurisprudence expressly sought to overcome.

The contention that the starting point of 'law as rules' is the practitioner's perception of law requires amplification. This perception is one that is ideologically mediated, that is to insist that lawyers and judges have their commonsense concept of law given through the ideological perspective within which they operate. This ideology asserts the neutrality and impartiality of the role and function of legal professionals. It is within his ideological context that legal professionals see themselves as the technicians of legal rules.

Two consequences stem from the perception of law as rules; on the one hand it gives rise to a strongly practical orientation and on the other to a general theoretical weakness.[110] The desire to render useful service to the practitioner has been seen as influencing Pound's concerns; it will be seen to be even more pronounced in the case of American legal realism. This concern is at the root of his social engineering perspective. It expresses itself in the overriding concern with the efficiency of legal rules. The preoccupation with the evaluation of legal rules arises within the context of assessing them as more or less successful instruments or techniques for the realisation of the normative or purposive content of legal rules.

Sociological jurisprudence intervenes where the legal system is perceived as malfunctioning, that is where it exhibits a gap between purposively defined goals and the social consequences manifested in 'the law in action'. This orientation underlines the client status of legal academics to practitioners; the legal theorist is called upon to justify his field of interest in terms of the imperatives of legal practice.

The theoretical weakness of sociological jurisprudence does not stem simply from the particular defects or contradictions within the theory propounded. Rather they arise from a general lack of attention to the theoretical enterprise itself. The theoretical content arises from *ad hoc* theorising as the need to provide an account or explanation of observed characteristics of legal systems. Theory has a largely descriptive function; it is seen as a means of 'making sense' of the observed phenomena. It is in this lack of attention to theory that the failure to develop a sociological theory of law is to be located. The sociological enterprise is focused on the analysis of the social context of legal rules and this orientation, coupled with the focus on the purposive character of legal rules, goes hand in hand with utilitarian social philosophy.

The sociological claims of sociological jurisprudence stem not from the fact that it advanced a sociological theory of law but from he fact that it adopted social utilitarianism. The fundamental theoretical error was the belief that the utilisation of concepts such as 'social interest' constituted a fundamental break with the theoretical and methodological individualism of Benthamite utilitarianism. The result was that social utilitarianism offered no such automatic transition from nineteenth century individualism to a sociological orientation seen as befitting the twentieth century.

Sociological jurisprudence provided an adequate basis for the law reform movement that was in harmony with the practical predisposition of the sociological movement with its emphasis on the purposive character of legal rules and its empirical critique of the malfunctions of the existing legal order. It did not provide the theoretical framework within which it could realise its claim to advance a sociological theory of law.

3 American Legal Realism

INTRODUCTION

With apologies to Eldridge Cleaver we may identify American Realism as a
way station between sociological jurisprudence and contemporary behavioural sociology of law. This characterisation implies a treatment that is
radically different from the conventional jurisprudential discussion of the
realist movement. My concern will not be the debates between realism and
contemporaneous trends in jurisprudence.[1]

The focus of this chapter will be more narrowly drawn. It is a view of
Realism as an important stage in the transition between the primarily
jurisprudential frame of reference of 'sociological jurisprudence' to the
predominantly sociological orientation of modern 'sociology of law'. Both
historically and intellectually, it will be argued, American legal realism
provides the bridge between sociological jurisprudence and the sociology
of law. In addition to the somewhat passive role of being a bridge I shall
argue that an understanding of the movement is necessary in order to
understand the specific form which characterises contemporary American
legal sociology. In particular it will be argued that the predominant
behaviouralistic stance of modern sociology of law has its roots, not only
in the American sociological tradition, but more immediately in the legacy
of American legal realism.

While the objectives of the present chapter are assisted by the
narrowing down of its terms of reference as outlined above there remains
the not inconsiderable problem of how the exposition is to be developed.
All are now agreed that Legal Realism does not constitute a 'school', rather
a 'movement'. As Cahill remarks 'In truth, Legal Realism is less a
description than a slogan and carries emotional connotations rather than

precise meanings.'[2] Rather than attempt to chart its many variations and permutations,[3] two related concerns will be focused upon. First to determine what, if anything, constitutes the sociological premisses of the movement and to examine these in the light of their relationship to sociological jurisprudence and American sociology of law. Second to examine what methods of study and work were distinctive of realism. The concern will be to uncover the theoretical basis and the methodology of the realist movement.

Since Realism was only a generalised trend, to attempt to identify a core of theory or method runs the potential danger of lapsing into the production of a bastardised view of realism representing only its lowest common denominator. To avoid this pitfall it is the intention to concentrate primarily on Karl Llewellyn. This selection rests upon two criteria, firstly that he is widely, if not universally recognised as the most important figure of the realist movement and secondly that his views represent the 'centre' of the movement, in that the diversity of realism was such that it had a 'left' and a 'right';[4] in so far as this is true Llewellyn constitutes a uniquely representative position but, as will emerge, one that was by no means static and, in these rather simple terms, moved towards the 'right'.

However it would be artificial to select one man as the embodiment of the whole movement.[5] While the central concern will be with Llewellyn other 'members' cannot be excluded. Indeed they play an integral part in the general treatment since it will be argued that the different 'wings' of the movement have found their reflection in the variations within contemporary sociology of law.

THE SOCIAL CONTEXT OF AMERICAN REALISM

The treatment of the Realists in standard jurisprudential texts tends to suggest a marked break with the previous stage of jurisprudential thought. Thus for example attention is frequently focused on the sharp polemical debate between Pound and Llewellyn.[6] Sociological jurisprudence stands astride the social divide of the First World War. The two strands are considerably intermingled during the subsequent decades. While there did exist distinguishing features the general case to be argued is in favour of seeing an overriding unity whose different forms and expressions are to be accounted for by reference to the different social and intellectual forces operating.

Sociological jurisprudence came of age in the first decade of the century. It reflected, like so many other areas of social thought, the declining faith in the economic and social philosophy of laissez-faire. The stupendous economic growth from the close of the Civil War had brought in its wake the rise of the giant monopolistic enterprise, massive disparities of wealth, rapid urbanisation with its concentration of social problems and increasing conflict between agrarian and industrial interests. Neither the society as a whole, nor the law, could as assuredly be regarded as a self-regulating mechanism. As Llewellyn later observed 'with the turn of the century the emotional revolt of labourers, farmers and small business-men had worked its way into the thinking of intellectuals.'[7] By the end of the nineteenth century state involvement had increased substantially. In Poundian sociological jurisprudence the reality of the conflict, and the subsequent need for regulation, finds expression in the clash of individual and social interests. The social interest model presumes that the interests are, in the long run, compatible but gives primacy to the social interest. Poundian theory is the reflex of the conservative progressivism of The-odore Roosevelt, explicitly structured within the framework of a capitalist economy and seeking to give a new 'socialised' form to the traditional individualistic creed.

The specific orientation of this tendency towards reform in both political and legal fields was a conscious recognition of the pace of social change.[8] Wise and far-thinking advocates of the '*status quo*', of whom Theodore Roosevelt and Woodrow Wilson were the best examples,[9] recognised the necessity of making far-reaching concessions, in particular to labour, in order to preserve the main features of the existing order. Hence there was widespread recognition of the inescapable necessity of increased state intervention. Realism similarly embodied, along with sociological jurisprudence, the conscious espousal of policy-oriented inter-vention by the state. It was the difficulties encountered in persuading the legal establishment of the necessity of this new conservatism that led to the clash between the judiciary and the state that came to a head in 1936. The espousal by Realists of a favourable response to socioeconomic legislation, which alongside their advocacy of judicial activism, was in essence a plea for a readjustment of the legal order to social developments.

Legal realism carries forward much of this orientation. Its insistent emphasis on 'social change' was in keeping with the pluralistic political ideology of the period. However the basic soundness of the social system was never doubted; faith in the efficacy of human effort still abounds, but a more strenuous effort to correct social imbalance and distortions is necessary. The sharpening of the social conflict of the pre-war years, both between labour and capital and between town and country, and the onward march of the trusts all resulted in realism being sharper in tone, more strident and urgent than had been sociological jurisprudence.

> Realism was the academic formulation of a crisis through which our legal system passed during the first half of this century.[10]

Yet significantly realism, even in its most polemical form, never became significantly radical; it presumed an unchanged constitution and a struc-turally unchanged legal system. Whilst urging and welcoming the advance of state intervention, particularly in the form of anti-trust and social legislation, it placed a preponderant reforming role at the feet of the judiciary. The heyday of Realism in the late twenties and early thirties coincided with the trauma of the Depression. While some evidence may be found that this experience deflated the inherently optimistic reformism of the earlier period, the literature of realism betrays little general doubt that the system could be reformed and adjusted to meet social need. The absence of any deeply rooted radicalism among the Realists is partially to be explained by the relative intellectual and social isolation of legal professionals, but also of importance was the relative absence of any cohesive socialist tradition, particularly of a theoretical expression, in the United States. The Realists to a man were liberals and reformers, very much part of the 'progressive' tradition. The overwhelming support and indeed substantial participation in the New Deal agencies of Franklin Roosevelt was very much a continuation of that tradition.[11]

However the very characteristics of the American legal system necessitated the Realists being rather more explicitly 'political' than for example English jurists have been.[12] The constitutional review powers of the Supreme Court have throughout the twentieth century, but most sharply during the New Deal, placed that institution in the centre of national politics. The New Deal legislation, in particular the National Industrial Recovery Act 1933, was effectively 'killed' by the Supreme Court. In the ensuing confrontation between Roosevelt and the 'nine old men' the Realists sided with the President and were in the main prepared to support his plans to reconstitute the membership of the Court.[13]

The realist movement has been characterised by the majority of commentators as 'radical' or 'left wing'.[14] Such labels need to be viewed in perspective. Even in the narrower focus of its relationship to other juristic trends it is far from proven that realism, other than in its polemical rhetoric, is more 'radical' than was sociological jurisprudence. The commitment to capitalism, to individualism and generally to the existing social order remains. The battle waged by the Realists was against the conservative traditions dominant in the judiciary and the profession;[15] they sought to drag the legal establishment into the twentieth century and to do so they were prepared to use stronger language than had been used before. The massive social and economic changes that American society experienced added a sense of urgency to the task.

THE INTELLECTUAL ORIGINS OF AMERICAN REALISM

American realism was a natural continuation of the trends that had brought sociological jurisprudence into existence. Yet the realist movement only took form and character in the process of sharply distinguishing itself from Poundian sociological jurisprudence. It is a common feature of intellectual movements that they develop in conflict with those that retrospectively they may be seen to have most in common with. It is however significant that Pound's undeniably impressive edifice of sociological jurisprudence should fail to attract a substantial following and undergo concrete development.[16]

Sociological jurisprudence lost its initiative and rather petered out after 1918 despite the continuing personal contribution of Pound himself. This assessment must however not be taken as denying the considerable generalised impact of the sociological tendency.[17] Sociological jurisprudence failed, or more accurately failed to realise its potential, because, in its Poundian articulation, it was very heavily oriented towards the nineteenth century philosophical currents of juristic thought. Its programmatic content, as symbolised by the call for 'social engineering', was very loosely formulated and it did not offer any concrete line of action or research, despite the fact that Pound had explicitly advanced a 'programme' to be undertaken under the banner of sociological jurisprudence. Thus for example the line of research most closely associated with sociological jurisprudence, the Cleveland Project,[18] ended up as a rather dry but voluminous exercise in data collection.

The criticism of Pound made by those who became identified as Realists was not to attack his theoretical framework or indeed his programme, but rather to complain about the reins which he kept upon the exploration of its implications and practical applications. Thus Jerome Frank remarked of Pound that 'while brilliantly elaborating it [Holme's views] in some limited directions, he nevertheless repressed it, obstructed its full growth.'[19] Oliphant expressed the objectives of the Realists as being to make 'a sociological jurisprudence a fact rather than a mere aspiration.'[20]

What the Realists demanded, in the light of their heightened consciousness of the need for reform, was a more activist programme. Pound offered a system of thought, the possibility of a comprehensive legal theory; the Realists tended to be impatient with general theory which did not lead to direct practical application. Further, although he went into battle against legal traditionalism, Pound failed to kill the dragon; the Realists wanted a sharper conflict and a more certain victory using fewer of the opponent's weapons. Hence the Realists appeared more prepared to dispense with traditional jurisprudential armour.

The consequence of the dissatisfaction with Poundian sociological jurisprudence was that the Realists drew their primary intellectual stimulus not from previous juristic development but rather self-consciously sought to build a theory of law upon pragmatic philosophy. The crucial link between the Realists and pragmatic philosophy was provided by Oliver Wendell Holmes.[21] His role is central not only because of his eminence amongst legal professionals,[22] nor simply because of the important part he played, along with Pound, in attacking traditional jurisprudence, but specifically because of his direct and close association with the leading figures of pragmatism. Holmes was a founder member of the 'Metaphysical Club' at Harvard along with C. S. Pierce, and William James.[23] His importance was that he gave early articulation in the field of law to a pragmatic orientation. The major Realists are explicit in their acknowledgement to the pragmatists, their writings carrying numerous references to Holmes and James, to C. S. Pierce and later to Dewey.

Holmes was canonised by the Realists; they saw themselves as his legitimate heirs and resisted the claims of sociological jurisprudence to derive title from him. Their contention was not without foundation because in his writings and judgments there were in embryo many of the ideas and attitudes which became the hallmark of Realism. Holmes had stressed the importance of extra-legal and subconscious factors in the judicial process; his relativistic view of legal certainty, 'I will admit any general proposition you like and decide the case either way',[24] underlies the Realist's 'rule skepticism' and gives rise to the abiding concern with prediction. Many of Holme's best known aphorisms are taken up by the Realists as their starting points; perhaps most central of all being his contention that 'the life of the law has not been logic; it has been experience.'[25]

It was suggested above that the Realists built a theory of law on a pragmatic basis. Such an assertion requires qualification. The type of 'theory' they articulated was very different from that which had preceded them. Pound had sought to construct a general theory that was capable of embracing every facet of legal phenomena; it was in the strict sense a 'general theory'. The relativistic empiricist implications of pragmatism manifested themselves in a disavowal of 'general theory'. The Realists did not exclude theory, indeed both Frank and Llewellyn continually stressed its importance; rather they sought to test theory in the acid bath of pragmatism, namely to question whether the theory was useful, to ask whether it contributed to an immediate furthering of the grasp of reality.

It has been observed previously that jurists in the Anglo-American tradition have been timid beings, feeling the need to justify their abstract theoretical concerns in the overwhelming sea of vocationalism. They have continually sought to be 'useful'. So too the Realists, but they were reinforced by a stronger philosophical prod, pragmatism required it of them; pragmatism provided a rationale for a result oriented, instrumental perspective.

While pragmatism provided the intellectual underpinnings for realism it was the climate and predispositions of pragmatism rather than as full-blown philosophical system that it was relied upon. The Realists imbibed certain key emphases from their philosophical mentors. Firstly a generalised ethical relativism; this in the main being the cause of the most sustained juristic onslaught upon the Realists.[26] Yet it must be insisted that their relativism was of a partial character and that in practice it was confined to a 'democratic individualism with changing content'. Secondly they carried over a pluralistic theory of causation; they had a horror of any view which propounded a single major causal factor. This was linked directly to the empiricist orientation necessitating the recognition of causation as a complex interplay of variables. These positions were associated with a generalised faith in the efficacy of effort which in turn derived from a view of human behaviour and institutions as mutable.

The end product is that the primary influence upon the movement was the lowest common denominator of philosophical pragmatism. As Shuman observes 'in the realism of the 1920s and 1930s ... the underlying pragmatic philosophy is largely a refined (and sometimes not too refined) commonsense humanism.'[27] It is noticeable that Llewellyn in particular made large play upon the appeal to commonsense; his demand for 'horse sense' as a means of approach to legal phenomena, while being an understandable reaction to conventional legal dogma, renders the philosophical basis of realism fragile in the extreme.

The major area in which American realism manifested a continuity with jurisprudential tradition was that, consistent with pragmatism, it was unashamedly positivist. Holmes's seminal formulation of the concept of law as 'the prophecies of what the courts will do in fact, and nothing more pretentious, are what I mean by the law'[28] was taken up and echoed time and time again by leading Realists.[29] Their view, despite the fact that both Llewellyn and Frank sought to redefine their position to avoid difficult philosophical implications,[30] nevertheless remained a rather simplistic positivism.

One of the distinctive features of realism was its pronounced 'modernism', apparent in the extent to which it took cognisance of contemporary developments in other fields of human learning. These influences were by no means uniform some exponents being more influenced than others and some being influenced by different aspects of contemporary scholarship.[31] The differences that existed amongst the Realists themselves can largely be accounted for in terms of the differential impact of other strands of enquiry. Thus developments in psychiatry and psychology had a marked impact upon Frank who drew heavily from both Freud and Piaget, and in a rather different form both Underhill Moore and Herman Oliphant were influenced by psychology.[32]

Of rather more general importance was the impact of developments within the natural sciences. The edifice of Newtonian physics had been crumbling for some time and the impact of the concepts of relativity and indeterminacy was taken up by the Realists; none more so than by Frank who explicitly shows evidence of the influence of Mach, Planck and Heisenberg. The extreme relativism of Frank's position, the major manifestation of which was the insistence that the major source of uncertainty in legal phenomena stemmed from fact indeterminacy, resulted in him distinguishing between the 'rule' and the 'fact skeptics' amongst the Realists. The extent of this influence was such that it resulted in his categorical repudiation of the general concern of the majority of Realists with prediction. Frank insisted upon the "ineradicable mutability of law".[33] He repudiated the possibility of a 'legal science', based on the model of the natural sciences, and asserted 'that predictability of most specific decisions is (and will doubtless remain) impossible.'[34]

Superficially the divergence between the rule and the fact-skeptics, as manifested in the respective positions taken to the possibility of prediction, appear to be of such an order that it is difficult to see these two streams as part of the same movement. However it is suggested that the gap is by no means so wide; at root the differences stem from the extent of the emphasis placed upon factors tending to produce uncertainty in the judicial process.

Taking Llewellyn and Frank as representative of the two trends they were united in their onslaught upon the formal syllogistic judicial method. Both insisted that the judicial decision was the resultant of a complex of interacting factors; Llewellyn believed that these factors could be 'held down' and marshalled into a valuable predictive device.[35] He was aided by his conscious orientation to the decisional process of appellate courts which resulted not from a narrow adherence to tradition, to the 'upper court myth', but because his concern was with the 'trouble case', the case which posed a new question requiring a new solution. In other words his concern was with the process of change and growth in law and, here Llewellyn is at his weakest, he assumed that such cases fairly automatically advanced to the appellate stage. He explicitly accepts much of Frank's demonstration of 'fact uncertainty', but neatly, though not very convincingly, avoids the problem by noting that the appellate court deals with a 'frozen record'.[36]

Frank on the other hand self-consciously taking the 'what the courts do' perspective focuses his attention upon the trial courts and quite consistently observes an ever more profound degree of uncertainty. *But* his repudiation of 'prediction' is circumscribed: it is the repudiation of prediction in the natural science context — prediction in a broader sense, as an 'art' is the indispensable craft of the practitioner, but it should never be confused with or elevated to the level of science. To do more would be to return to the rigidities and formalism of traditional jurisprudence. This is fundamentally the same position that Llewellyn arrives at in *The Common Law Tradition*. Hence both Llewellyn and Frank start from the assertion of lack of certainty in law; while Frank's greater emphasis on the indeterminacy principle results in different emphases their positions are not as antithetical as has sometimes been suggested.

THE THEORETICAL FRAMEWORK OF AMERICAN REALISM

As indicated in the Introduction to this chapter the concern is with the nature and degree of American realism's contribution to a sociologically oriented approach to law. As a consequence it is not our concern simply to give an account of this juristic tendency, but rather to assess it in terms firstly of the explicitly 'sociological' jurisprudence associated with the name of Pound, and secondly in its connections with the self-conscious creation of a 'sociology of law' that arose in the United States after the Second World War. The concern with the 'theoretical framework' allows us to make a judgment upon the extent to which realism was 'sociological' and to determine the type and direction of that sociological content.

American realism was a movement without a clearly articulated theoretical foundation. There was a tendency to exhibit a distrust for theory. This hostility to theory is least evident in Llewellyn and we are therefore able to find a rather more coherent theoretical stance in his writings.

Since the Realists themselves failed consciously to articulate their theoretical premises it is necessary to proceed by attempting to reconstruct them. The problem is compounded by an explicit denial of a theoretical basis; thus even Llewellyn in his later years was still writing 'Realism is *not* a philosophy, but a technology . . . . What realism was, and is, is a method nothing more.'[37] This approach rests on the assumption, to be examined more fully later,[38] that it is possible to have a 'method' that exists independent of a theoretical basis. In addition however the intellectual context in which realism was generated to a considerable extent produced this atheoreticism. Realism was highly reactive and was drawn together as a movement around the negative bond of the attack on legal traditionalism. The jurists of the 1920s and 1930s were conscious that, despite the pioneering work of Holmes and Pound, of Brandeis, of Chipman Gray and Bingham,[39] little had changed in the general orientation of the majority of judges, legal practitioners and academics. As a consequence Realism started in a highly polemical context.[40] The radical debunking facet of Realism was manifested in the ventures into the production of satirical journals, the *Harvard Law Revue* and the *Yale Law Jumble*. As a natural (but not a necessary) consequence 'the realist movement has suffered, like most evangelisms, from its own exaggerations.'[41]

The confrontation with legal traditionalism had the consequence of the Realists defining themselves negatively and resulted in a failure to elaborate the theoretical foundation upon which they might have built an alternative approach. This failure in some large measure accounts for the failure of the movement to coalesce into a 'school' and resulted in the process of decline and fragmentation that set in during the thirties. It was only Llewellyn in his more explicitly sociological work who manifests an awareness of theory.[42]

Realism and the positivist tradition
The corner-stone of the realist position was a positivist perspective.
> Lawyers, like the physical scientists, are engaged in the study of
> objective physical phenomena . . . . As lawyers we are interested in
> knowing how certain officials of society . . . have behaved in the past
> in order that we may make a prediction of their probable behaviour
> in the future.[43]

Their position is not of a very sophisticated character, reflecting a strong
orientation to a model of the social sciences based narrowly on the natural
sciences which are presumed to be largely inductive in their methods. It
may be noted, pending further elaboration,[44] that this positivism leads
directly into behaviouralism.

   Their positivism is also very closely related to the basic 'what the courts
do' definition of law so commonly utilised by the Realists. It accounts in
large part for the accusations that have been levelled at them that they
neglected the normative character of law. This criticism largely misses the
point since what the Realists were concerned with was not to deny the
import of rules, but rather to achieve a value neutrality that they felt was
necessitated by their efforts to emulate the natural sciences. One therefore
finds Llewellyn saying that the Realists 'want to check ideas, and rules and
formulas by facts, to keep them close to facts.'[45] What is clear is that
there is none of the strict positivism of Durkheim; the relationship
between 'norms' and 'facts' is skated over by saying that they must be
'kept close' with no consideration of the implications of this injunction
nor of how it is to be achieved. It results in him taking a surprisingly
narrow view of the sociological approach. He suggests that a 'sociologist is
content to see and describe what happens';[46] and to argue that realism is
'a descriptive sociology of law.'[47]

The realist model of society
The Realists operated with a model of society that bears very close
resemblance to that which underlies Pound's interest theory.[48] It utilises
an 'economic man' construct relying on some of the traditional concepts
of classical political economy, in particular the notion of 'scarce resources'
which is applied beyond the purely economic field. Human societies are
viewed as constituted of individuals acting through the agency of groups
which advance wants and desires which are asserted as interests. The
interests, asserted as 'claims', cannot all be fulfilled since social as well as
economic 'resources' are scarce. Llewellyn argues that
> law operates under the principle of scarcity. The energy available for
> social regulation at any time and place is limited . . . . Because of this
> fact, control by law takes on the aspect of engineering. We require
> . . . to invent such machinery as, with least waste, least cost and least
> unwanted by-products, will give most nearly the desired result.[49]

The perspective is thus a form of social utilitarianism. While in the other social sciences this position was in retreat by the twentieth century it appears in an unqualified and uncritical form in the writings of the Realists. Its significance is that it lends itself to a functionalist interpretation which as will be seen is particularly pronounced in Llewellyn.[50]

This economic model reflects the considerable influence, particularly on Llewellyn, of William Graham Sumner, the social Darwinist.[51] Whilst at Yale, where Sumner's influence was still strong, Llewellyn formed many of his sociological ideas. He very soon discarded the more mechanical evolutionism, but his continuing influence is attested by the fact that he, and for that matter Frank, refers more frequently to Sumner than to any other sociologist. It is significant that in the other social sciences the social Darwinist legacy was already being discarded whilst among lawyers turning towards the social sciences this should still have a substantial influence. It may also be observed that there exists an important intellectual congruence between the economic model of society, social Darwinism and utilitarianism.

Utilising the scarce resources model leads to a stress upon law as a distributive mechanism. The social cake (economic and social) is conceived as being of fixed size; the groups within society press their claims either to have a slice or to have a bigger slice. The law plays a part in guiding the hand of the carver, not so much in determining the size of the slices but at least in ensuring that this be done in accordance with some known principles.

The Realists take this equilibrium model and within that framework lay considerable stress on the fact of social change. While Pound's work constantly revolves around the 'change versus stability' polarity they bring change even further into the foreground. The extent, both quantitatively and qualitatively, of social change is such that their social model is one of a changing equilibrium, that is a dynamic equilibrium model. Despite the massive social and economic upheavals of the period they did not seem to doubt that the basic social equilibrium could be maintained. Their confidence in the manageability of social change is a reflection of the pervading faith in the efficacy of human effort derived from the pragmatic philosophical basis.

The utilisation of an interest theory within the context of an equilibrium model results in the Realists adopting a pluralistic perspective. Social groups compete in advancing their claims although some are stronger and better organised; they are perceived as operating within a competitive market situation. They were prepared to recognise that a more active intervention, whether by the state or the judiciary, was necessary to give a fairer weighting to the claims of certain groups; yet in essence they saw the existing social order as capable of giving adequate recognition to the competing social groups. Llewellyn for example asserted that unless a social system was able to resolve competing claims 'the group or society blows up or dribbles apart or starves or perishes in civil conflict.'[52] He is committed to an equilibrium model with a pluralistic content in which inherent antagonistic conflict is logically incompatible with the social model adopted.

This position is reflected in the political positions they adopted. They were almost exclusively liberal, with a pronounced tendency to favour the Democratic Party, witnessed by their substantial participation in the administration of New Deal agencies. None of them explicitly adopted a degree of radicalism that took them outside the rather limited two-party structure of American political life. Certainly the majority would have wished to tip the fulcrum of the social equilibrium towards the disadvantaged, whether it be labour, the poor or the ethnic minorities; but none challenged the ability of the capitalist social system to resolve these problems.[53]

Realism as functionalism
One of the most distinctive features of American realism is the functionalist stance that was adopted. This trend to functional analysis was already asserting itself in the broad field of American sociology in the 1930s.[54] Its root lies in the instrumentalist position adopted, of viewing law as a means to an end. This is stressed by Llewellyn as being one of the key common characteristics of Realism.[55] The adoption of this position provided a happy release from the formalistic debate which has dominated traditional jurisprudence about the 'definition of law' which Llewellyn and Frank in particular came to regard as sterile. The instrumentalist orientation also served to assert their concern with a 'contextual approach' to law, that is its relation to the wider social structure. Further instrumentalism is very much in keeping with their anxiety to be practical, to orientate themselves to the needs of practitioners. Beyond this it assisted them in escaping from the narrow normative approach of traditional jurisprudence by allowing attention to be focused upon the consequences of law for social behaviour.

From an instrumentalist position it is a short, but nevertheless decisive and to some degree an irrevocable step, to functionalism. It is significant that a fairly explicit functionalism was common to the major figures of the movement. As will be illustrated it is central to Llewellyn's work. In Frank the whole discussion of the 'basic legal myth' and the associated 'legal magic' is couched in terms of an examination of their functional consequences for the legal system. Again Thurman Arnold's concern with the role of symbolism within legal institutions is consciously functionalist. Felix Cohen with his very close proximity to the Realists went as far as to renounce the realist label and to elaborate a 'functional jurisprudence'.

Llewellyn's functionalism becomes more conscious and articulate as his work develops. As early as *The Bramble Bush* his functionalism becomes explicit. At this stage he presents a fairly simple model in which law has a dual function; firstly conflict resolution, and secondly conduct guidance or channelling. 'The court decision reaches out beyond the individual case and enters into moulding and channelling the action of the community.'[56] The former function is clearly seen at this stage as primary, its primacy being captured in his analogy of law as 'the maintenance department of society'. This generalised concern with function expresses itself sharply in the major paper 'A realistic jurisprudence − the next step'.

I have argued that the trend of the most fruitful thinking about law has run steadily towards regarding law as an engine . . . having purposes, not values in itself.[57]

The functionalism becomes more developed as he turned his interest towards legal anthropology. The dual influence of Sumner and Weber focused his interest upon 'primitive law'. It became more specific under the impact of Malinowski's *Crime and Custom*.[58] His dissatisfaction with the generality of Malinowski's work and its many unasked and unanswered questions advanced his interest. During the early 1930s he supervised Adamson Hoebel's graduate studies and doctorate on the law-ways of the Comanche. In 1935 they adopted the joint project which was to materialise as *The Cheyenne Way*.[59] While Hoebel did virtually all the field work,[60] Llewellyn's contribution, and it was a major one, was to devise the 'theory of investigation' and was responsible for the general theoretical and jurisprudential matrix within which the field work was placed. 'This was a meeting of realistic jurisprudence and functional anthropology.'[61]

The Cheyenne Way is arguably the most important work to have been produced by Llewellyn. That contention is certainly true if importance is to be assessed in terms of the resulting intellectual impact. The 'trouble case' method,[62] the observation of what other cultures do about disputes, which they pioneered against the normative approach which largely contented itself with asking for verbal formulations of rules, remains the primary method in legal anthropology. This influence finds its clearest expression in the work of Max Gluckman[63] and of Bohannan.[64]

Aside from its importance in the development of legal anthropology *The Cheyenne Way* also constitutes an important advance in Llewellyn's formulation of his functionalist theory. This theory takes the form of 'the law-jobs theory'.[65] The law-jobs theory emerges in its basic form at this stage although it underwent some subsequent development.

The law-jobs theory is one about 'society as a whole'. For human groups and societies to survive there are certain basic needs that must be met; it is within this context that the wants and desires of individuals and groups, their 'divisive urges', assert themselves. The conflicts produced are inevitable but are at the same time inimical to group survival. Hence conflict resolution and prevention are a pre-condition for group survival. These necessary tasks are more broadly conceived than the earlier formulations about 'conflict-settlement'; they express themselves as six 'law-jobs' which term is employed as shorthand for 'functions of law'. These functions include the disposition of trouble cases and the preventive channelling and orientation of conduct, but go on to include, for example, the allocation of authority. Also included are 'law-jobs' of extreme generality, for example 'the net organisation of the group or society *as a whole* to provide cohesion, direction and incentive'. The law-jobs then are conceived as imperative necessary conditions for 'groupness'.

> The law-jobs entail such arrangement and adjustment of people's behaviour that the society (or the group) remains a society (or a group) and gets enough energy unleashed and coordinated to keep on functioning as a society (or as a group).[66]

As he develops the law-jobs theory its functionalism becomes more extreme; the law-jobs are presented as universal, applicable and necessary to all groups and to all societies.

> The law-jobs are in their bare bones fundamental, they are eternal.[67]

Llewellyn thereby, apparently unwittingly, stumbles into a major theoretical deficiency of functionalism of imposing on disparate phenomena, from different societies and different historical periods, an *a priori* unity.

The law-jobs theory is embellished with a collection of related concepts, such as 'law-ways' (behaviour, practice or conduct involved in the fulfilment of law-jobs),[68] 'law-stuff' (any phenomena in the culture which relates discernibly to the legal).[69] His fifth law-job is that of 'juristic method' which involves the ways, the mechanisms and the institutions through which the law-jobs get done. As he develops his theory this function becomes more specific and comes to occupy an increasingly important role within the theory as a whole. By the time he wrote 'Law and the social sciences'[70] he is discussing the 'law-work' or 'law-craft' that operates within the institutions to fulfil the other law-jobs.

This concern with 'craftsmanship' in law provides a major mediating theme in Llewellyn's work. His exuberance and enchantment with the 'success' of the Cheyenne in resolving trouble cases is thereby linked with his espousal of the 'Grand Style' as the appropriate craft technique for appellate judging under contemporary social conditions for which he argues mightily in *The Common Law Tradition*. In a very significant sense his elaboration of a theoretical edifice, which comes to place increasing significance on the craft of judging, comes full circle back to the traditional concerns of jurisprudence. The concern with the 'judicial process' has been central in Anglo-American jurisprudence and his self-conceived major work *The Common Law Tradition* is devoted exclusively to its study, indeed is even narrowed down to a consideration of the appellate judicial function. It is not therefore that there is any break or fundamental departure in his work, but rather that his concern with the elaboration of a theoretical framework leads him back to a concern, albeit in a new guise and with a new conceptual framework, with the most traditional of jurisprudential questions.

There is a further facet to the evolution of the law-jobs theory.

Included in its early formulation[71] is reference to the institutional structure within which law-jobs are developed. But he comes to strengthen this aspect by explicitly advancing an 'institutional' analysis. The institution is conceived as 'organised activity, activity organised around the cleaning up of some job.'[72] It is therefore a behavioural approach to the institution which he contrasts to the normative approach to institutions as exemplified in the sociology of Kluckholn and Talcott Parsons. It is very much within the positivist frame of reference; in essence what Llewellyn succeeds in doing is in translating Holmesian juristic positivism into sociological positivism.

Llewellyn added a further dimension in the late 1940s when he abandoned attempts to keep the law-job approach confined to the purely 'legal' and found it necessary to advance the 'law-government' concept since he found the law and governmental functions to be inseparable intertwined. He describes 'law-government' as follows:

> The chart picture of the single institution would be a long ellipse with two imaginary foci. The one focus (never found alone) would be complete regularity utterly independent of judgment or person; the other (never found alone, either) would be non-recurrent action determined utterly by the particular acting official's idiosyncratic and also non-habitual choice. The 'law' phases of law-government are closer to the first focus; the more purely 'government' phases are closer to the second.[73]

This was the closest that Llewellyn was ever to come to the elaboration of a general theoretical framework. It is significant that he never gave it a rounded presentation; a work under the title *Law In Our Society* which attempted this task was never completed for publication. Twining reports that shortly before his death he was again working on an attempted general theoretical presentation of his views.[74] The later period of his working life was concerned with two major projects. The first, which has contributed greatly to his reputation particularly in the United States, was his return to his early specialism in commercial law manifested in his major responsibility for the Uniform Commercial Code.[75] This project occupied him throughout the 1940s and into the early 1950s. The second major undertaking was the preparation and writing of *The Common Law Tradition*.

The Common Law Tradition remains Llewellyn's major jurisprudential work. Yet it is in many respects a very disappointing exercise. It is full of very real insight into the judicial process reflecting his considerable and diverse experience. It is the most sustained and substantiated indictment of traditional judicial ideology, the 'formal style'. It contains many potentially valuable ideas in particular the classification of the 'steadying factors' that promote 'reckonability' in the appellate judicial process. But, and indeed it is a very large 'but', the great disappointment is that it fails as an application of his broader theoretical perspective epitomised in the 'law-jobs theory'. By the time he wrote this study his theory existed in a fairly consistent form and one would have expected that it would have suffused and informed that work. What materialised was a very partial and uneven reflection of that theoretical position.

Instead of viewing the appellate function in terms of the wide perspective of the whole range of law-jobs he instead takes up only one facet, and that a traditional jurisprudential one namely the concern with craftsmanship in law. His illustration and commendation of the 'Grand style' is a plea for a conscious and articulated extension of a trend in appellate decision-making which he detects as characterising the contemporary appellate bench. What impresses him about the 'Grand style' is that it promotes reckonability while at the same time allowing for the creative utilisation, in the name of the humanisation and individualisation of justice, of the potentials for judicial creativity contained in the 'leeways of precedent'.

The Common Law Tradition in its failure to carry forward and apply his functional theory of law is the clearest evidence of the deficiencies of that theoretical position. Despite the considerable length of the book there is a complete failure to give any consideration to the interrelationship of the factors which impinge upon and determine the outcome of the judicial process and at the same time a virtual absence of consideration of the role of extra-legal factors on the decision-making process. This is the more surprising because a common core of the critique by both sociological jurisprudence and realism of traditional jurisprudence was of its formal rule-bound horizons and its failure to take cognisance of the extra-legal in the determination of the legal. Thus in a very real sense *The Common Law Tradition* was a renunciation of sociological jurisprudence in general and legal realism in particular. That judgment must be qualified by the proviso that from the work can be extracted and compiled an extremely useful essay on the development and role of judicial ideology.

A functionalist position is in some respects self-evident and all social sciences are at a general level necessarily functionalist. That phenomena are to be explored not as 'things in themselves' but through their effects and consequences and through their relationship with other facets of reality. But functionalism that goes beyond this level of generality, as does that adopted by the Realists and by Llewellyn in particular, gives rise to a number of deficiencies.

Functionalism is an analogy and as such it is a mechanical analogy. Thus for example few difficulties arise if we define the 'function' of a bicycle chain as being the transmission of motive power from pedals to wheels. But the relationships which subsist between social phenomena rarely have this simple cause and effect character. Hence to adopt the functional analogy often detracts from the central methodological problem of the social sciences, namely to grasp and be able to give expression to the complexity of the interaction and interrelationship between the constituents of the social totality.

This tendency to simplistic reduction is compounded by the fact that invariably the adoption of a functionalist perspective goes hand in hand with the utilisation of an equilibrium model. Functionalists can and do differ amongst themselves as to the degree of stability they posit for the social equilibrium. Thus for example with reference to the Realists contrast the positions of Frank and Llewellyn. Yet all rests upon the dubious assumption that there is detectable some optimum functioning of the social system, or a part thereof, which is essential to the preservation of that equilibrium. Any departure from that optimum balance is regarded as producing negative consequences for the stability or preservation of the system as a whole. Hence the application of a functionalist perspective tends to import some preconception of how the system ought to operate.

The further and more unacceptable consequences of the functionalist position is that it renders analysis static. His suggestion for example that a society could 'blow up' or otherwise perish implies that the operation at an optimum level of the legal order becomes a necessary condition for the survival of the whole.[76] Hence every facet of the present is seen as necessary and inevitable and social change is consequently perceived as potentially destructive. There exists therefore a certain conflict and inconsistency between his functionalism and his otherwise strong emphasis upon the significance of social change for the legal system. Further the universalism claimed by functionalism is an unsupported assertion which carries the dangerous implication of being likely to result in the misleading imposition of uniformity upon the diversity of social reality.

In the final analysis he ends up by not advancing upon the sociological jurists. He did not achieve more than giving vent to the desire for a view of law in its social context. The realisation of that aim, with the major exception of *The Cheyenne Way*, eluded Llewellyn.

Behaviouralism in American realism

The whole of the realist movement had a pronounced leaning towards behaviouralism. At root this tendency shares common bonds with positivism and functionalism. Therefore the behaviouralist content of realism had a marked impact on their theoretical perspective and the methodology adopted. But its consideration has a further and more substantial importance in the context of this study. The contention will be developed that the importance of Realism to the emergence of contemporary sociology of law lies in its historical role as a bridge between generalised sociological jurisprudence and the very pronounced behaviouralism that characterises a major tendency in contemporary American sociology of law.

Within the corpus of the realist movement behaviouralism manifests itself at two levels. The first, the more general, is the advocacy of a behaviour orientation to the study of law. The second, and more specific, is the adoption of a specific methodology of enquiry.

The general 'behaviour orientation' is found in the majority, if not all, of the Realists. Thus Llewellyn argues 'the focus of study . . . should now be consciously shifted to the area of contact, of interaction between official behaviour and the behaviour of those affected by official regulatory behaviour.'[77] Similarly Yntema asserts 'the most (not the only) significant aspect of the relations of law and society lie in the field of behaviour.'[78] Herman Oliphant is even more overtly behaviouristic in arguing that judicial decisions should be viewed as 'responses to the stimuli of the facts of concrete cases.'[79] Jerome Frank attacks legal formalism that finds its expression in the insistence that decisions are a result of the application of rules to facts which he reduces to 'Rules' x 'Facts' = 'Decision'; he substitutes a behaviour model, 'Stimuli' x 'Judge's Personality' = 'Decision'.

The general realist movement contained a grouping who took the behavioural approach further. This group was in the main composed of those who broke away from the Columbia Law School in 1928.[80] It included Herman Oliphant, William Douglas and, to a lesser extent, Hessel Yntema. But the individual from the same stable who took the behaviouralist approach furthest was Underhill Moore. Moore, particularly in his collaboration with Callahan,[81] wrote under the influence of behaviouristic psychology.[82] Their most famous study was of the impact of driving and parking ordinances upon motorist behaviour in New Haven under conditions that approached those of a controlled experiment. The work was based on the premise that 'a proposition of law is nothing more than a sense-object which may arouse a drive and cue a response.'[83] The purpose of the work was not so much to establish any causal theory of motorist behaviour, but to demonstrate that human conduct as affected by legal regulation is susceptible to measurement in quantitative form.

The study itself goes very much further than did other Realists in the search for an empirically grounded approach to the study of legal phenomena. The authors assembled an impressive mass of statistical data yet it is by no means certain that they produced a method of study that has wider applicability. The real danger of the methodological position adopted is that it can result in the approach being reduced to a narrow empiricism.[84] Yet these works were undoubtedly influential on a new generation of behaviouralists, particularly those working in the field of judicial behaviour.

> When one compares the assumptions and concepts of contemporary legal behavioralism with those of the realists one is struck by the amazingly similarity.[85]

The proximity between the Realists and modern behaviouralism is very forceably demonstrated by their mutual concern, even perhaps obsession, with prediction. The strictures of behavioural methodology tend to shy away from causal explanation and, as part of the wider utilitarian tradition, to be concerned with the production of 'useful results.'[86]

METHODOLOGY OF AMERICAN REALISM

The Realists give much greater emphasis to 'method' than had been usual amongst jurists and certainly more so than the sociological jurists. What realism was, and is, is a method nothing more.[87]
If the Realists were so insistent on the importance of method then some premium must be attached to trying to establish what that method was. Llewellyn presented it as follows:

> The only tenet involved is that the method is a good one; 'see it fresh', 'see it as it works' — that was to be the foundation of any solid work.[88]

The formulation is singularly unhelpful and uninformative; who would wish, or for that matter be able, to deny that they wished to 'see it fresh' or to 'see it as it works'? If that is all there is to the realist method then we are all Realists.

There is a continual assertion by the Realists of the Holmesian dictum to see law in action. But again, who will deny the importance of law in action? One needs no specific label to espouse such a cause. The explanation of the banality of such formulations of the 'realist method' lies in their reaction against legal traditionalism.

Since the Realists founded themselves on what, through contemporary eyes at least, is such an unexceptional premise it may be useful to examine where this 'method' led them. The answer must take account of the internal differences within the movement. As has been observed above it took some, Underhill Moore in particular, to a relatively formal and rigorous behavioural methodology. For the majority, under the influence of 'scientism' and full of the zeal to found a 'legal science', it resulted in nothing more than a general advocacy of an empirical approach. This was in part induced by the feeling of relative intellectual insecurity that jurists in the vocationally oriented world of law. The general desire to be useful led the Realists, afflicted with the Anglo-American obsession with the judicial process, to the objective of prediction. It is not that prediction is not worthwhile, but that if it is confined within a narrow empirical approach it becomes a substitute for the quest for 'explanation'.

The empiricism implied in the general orientation of Realism, coupled with positivism, led the Realists to desire 'hard facts' as the necessary raw material for legal enquiry. Thus for example Yntema in discussing the preconditions for the creation of 'legal science' places primary emphasis upon the need for more and better 'judicial statistics'.[89] As a consequence a vast amount of intellectual energy was burnt up in the collection of data.

The central deficiency of empiricism is not that the collection and utilisation of factual data is in itself undesirable; indeed such activity is a necessary condition for the development of social science method. But the empiricists believe incorrectly that it is a *sufficient* condition. Data collection becomes an end in itself; it becomes a purposeless and undirected activity. In brief this is how the energy of the majority of the Realists came to be absorbed. This was particularly true of those who came together to form the nucleus of the short-lived John Hopkins Institute for the Study of Law.[90] The Institute was established in 1928 but was one of the first victims of the cutting off of academic finance as a result of the Great Crash. Short-lived though the Institute was the characteristics of its work were clear. It embarked on a programme of empirical studies of judicial administration in Maryland, Ohio and New York State. These studies did not go much beyond the compilation of judicial statistics despite the Institute's professed objective of concern with the 'human effects of law'.[91] Another group of Realists centred on Yale working in collaboration with the interdisciplinary Institute of Human Affairs produced further empirical studies.[92]

All that may be said of these studies, which both individually and collectively failed to make any marked impact, is that the Realists may be credited with having made the use of statistics and statistical method a regular and accepted part of the study of legal phenomena.[93] In adopting a rather narrow empiricism the Realists were in keeping with a general trend throughout the social sciences, and in particular sociology, during the period.

Llewellyn himself never became an empiricist. The nearest he came to it was his study on divorce.[94] While he did use some statistical data the articles as a whole are a rather strange mixture of statistical, descriptive and intuitive analysis. As Twining comments 'his own natural tendency was towards intuitive and commonsense 'realism' rather than to 'scientific' research.'[95] This caution with respect to scientific method arises from his strictures on the impossibility of a direct application of 'natural science' method in the formulation of the social sciences. He characterised social, and therefore legal, studies as being at a 'pre-scientific' stage and at one point designates them as 'pre-pre-scientific'.

It is therefore difficult to put one's finger on anything that is distinctively the 'Llewellyn method'. He was an exponent of common-sense, of 'horse-sense', as being the means to achieve the Realist objective of 'seeing it fresh'. What he practised was a brand of non-empirical empiricism in which intuitive and descriptive techniques dominate. This is in reality the absence of method rather than a method. Yet the contradiction remains that throughout his writings he maintained an explicit advertence to method; thus for example alongside the advocacy of 'horse-sense' is an insistence on the need for 'conscious toolmaking'[96] and for 'sound theory' in general. His reluctance to apply a more rigorous approach is revealed in his observation that 'I must come up with tools of analysis which any thinking man of law can understand both in their nature and in their use.'[97] It is this subservience to the stage of development of the legal profession in general, and the ever present desire to be 'useful' that gives rise to the self-restriction inherent in the above quotation.

His most important and developed application of method is to be found in *The Cheyenne Way*. The development and application of the 'trouble case method' had, as already observed, a profound impact on legal anthropology. The method is consistent with his general theoretical perspective. The occurrence of 'conflict' within a social group or a society imposes the necessity for a mechanism exhibiting regularity and authority to intervene to mitigate the danger to the social equilibrium. The 'trouble case' is explicitly referred to, not as the everyday run-of-the-mill conflict, but as the difficult case; 'the trouble case is the case of doubt where the normative system is being stretched.'[98] While the 'trouble case' has important attributes, which have been widely recognised, the method is not without problems. It produces a certain tendency to focus attention on the first of the 'law-jobs' i.e. conflict resolution and the fifth, the 'juristic method', and in so doing distracting attention from the other functions of law. If one concentrates attention upon the 'trouble case', the difficult problematic case and ignores the routine, it is the latter which in the main can be expected to contribute most to and to be most revealing about the general character of the normative system. The 'trouble case method' is therefore the perpetuation of the 'upper court myth'; that is it treats the exceptional and ignores the average, the majority of conflicts and their consequences. Despite these strictures this method stands out as his most distinctive contribution in the field of method.

What emerges is his consciousness of problems of methods, some genuine constructive thought in the field but overall a pervading sense of looseness and eclecticism pervading his work as a whole. This characteristic is repeated with reference to the use he makes of contemporary developments in sociology. There is evidence that he read widely in the disciplines of sociology and anthropology. He did not derive any distinctive sociological orientation while at the same time he felt justified in attacking sociological jurisprudence as 'bare of most that is significant in sociology.'[99]

He was undoubtedly influenced by Weber and much of his concept formation and exposition is in the 'ideal type' method.[100] Similarly his definition of law presented in *The Cheyenne Way* has a distinctively Weberian flavour.

> As soon as the course of behaviour shows, recognisably, authority in procedures or persons for cleaning up trouble cases, or authority in standards whose infraction is met not only by action, but by action carrying the flavour of the *pro tanto* official, at that point peculiar institutions called 'legal' have become perceptible in the group or culture.[101]

He admitted his work was 'peculiarly indebted'[102] to both Weber and Sumner and in *The Common Law Tradition* acknowledges also the influence of David Reisman. His utilisation of the concept 'institution' is directly sociological in formulation and application; so also does the discussion of judicial office throughout *The Common Law Tradition* bear marks of familiarity with sociological 'role theory'.

Thus while Llewellyn was undoubtedly the most accomplished and wide-ranging of the Realists he never succeeds in formulating and applying a theoretical structure which can be said to amount to a systematic sociology of law. Indeed in some important respects he moves gradually away from such a possibility. His early 'law-jobs' theory had at least the merit of theoretical comprehensiveness, but by the end of his career, although still toying with the idea of further elaborating a theoretical synthesis, his sociological features are limited to the presentation of a 'theory of the crafts of law'.

WHAT PRICE REALISM?

The realists have been considered here as a mediation between the juristically oriented sociological jurisprudence of the earlier part of the century and the more recent development of sociology of law as a specialism. That they were an important link is demonstrated by the proximities between contemporary trends and key facets of Realism in particular the pronounced functionalism and behaviouralism of Realism. What is much less certain is whether, aside from providing a link, the Realists made any distinct substantive contribution.

In some respects realism represents a retreat from the achievements of Pound's sociological jurisprudence. The latter succeeded in elaborating a theoretical framework which allowed investigation of multiple facets of legal phenomena to be integrated within this general theory. The nearest comparable achievement by the Realists was Llewellyn's 'law-jobs' theory; but this theory he himself, with the exception of *The Cheyenne Way*, never applied as a whole nor was it taken up and used consciously by others. Indeed the extreme functionalism of his theory made such a sustained application improbable. For while functionalism was the dominant mode of American sociological thought spanning the Second World War it fell increasingly into disfavour thereafter.

Further the Realists exhibit a contradiction nowhere more clearly expressed than in Llewellyn himself. They were much more strident than their predecessors in calling for a scientific base to legal science as part of the wider social sciences. Yet faced with the difficulties implicit in the working out of what constitutes a 'scientific' approach to social phenomena they lapsed into a facile scientism, namely empiricism. Yet even in this they were not consistent and their empiricism was rarely very rigorous or sustained.

Neither realism nor sociological jurisprudence succeeded in breaking out of the dominating preoccupations of the juristic traditions from which they emerged the central feature of which was the obsessive concern, within Anglo-American juristic thought, with the judicial process.

Despite their failure to generate, and then to operate, through a consistently sociological perspective the Realists had a very substantial impact upon legal scholarship and legal education. Their onslaught on legal formalism, as part of a generalised 'revolt against formalism',[103] consolidated the efforts of earlier sociologically oriented jurists. Realism marked the 'final victory' over legal formalism in the field of jurisprudence. Jurisprudence since the 1930s while for example still remaining predominantly in either the analytical or natural law tradition no longer operates in the isolated and metaphysical world of pure law. Thus for example important figures like Morris Cohen and Lon Fuller while hostile to the Realists in very many respects adopt axiomatically a law-in-action, law-in-society perspective.[104] In a very real sense we *are* all Realists now if only in the most general context of recognising the need to view law in its social context.

Their impact on legal education is no less important. The overwhelming adherence to the 'cases and materials' method is very firmly established and is a direct legacy of the Realists though the mere adoption of the form does not necessarily mean that the substance of legal education has changed markedly from the Langdellian case study method. The absence of a realist camp in English jurisprudence may be a contributory factor in explaining the absence of any similar changes in English legal education.

The overall substantive contribution of the Realists are not in themselves of very great historical importance. Though they appeared very polemical and iconoclastic at the time they can in perspective be seen as part of a longer trend that resulted in the break with the traditionalism of nineteenth century British and American legal thought. The specific contribution of the Realists to the development of sociology of law was that in articulating this revolt against formalism they utilised, albeit patchily and inconsistently, the materials and methods of the social sciences. Their espousal of empirical methods, their functionalism and behaviouralism created the base, in association with parallel developments in the other social sciences, upon which modern American sociology of law has developed.

4 Emile Durkheim–Towards A Sociology of Law

INTRODUCTION

Sociology is like a river. It self-evidently exists and it moves. But as with a river its source is illusive and challenging. This is even more evident when our subject is not sociology as such but one of its sub-divisions, the sociology of law. Sociology as an area of enquiry emerged out of political and social philosophy. A similar historical indeterminacy exists with reference to the sociology of law. It would be perfectly legitimate to trace its subject matter and its concerns to classical political philosophy in the persons of Hobbes or Locke or Rousseau. It would be even easier to trace its geneology to Montesquieu with his very specific treatment of law.

Fascinating though the quest for sources may be there is a way in which this quest can become the pursuit of an object that continually retreats into the past. Tempting though this enquiry may be there is a sound realism that insists that a subject is not to be defined exclusively by its origins. Without therefore wishing to deny that many of the common objects of enquiry for both jurisprudence and sociology of law can be located in the traditions of political philosophy, we may follow the injunction of realism.

Durkheim is unambiguously a major sociological figure, but significantly his work provides a bridge backwards to social philosophy. He is also the first amongst the sociologists to devote substantial attention to law as a social phenomenon. We do not therefore need to assert that he was the originator of sociology of law; it is sufficient that he provides us with a substantive sociological treatment of law.

Durkheim remains an undisputed giant amongst social scientists. His influence has been such that the development of sociological thought in the twentieth century would be impossible to relate without reference to his contribution. His major significance lies in the fact that he demarcates more sharply than his predecessors the parameters of sociology as a distinct and autonomous field of intellectual enquiry.

The main purpose of this chapter is to consider how far his thought may be considered as developing, or contributing towards the development of, a sociology of law. It is possible to show that he gave considerable attention to law; this treatment is not only of quantitative significance, but it will be argued it is qualitatively important in his general sociological theory. But in order to make his treatment of law more accessible it is necessary to commence by setting it in 'the context of his general sociology. It is necessary to do so because the consideration of law does not constitute a neat and self-contained area in his work; it is not only spread widely throughout his diverse writings, but occupies an important role with the major concerns which motivate his sociology.

DURKHEIM'S SOCIOLOGY

Durkheim left behind him no general treatise on sociology. The titles of his major works indicate the very considerable range of subjects with which he dealt. Yet despite the diversity of his subject matter there exists a substantial unity to his thought. This unity is derived from his overriding and continuing concern with the nature and source of social cohesion or social integration. Running through all his works is a concern with the question: what is it about human society with its ever more complex interrelationships, structures and institutions which ensures not only its continuity and cohesion, but also its transformations? He manifests a persistent desire to account for the reality of the complex and arbitrary actions of individuals pursuing narrowly conceived individual ends but which nevertheless become welded into an entity which exhibits characteristics of stability and continuity. Simply, Durkheim's concern is with what holds society together; his object of inquiry is the social order.[1]

The explanation that he provides of the fascinating reality of 'society' changes considerably over the duration of his intellectual life yet the fundamental question which he poses remains the same. Durkheim's work manifests the continuing affirmation of the primacy of the 'social'.

Man is man only because he lives in society.[2]

It is within society that the reality of human existence is to be found.

Collective life is not born from individual life, but it is, on the contrary, the second which is born of the first.[3]

This affirmation of the primacy of the social leads him to adopt a consistently anti-individualist approach. Much of his first major work *Division of Labour* is given over explicitly to an attack upon Spencer, but it is one that we may read as a general critique of all individualist thought.

He insisted that it was impossible to explain the evolution of human society by reference for example to the desire of men for 'progress' since these apparently isolated, private ends are in fact social products. Alongside his emphasis upon the social stands the prevailing positivism of Durkheim's thought. Positivism marked an important stage in the development of the social sciences and its major premise is the very assertion that it is possible, that is logically or methodologically, to speak of social *science*. What was asserted was the possibility of scientific study of society. Espousing the cause of scientific method he insists upon the social sciences basing themselves upon the study of data that has an objective reality, that exists independent of the consciousness of the observer. Yet a social scientist who interprets this restriction as encompassing only material subjects would render it extremely difficult to say anything meaningful about social reality. Some of the more extreme variants of positivism have taken this approach and sought to explain social phenomena in ecological or biological terms. Indeed Durkheim's early work, with its emphasis upon morphological factors exhibits certain of these characteristics; for example the use of the forms of 'density' in accounting for the evolution of the division of labour exhibits a marked degree of naturalism.

However the characteristic of people as conscious, sentient beings largely invalidates all approaches which take no cognisance of this element. Yet once conceded that any understanding of human society requires the recognition of human consciousness and self-consciousness it is but a short step to a purely subjective, and hence introspective, analysis. Durkheim insists upon the possibility of defining a subject matter for sociology which encompasses non-material 'reality', yet which at the same time meets the criteria of scientific objectivity. In so doing he makes what is perhaps his most distinctive and enduring contribution to sociological positivism. His positivism is contained within the injunction: 'The first and most fundamental rule is: consider social facts as things.'[4] This methodological prescription is of such importance to his subsequent treatment of legal phenomena that it is necessary to elaborate upon it more fully. A social fact is to be distinguished by two features, its autonomous existence and its coercive power. Thus he defines social facts as 'ways of acting, thinking, and feeling, external to the individual, and endowed with a power of coercion, by reason of which they control him.'[5] The coercive character of social facts is to be found in the fact that their violation is met with sanctions, or at least resistance. Law constitutes a paramount example of a 'social fact' since it manifests both externality and constraint and, as will be demonstrated, explains in large measure the attention that Durkheim gives to law.[6]

Durkheim's methodology is based upon an epistemology that asserts that in studying a social phenomenon we must search for its 'observable manifestations'.[7] This leads him to adopt the proposition that it is necessary in order to study some social phenomena to approach them indirectly through some visible intermediary. The importance of this methodological device will become apparent when we discuss the role that the analysis of legal phenomena played in *Division of Labour*.[8] For Durkheim law was a 'visible symbol' and this in large measure accounts for the attention which he devoted to its study.

One further important implication of his concept of 'social fact' is that it provides him with a mechanism for bridging the gulf that divides the natural and social sciences. It provides him with a means of coping with the 'subjective' in social action. He defines the major manifestations of the subjective or mental element, namely values, sentiments and opinions, as 'social facts' and hence capable of objective, scientific treatment on the grounds that they exercise constraint upon social behaviour. Durkheim, consistent with his anti-individualism, focuses attention on the collective aspects of these 'social facts'. He endows shared values, sentiments, and opinions with an autonomous existence that is independent of the individual bearer; they are 'collective representations'.

> Society is not a mere sum of individuals. Rather the system formed by their association represents a specific reality which has its own characteristics.[9]

If society exists in its own right, independent of the individuals who constitute it, so too do the ideas and values. Thus he introduces his famous concept 'conscience collective'.[10] He also relies heavily on the notion of 'collective representations'. Apart from stressing their general importance in his sociology, two particular aspects of these concepts need to be emphasised.

Firstly they manifest what may be characterised as the reification of society by Durkheim. Starting with the positivistic premises indicated above he succeeds in reifying society, but he goes considerably beyond this; not only does society have an autonomous existence but it also has an independent power over individuals.

> The individual finds himself in the presence of a force which is superior to him and before which he bows.[11]

> Society commands us because it is exterior and superior to us.[12]

In his later works the reification of society becomes transformed into a tendency to deify the state. He produces a brand of statism in which the citizen is enjoined to fulfil a duty of obedience to the state as the embodiment of society.[13] Yet his statism is not a return to conceptions of an absolutist state; it bears much closer resemblances to Weber's authoritarian version of democracy; the state is presented as a specialised agency 'qualified to think and act instead of and on behalf of society.'[14]

Secondly we find that his treatment of the 'conscience collective' reveals itself with increasingly metaphysical trappings. He posits an existential reality that only just falls short of a 'group mind' concept:

> The group thinks, feels and acts quite differently from the way in

which its members would were they isolated.[15]

He frequently uses formulations such as 'the diffuse soul of society',[16] 'society thinks of itself',[17] 'collective thinking'.[18] Yet at the same time he recognises the dependence of the collective upon the individual. The result is that he ends up with the distinctly ambiguous formulation 'it is the aggregate which thinks, feels, wishes even though it can neither wish, feel nor act except through individual minds.'[19]

The reaction against individualism, especially against the economic individualism of classical political economy, leads him to identify the essence of the social in the existence of an ideological community.

> In short, social life is nothing but the moral milieu that surrounds the individual — or to be more accurate, it is the sum of the moral milieus that surround the individual. By calling them moral we mean that they are made up of ideas.[20]

Durkheim sets out with a strongly naturalistic position and in many instances comes close to materialism, but his attempt to pin down a social essence brings him to an unambiguously idealist position. Society exists only by virtue of the reality of common values, ideas and beliefs.

The general development of his thought, which has a marked bearing upon his treatment of law, departs from the more conventional positivism of *Division of Labour*. In this work he posits social solidarity as a product of changes in the morphological basis of society with the form of social solidarity thereby produced being reflected in the 'conscience collective', whereas, in his later works, the 'conscience collective' has achieved much greater autonomy and causal determinacy. Indeed it has *itself* become the foundation of social solidarity. Embodied in *The Elementary Forms of Religious Life*[21] and in *Moral Education*[22] is the quest for a new secular morality which will provide the foundation of social cohesion in the void resulting from the decline of religion in modern society.

It is this concern with social order and the means of securing social stability within modern society that has led a number of writers to stress the inherent conservatism of Durkheim's thought.[23] But this label of conservatism fails to capture the contradictory character of his position. He remained politically committed to 'modern society' founded upon an advanced division of labour and individualism. However the conditions for securing and advancing modern society always remained problematic and he was led to analyse the conditions of stability against the joint assault of anomie and the forced division of labour. It is the programme he put forward to ensure social integration, occupational groups as the bearers of the new secular morality, that links him to nineteenth century French conservatism.[24]

Another characteristic of his sociology is a persistent 'primitivist' reductionism; that is, the adoption of the view that, if the social scientist is able to study a social phenomenon as it exists in a primitive or simple society, his search for the essence or fundamentals of the phenomenon will be aided by the fact that it is likely to exist in such a form as to be more directly observable. The central or permanent characteristics will exhibit themselves unencumbered by the subsequent encrustations that arise in a complex society. This orientation explains his interest in primitive legal systems. Such a method of study lays itself open to serious objections. It rests on the assumption that the 'advanced' form of a social phenomenon is merely a more complex variant of its 'simple' predecessor. Such a thesis founders on the primary weakness of functionalism that implies the existence of a set of core or universal functions. While Durkheim avoids the worst reductionism of functionalism he cannot avoid an essentialism which rests upon a view of society as an ideological community existing as a system of shared values.[25]

DURKHEIM'S SOCIOLOGICAL ANALYSIS OF LAW

Introduction

Durkheim's interest in law is perhaps best characterised as tangential or indirect. He is not specifically interested in law for its own sake in the same way that he is for example interested in religion. He does not set out to develop a sociology of law. Yet it must not be thought that his treatment of law can be regarded as an unimportant or residual aspect of his work. His discussion is tangential in that he sees law as a prime example of the concretisation or objectification of social norms and values. Law is the example par excellence of the 'social fact'. Most of the illustrations he uses in *Rules* of the social fact are drawn from law. For Durkheim law is a visible symbol of all that is essentially social.

His consideration of law and legal phenomena is spread widely through-out his writings. Of particular importance is the study of the relationship between law and social solidarity in *Division of Labour*. In his method-ological treatise *Rules* he relies heavily on law to provide examples and analogies to support the framework of his method. In a number of places he gives considerable attention to the institution of contract particularly in *Professional Ethics*. The nature of crime is a recurring theme to be found in *Division of Labour*, *Rules* and *Suicide*[26] and receives specific and detailed treatment in 'Two laws of penal evolution'.[27] In addition the journal *Année Sociologique*, which he founded and edited, dealt with law, legal institutions and legal sociology right up to the outbreak of the First World War.[28]

Yet despite the considerable volume of Durkheim's writing on law it cannot be said to amount to a 'sociology of law'. His concern is not with elaborating a general framework or method for the sociological analysis of law; rather he used law to advance his more general sociological interests. However his interest in law resulted in the school that formed around him developing a considerable interest in the study of law as a social process.

The work of George Davy, Marcel Mauss and Maurice Hauriou was very much influenced by Durkheim. Many of his formulations and methods of presenting questions constitute an important background to subsequent debates and discussions. The two most obvious examples are the anthropological debate about 'primitive law',[29] and the criminological discussion about the nature of crime.

Law and social solidarity

Law plays an important role in Durkheim's first major work *The Division of Labour in Society*. In this book he sets out to explore the nature and origins of 'social solidarity' and the transformations it undergoes. In undertaking this study Durkheim was reacting explicitly against methodological individualism (particularly in its utilitarian form) and the notion that social 'progress' could be accounted for in terms of the pursuit of individual self-interest.

He was engaged in a debate with French socialism. Zeitlin is wrong in characterising this as being a 'debate with the ghost of Marx'.[30] What is true of Weber as a consequence of the influence of Marxism upon German social democracy is not true in the case of France where Marxism had only very limited influence during this period on French socialism. We find a whole number of points in *Division of Labour* and elsewhere at which he advances positions that almost have a Marxist flavour. The parallel with Marx is the desire to penetrate beneath consciousness to seek for structural or 'profound' causes. Beyond this the parallels are few. Politically Durkheim's general commitment to a meritocratic industrial capitalism separated him from Marx and led him to decry 'the sad conflict of classes'.[31] Thus Durkheim's notion of 'forced division of labour' bears close similarities with Marx's notion of 'class struggle'. Yet there is the profound difference; for Marx this was a natural and inevitable consequence of the division of labour, but for Durkheim it is an abnormal or pathological form to which he devoted little subsequent attention.

Whereas Marx pursued the analysis of the division of labour in terms of the development and transformation of social relations in the production of material life, Durkheim attributed some causal significance to certain morphological factors. Although these factors subsequently disappeared from his sociology the advance in the division of labour is in the first instance related to the increased 'moral density', that is to the increase in population and its greater concentration manifesting itself in a higher level of interaction outside of kinship systems.

Durkheim advances the thesis that human society produces two distinct forms of social solidarity, namely 'mechanical' and 'organic solidarity'. His types of solidarity are polar types. Yet he also sees them as part of an evolutionary continuum marking the distinction between primitive society, with a minimal division of labour, and advanced society, with a more extensive division of labour. At the same time he insists that any particular society in this evolutionary process contains within it elements of both forms of solidarity.

Mechanical solidarity is characteristic of simple societies with only a very limited division of labour. Society is characterised by a prevailing 'sameness' or 'likeness'. The members are completely enveloped in the similitude of activities and as a consequence share the same values and ideals. This uniformity of values and ideas constitutes the 'conscience collective'. Under mechanical solidarity 'collectivism' is highly developed and valued and 'individualism' is only weakly present and usually suppressed.

Organic solidarity is characterised by the existence of an advanced division of labour. The society thus formed is marked by 'interdependence' in which the economic and social activity of the society is highly specialised and in which complex patterns of mutual dependence exist. 'Sameness' thus gives way to 'differentiation'. The 'conscience collective' weakens and is replaced by differential moralities forming around different occupational categories, constituting what Durkheim called 'occupational morality'.[32] In his later works he presents these occupational moralities as playing a major role in providing the basis for the secular morality that is necessary for the maintenance of social cohesion after the eclipse of morality derived from religion. Collectivism declines and is replaced by individualism which is able to flourish amidst increased social tolerance resulting from the growth of 'mutual indifference'.[33]

Durkheim recognised that his types of social solidarity were extremely broad and did not lend themselves to exact observation. It was in his view necessary to find some more precise and measurable external symbol.

This visible symbol is law.[34]

> Indeed social life, especially where it exists durably, tends inevitably to assume a definite form and to organise itself, and law is nothing else than this very organisation in so far as it has greater stability and precision . . . . We can thus be certain of finding reflected in law all the essential varities of social solidarity.[35]

He provides us with the following general formulation of the relation between law and social solidarity.

> Since law reproduces the principal forms of social solidarity, we have only to classify the different types of law to find therefrom the different types of social solidarity which correspond to it.[36]

In his defence of his doctoral examination of *Division of Labour* he claimed that he had discovered a constant index of the division of labour in the legal system and that this relation was explored through 'purely scientific method'.[37]

Before turning to his classification of the different types of law it is worth noting that apart from this explicit utilisation of law as a tool for the observation of the central reality of social cohesion, his general method lends itself to a 'legalistic' formulation. His picture of society is that of the individual confronted by a system of exterior rules which exercise constraint upon his behaviour.

After asserting the general relationship between law and social solidarity he indicates his method of enquiry.

To proceed scientifically, we must find some characteristic which, while being essential to juridical phenomena, varies as they vary.[38]

The key variable that he selects is that of 'sanctions'. He argues that law exhibits two main types of sanctions. These he calls 'repressive' and 'restitutive' sanctions and on this basis he speaks of 'repressive' and 'restitutive law'.

Repressive law is characterised by the fact that its sanctions may be subsumed under the concept of punishment. It is synonomous with the more conventional designation criminal law (although he also includes within the concept certain elements of administrative law and what he loosely calls state law). Repressive law is associated with the existence of strong and enduring social sentiments; its violation gives rise to sanctions that impinge upon the fortune, liberty and life of the individual and also upon his honour. Since repressive law is diffuse its existence is not dependent upon the existence of any special judicial machinery but rather he sees it being enforced by the collective as a whole. In order to expound his concept of repressive law he embarks upon a protracted discussion of the nature of crime and punishment to which it will be necessary to return.[39] Restitutive law, 'consists only of *the return of things as they were*, in the re-establishment of troubled relations to their normal state.'[40] This category embraces all civil law, procedural law and most of administrative and constitutional law. We see that, while there are close parallels, he departs from the more conventional distinctions between civil and criminal law and between public and private law. This he does explicitly, for example, he rejects the utility of the distinction between public and private law. 'We believe that all law is public, because all law is social.'[41]

Restitutive law is concerned with the adjustment of social relations which arise from the differentiation of social labour. They are therefore not a product of the 'conscience collective', and hence do not involve the same strong sentiments. Thus there is no disgrace or loss of honour associated with the imposition of restitutive sanctions.

He further subdivides his classification of restitutive relations in that he distinguishes between negative and positive relations. Negative relations are concerned with 'abstention'; they reflect a form of social self-limitation and are particularly concerned with the relations between persons and things. Thus property law is negative and so also is tort law in that it is concerned not with the provision of any positive rights, but rather it consists of injunctions about 'not harming'.[42]

Positive relations differ in that they arise from cooperation and reflect that cooperation which is a necessary consequence of the division of labour.

The contract is, *par excellence*, the juridical expression of co-operation.[43]

Also added to this category are domestic and commercial law and further both procedural and administrative on the basis that they also reflect cooperation in that these aspects of law serve to fix the respective roles played by the parties in the social process.

The increased complexity and subdivision of restitutive law is consistent with his view that it corresponds to a higher stage of the division of labour. Both the substantive content and the machinery for its enforcement take on more specialised characteristics. He regards the development of restitutive law as being part of a process towards a 'law of positive cooperation'.

His application of the repressive-restitutive law dichotomy suggests a very direct, in fact a quantifiable, application. The method suggested is that 'it will suffice, in order to measure the part of the division of labour, to compare the number of juridical rules which express it with the total volume of law.'[44]

He is here presenting a model in which the two forms of social solidarity exist as ideal types; the particular position which any given society has reached lies on a continuum between the polar types. This position is to be determined by calculating the relative percentage or volume of repressive and restitutive law. He himself nowhere carries out this exercise. Neither does he provide any further methodological advice for such an undertaking. It is not a very clear instruction to the researcher to ask him to count the 'number of juridical rules'. Hidden within this superficially straightforward exercise are endless methodological problems; in particular it would be necessary to ensure that an efficient operational definition of law was found which allowed phenomena to be measured at the same level. For example many statutes contain a relatively small number of 'general' rules, but a much larger number of sections which stand in relation to that general rule are definitional, qualifying, limiting, etc. If one wished to count merely general rules it would be necessary to have available some criteria by which they could be extracted. Alpert, one of Durkheim's most consistent admirers, has attempted such an undertaking; basing himself on Durkheim's descriptive evidence he produces a table in which he tabulates the percentage composition of restitutive and repressive rules within a number of legal systems. The result is a typology of the stages of legal evolution which correspond broadly with Durkheim's stages of social evolution. But the connection is only of the most general character and the method does not constitute the precise method that Durkheim would appear to suggest.[45]

Durkheim posits a mirror image relationship between law and social solidarity. This rests upon the unsubstantiated assumption that law embodies the content of all normative systems and necessarily denies the possibility of conflict between legal norms and other normative systems; and such conflict could only be regarded as temporary and abnormal. It therefore follows that the use of law as an empirical index of social solidarity is a dubious undertaking.

Durkheim's evolutionary thesis of transition from repressive to restitutive law may also be assessed at the empirical level. To what extent does his model account for the known facts of the evolution of law? A cautionary note is necessary: the breadth of Durkheim's thesis invites an excursion into the wider debate about the evolution of law and legal systems. Attractive though such an invitation is, it is beyond the scope of the present concerns.

For convenience we may isolate three aspects of his thesis. Firstly to enquire whether it is valid to describe primitive law as 'repressive'. Secondly to assess whether the law of advanced societies marks a transition to restitutive law; and finally whether this is associated with a relative decline of repressive law.

His characterisation of primitive law as repressive has been at the centre of the anthropological debate about the nature of primitive law. We may deliberately avoid entering the debate about whether or not primitive societies can usefully and meaningfully be said to have 'law' before the emergence of legal institutions as such. If primitive societies have no 'law' then there can be no question of it being repressive. If however we admit the legitimacy of the concept 'primitive law' then it is clear that the overwhelming weight of currently available evidence runs against Durkheim. What may be termed the 'classical debate' in the anthropology of law involving Malinowski,[46] Hogbin,[47] Radcliffe-Brown[48] and Hoebel[49] went very much against Durkheim. The closest to Durkheim was Radcliffe-Brown with his emphasis on a distinction between 'public' and 'private' delicts.[50] The more recent contributions of such anthropologists as Gluckman,[51] Bohannan[52] and Pospisil,[53] while being anxious to stress the diversity of forms of primitive legal systems, offer no more support to Durkheim. Diamond has attempted to collate a large quantity of existing evidence; he argues that in the early stages of development repressive law was restricted to a very small number of offences such as incest. The general characteristic of early law is that of a regulated or semi-regulated system of private vengeance or feuding.[54]

Alpert attempted to rework Durkheim's empirical evidence and therefore relied exclusively on societies actually mentioned by Durkheim.[55] These show some support for Durkheim's thesis, but it is important to note that the majority of these societies are ones which exhibit fairly well developed state institutions. The evidence accumulated by Diamond[56] and the argument advanced by Seagle[57] indicates that the rise of repressive law can be associated with the emergence of economic class divisions and state forms after earlier pre-state stages of development which exhibit predominantly non-repressive forms of social regulation. This evidence cannot be regarded as providing any support for Durkheim since he himself repudiated any direct connection between stratification, the state and repressive law. He vastly overstates the role of repressive law in primitive societies.

The study of Schwartz and Miller brought together available anthropological data and subjected it to fairly sophisticated analytical techniques.[58] They argued that the form of primitive law and the nature of the sanctions relied upon were not very useful criteria. They contended that a comparison of legal development with institutional developments was more revealing and showed that forms of mediation and conciliation were characteristic of societies with the lowest division of labour. Again this evidence sharply contradicts the Durkheimian thesis. It may safely be concluded that the balance of evidence points to the fact that Durkheim was quite simply wrong in his characterisation of primitive law.

His contention that advanced societies exhibit restitutive law is less directly open to contention. There has occurred a very substantial advance in the volume and social significance of law relying on restitutive sanctions. The growth of restitutive law has taken the form of the development of new areas of legal regulation that were absent or underdeveloped in earlier stages. The most fundamental area of development is that which derives from the growth of property and its penetration into every sphere of social activity in more complex forms. The major expression of this development has been the expansion of contractual law, but it should be noted that this method of exposition focuses attention upon developments in substantive law. Yet his major contention relates to the changing form of legal sanctions. He posits a solution to the problem of the relation between form and substance at a very high level of generality by asserting an integration between form and substance with respect to changing types of social solidarity. What such an analysis leaves both unasked and unanswered is the nature of the process of mediation between form and substance, the way in which changes in specific social relations find legal expression which do not necessarily manifest a congruence between form and substance. Durkheim's thesis on the advance of restitutive law fails to provide an analysis of significant problems central to a theory of legal evolution; it is the omissions and the unasked questions that persist after an acceptance of the bare bones contention of the advance of restitutive law.

It is straightforward to point to a growth of restitutive law. It is less clear whether he saw this as an independent development or whether he sought to suggest that restitutive law actually replaced repressive law, that is whether a particular form of social activity is at one stage regulated by repressive law and at a higher stage of development becomes subject predominantly to restitutive law. If this construction is to be placed upon his thesis it is certain that he provides little or no supporting evidence.

Examples can be found, perhaps the most important being the general
abolition of penal sanctions for civil debt, but there does not appear to be
sufficient evidence to support a general pattern of substitution of penal by
restitutive sanctions.

At the most general level his theory posits a general advance of
restitutive law and a parallel decline of repressive law. The general
character of legal developments in advanced capitalist societies does
certainly indicate an increase in the volume of restitutive law, but it is less
obvious that repressive law has retreated. Changes in the forms and
severity of sanctions have taken place and certain traditional offences have
declined or ceased to exist. Yet an extension of the number and range of
offences carrying repressive, or at least non-restitutive, sanctions can be
pointed to. The analysis and classification of these new offences give rise
to some important questions which affect the Durkheimian analysis.

In some areas there has occurred an increase in the number of 'pure'
criminal offences, the most important area being that associated with the
increasing complexity of property in capitalist societies which has resulted
in an increase in offences concerned with the dishonest or fraudulent
dealing with property. Similarly as a result of the extension of state
activity and intervention in social and economic life a wide range of new
offences have been created. The most important area of expansion has
been with respect to what have been termed 'public welfare offences' or
'regulatory offences'.[59] This wide-ranging and constantly expanding category of offences are repressive in the sense that they make use of some, if
not all, of the sanctions asscoiated with repressive law. Yet these offences
diverge significantly from the Durkheimian definition of crime. Their
breach is generally not met with collective repudiation nor is there the loss
of honour that he saw as the hallmark of criminality. It may be noted in
passing that, particularly with respect to 'public welfare offences, but also
more generally with respect to the majority of minor offences, the
prevailing form of sanction has come to be that of the monetary fine
which again departs in important respects from the ideal type of a
repressive sanction. It may be that the pure type of punishment is no
longer loss of liberty but is increasingly economic in character.

While many of the developments referred to have only fully asserted
themselves in recent decades it is significant that these changes were
strongly indicated by the turn of the century. They serve to establish the
fact that the simple dichotomous characterisation of legal evolution is not
merely incorrect in significant respects but also that it misses many of the
distinctive features of modern legal evolution. Yet despite these criticisms
it remains true that the thesis retains, rather in the same way as does
Maine's status-contract dietum, a certain compelling force. The service of
such forceful and polemical theses is that they serve to concentrate and
focus the ongoing analysis of legal development. But like all such tight and
polar formulations they also serve to obscure other fundamental features

of the processes under examination.

What is most surprising about the thesis of the transition from mechanical to organic solidarity is the extent to which it totally fails to give any recognisable account of the broad sweep of the historical process. He is not alone amongst social theorists in seeking to explore the conditions that gave rise to 'modern society'. He was only slightly less obsessed than Weber by the 'uniqueness of the West',[60] but what is absent or repressed by Durkheim is any conception of intermediate stages between primitive and modern society. He was much less concerned than either Marx or Weber with the historical genesis of capitalist or industrial society; the conception of a specific process of transition is submerged under the more evolutionist notion of an advancing division of labour. The omission of transitional forms of society it will be argued has serious consequences for his treatment of the state.

The above considerations indicate that the particular relationship which Durkheim posited between law and social solidarity cannot be maintained. Yet at the same time it may be argued that while we are entitled to reject the specific thesis that he presents we would be foolish not to recognise that there remains a rather more general and enduring contribution in his analysis. What endures is the proposition that the type of law that exists within a particular society is intimately wedded to the form of its social structure. In societies with a low level of division of labour law is marked by its universalism, that is it deals with social relations that are encountered in common either in fact or potentially by all members of society. In societies marked by a high degree of differentiation law itself reflects this differentiation and specialisation. Yet if this is all that remains of Durkheim's thesis it must be freely admitted that he does little more than assert the social character of law and indicate that there is some developmental relation between the type of law and other features of the social system.

Taylor, Walton and Young see Durkheim as advancing a 'fully social theory'.[61] His superiority over the psychologistic theories that have dominated traditional criminology is not in dispute. However they seem unaware that the form taken by Durkheim's 'fully social theory' is one which leads directly towards holism. Since the whole (society) is more than the sum of its parts (individuals) the distinctive attributes of society are not present in its parts; hence society is seen not only as the source of its distinct characteristics, but also to be its own spontaneous cause.

As has previously been noted he tends to retreat from his dualistic model of social evolution in his later works, but it is never abandoned. He no longer utilises the distinction between mechanical and organic solidarity. Instead he concentrates upon the changing function and character of the 'conscience collective' as the source of social cohesion. He also drops his insistence upon law as the key index of social solidarity. He no longer places such emphasis upon the coercive character of social control.

In its place he increasingly emphasises that morality and religion constitute the decisive methods for the realisation of social solidarity. The 'social fact' or 'is' of solidarity induced through exterior constraint is replaced by the 'ought' of moral obligation.

The theory of crime

Durkheim's exposition of the relationship between mechanical solidarity and repressive law led him on to a detailed consideration of the nature of crime. His interest in the origin and function of crime was to endure despite the shift in his general emphasis indicated in the preceding section. This feature of his work is perhaps the most widely known aspect of his treatment of law and has played an important part in the general debate within criminology.

His starting point was to insist upon a very close connection between crime and the primary social values embedded in the 'conscience collective'. Thus 'an act is criminal when it offends strong and defined states of the collective conscience.'[62] This insight is developed in one of the most frequently quoted passages from his writing 'we must not say that an action shocks the common conscience because it is criminal but rather that it is criminal because it shocks the common conscience.'[63] The characteristic of crime does not derive from the quality of the act itself, but it is simply a consequence of the fact of violation.

> A sanction is the consequence of an act that does not result from the content of that act, but from the violation by that act of a pre-established rule.[64]

Crime for Durkheim is a universal feature of human society. It is in every sense of the term a social product. The social function of crime is the reinforcement of the values of the collectivity. The infraction of these values is seen as enfeebling and undermining the vitality of society. This vitality is reaffirmed every time there is a collective reaction against the violation of criminal law.

> Since it is the common conscience which is attacked, it must be that which resists, and accordingly the resistance must be collective.[65]

It is this collective reaction that, at an early stage in social evolution, facilitates the developing of an organised response to the violation of fundamental social norms. The power to react is vested in the hands of tribal chiefs and ultimately in the state. Once in existence the state acts to reinforce the 'conscience collective' and in defending it becomes entitled to punish those who attack the state itself. Durkheim exhibits a tendency to advance a naive 'social contract' theory of the state in which the collectivity is deemed to relinquish its function of repressing crimes to a body that acts on its behalf.[66]

Durkheim's view of the state is organic; it is seen as the concentrated expression of the collectivity. The political sociology advanced is consequentially of a most limited and even simplistic character. In spite of

Gidden's attempt to establish the significance of his political sociology he is forced to admit the essential deficiency of his treatment of political power.

Political power is implicitly assumed to be an outcome of a pre-established moral ascendancy of the state.[67]

As a direct corollary there is a consequential absence of any treatment of the relationship between law and the state. The state is treated simply as a means, as an instrument which is the authoritative guardian of the collectivity, accumulating to itself the means of organised coercion through which it imposes and carries out the punishment of offenders. Only in 'Two laws' do we encounter any fuller discussion of the relationship between crime and the state; and even here it is still somewhat cursory.

Central to Durkheim's definition of crime is the association between crime and punishment. His methodology leads him to define phenomena in terms of external characteristics. Thus if a certain set of acts all evoke the observable external reaction of punishment they must all have a common root and fall within the concept 'crime'. This is another example of what Keat and Urry describe as 'his curious method of definition, namely, classing together all phenomena that happen to share common external characteristics.'[68] In practice his definition of crime is by reference to sanctions. Durkheim defines punishment as 'a passionate reaction of graduated intensity that society exercises through the medium of a body acting upon those members who have violated certain rules of conduct.'[69] What he advances is an unapologetically expiatory view of punishment.

What we avenge, what the criminal expiates, is the outrage to morality.[70]

Durkheim goes a stage further and insists that the demand for vengeance aroused is socially necessary and functional.

It is an error to believe that vengeance is but useless cruelty . . . It consists, then, in a veritable act of defence, although an instinctive and unreflective one.[71]

Durkheim finds evidence of the expiatory nature of punishment, despite changing criminological fashions, in the minute precautions taken in most legal systems to proportion punishment as closely as possible to the conceived gravity of the offence.

What is problematic, if not fatal for his argument, are the implications that flow from the assertion of the organicist view of the state and legal institutions, as agents 'reflecting' or responding to the 'passionate reaction' of the collectivity. At a stroke the problem of power is abolished or, more accurately, it is buried. Within the ambit of his views it is impossible to admit the possibility of crime consisting to a greater or lesser degree of it being a repressive code enforced by one section of society against another or the possibility of there being a gap between the changes in legal sanctions and changes in public attitudes and opinions. There is a further assumption that underlies his account of crime. It rests upon what Hart has called the 'disintegration thesis' that unless society reacts to violations of norms through the imposition of sanctions social solidarity itself would be threatened.[72]

His essentially functionalist analysis is also apparent in *Rules*. The context is the attempt to delineate between 'normal' and 'pathological' social phenomena. If sociology is to contribute to social well-being it is necessary, he argues, to be able to distinguish the normal or 'healthy' facets since this will ensure 'the perfect adaption of the organism to the environment.'[73] His definition of 'normal' is simply constituted by 'those social conditions that are the most generally distributed.'[74] To conceive of widely distributed abnormal or pathological conditions would, except as a temporary aberration, be impossible. In terms of his organistic and functionalist view such a society would decay or collapse.

In order to illustrate the implications of this thesis he used the example of crime. Crime is deemed by laity and professionals alike to be pathological; an increase in crime is 'bad', the ultimate goal is conceived in terms of the elimination of crime. Durkheim however insists tnat the persistence of crime in human society must necessitate it being regarded as normal in the sense of it being an inevitable component of social life; although it should be noted that in *The Division of Labour* he had presented crime as a more pathological phenomenon, as 'the very negation of solidarity'. But he goes a significant step further and argues that 'it is a factor in public health, an integral part of all healthy societies.'[75]

The occurrence of crime is inevitable; this proposition rests on the assertion of the essentially statistical proposition that in every population some individuals must diverge from the collective type. The only conditions in which crime might be eliminated is when the 'conscience collective' completely dominates individual consciences, but such a society would be morally and socially static.[76]

Crime contributes to social health because if there were no violations of collective sentiments these sentiments would wither away. Their demise would occur because it would only be reacting against violations that the 'conscience collective' reinforces and revitalises itself. Punishment 'has the useful function of maintaining these sentiments at the same degree of intensity, for they would soon diminish if offences against them were not punished.'[77] What Durkheim achieves is a view of crime which challenges conventional wisdom.

> Contrary to current ideas, the criminal no longer seems a totally unsociable being, a sort of parasitic element. . . . On the contrary he plays a definite role in social life. Crime for its part, must no longer be conceived as an evil that cannot be too much suppressed. There is no occasion for self-congratulation when the crime rate drops noticeably below the average level, for we may be certain that this

apparent progress is associated with some social disorder.[78]

One further aspect of crime upon which Durkheim dwells is its historical roots. In a typically Durkheimian way he advances the view that its roots, and those of law generally, are to be found in religion. His evidence is that in early codes there is an admixture of legal and religious precepts. In a phrase which predates the famous exposition of religion as the sanctification of society he concludes 'but offences against the Gods are offences against society.'[79] A crucial part is played by ritual. The earliest form, negative ritual, gives rise to 'interdictions' that forbid certain acts. The function of these interdicts lies in his central distinction between the sacred and the profane. The infraction of the interdicts is not only met with supernatural sanctions, that is the belief that the deities will bring misfortune, but also with social sanctions. These social sanctions are of decisive importance and become more so as religious officials come to take responsibility for their administration. But Durkheim does not carry the analysis through and show how a separation arises between specifically ritual interdicts and emergent legal rules. But he indicates sufficient[80] to suggest that this is the historical pattern of evolution. Elsewhere he is content to assert the general relationship between law and religion.

Sociologists and historians tend more and more to agree on this common affirmation: that religion is the most primitive of all social phenomena. It is out of it that there have come, by successive transformations, all the other manifestations of collective activity, law, morality, art, science, political forms, etc.[81]

He undertook a detailed study of one area of criminal law. In *Professional Ethics* he presents us with a very characteristic analysis of homicide.[82] His starting point is that there are certain social rules that are universal and exist independent of any particular social system. He indicates the existence of three such rules enjoining respect for life, for property and for the honour of others. There are a number of parallels between his treatment of homicide and his more famous study of suicide. He utilises a two-stage model, closely resembling the mechanical-organic model (although the particular terms are dropped) in which the fundamental value orientation is the transition from collectivism to individualism.

In primitive societies homicide was treated as the highest breach of morality because it consisted in an attack upon the social order which itself has a sacred character and, in so far as homicide is an attack on the sacred, the individual life is enveloped and itself becomes sacred. Thus at this stage of social development the offence of homicide reflects the strength of collective sentiments.

The process of social evolution results in a decline in collective sentiments and the elevation of 'individual morals'. Yet homicide remains the supreme crime. He argues that this is because in civilised society it is now the *individual*, rather than society itself, which has become 'the object of sacred respect'.[83] The 'moral individualism' of civilised society finds expression in an especial abhorrence of murder. This is reflected in a general relative decline in homicide rates while at the same time many other offences of violence against the individual, and offences against property, have increased. As he does in *Suicide* he proceeds to an analysis of social statistics. He seeks to demonstrate that a strong 'state orientation' provides an explanation for an increase in homicide rates. In particular he stresses the tendency for homicide rates to rise sharply during wars; a similar increase is detected in periods of acute political crisis. He also demonstrates that homicide runs at a higher rate in Catholic communities than in Protestant ones; again he explains this in terms of a greater collectivist orientation present in Catholicism.

What the criticisms that I have made of his treatment of crime share in common is that they throw into sharp relief the absence in Durkheimian sociology of concepts of power and class. Their presence is rendered impossible, or at best marginal, by the dominant role of an organicist conception of state and society. The presence of the 'forced division of labour' remains unelaborated; it is a residual category signifying the absence of a 'natural division of labour' in which individuals occupy social positions upon biological meritocratic principles; it is a position that comes perilously close to social Darwinism despite his formal rejection of such an approach. The absence of the necessary theoretical categories makes it impossible for him to analyse structural dislocation and antagonistic social relations and as a consequence has fundamental significance for his theory of crime.

Crime, like religion, has as its object the collectivity. It is the response of the collectivity that underlines the social character of crime. Hence punishment and crime are definitionally integrated as 'graduated responses', that is they are necessarily in harmony. Crime is rendered non-problematic in that the integration of society is symbolically represented as the 'conscience collective' through collective representations and through the state as their agent. All that remains is to explain the actual incidence of deviance and criminality. The criminal status of some acts as opposed to others is non-problematic; the acts are either attacks upon society itself (religious criminality) or upon values that come to be protected by the collectivity (human criminality). Crime like suicide is natural because it is social; what is left open for the sociologist to explore is the incidence of deviance, to account for its particular forms and manifestations. This is the arena into which Durkheim projects the related concepts of anomie and egoism. These concepts have attracted much attention, to such an extent that many introductory treatments of Durkheim place anomie as occupying a central role. This is particularly the case for the reception of Durkheim into Anglo-American sociology through the agency of Talcott Parsons and Robert Merton. This importance is unwarranted; it is a concept that Durkheim uses to plug the holes in his oversocialised conception of the individual in society.

The organicist concept of both society and the state has important implications for his treatment of law and crime. For Durkheim the individual is dominated by society. This perspective excludes consideration of human domination, that is the domination of social groups or classes by other groups or classes. Hence the relationship between law and human domination is entirely absent as a focus of analysis; at best it attracts passing mention. When this absence is coupled with his failure to develop any treatment of transitional social and state forms between tribal and industrial society the consequences are far-reaching. For it is precisely within this historical and structural context that all of the most important features both of the content and the institutions of law that characterise modern legal systems are to be found. The absence of any concepts appropriate to this historical period is profoundly damaging not only for his treatment of social development, but also for its potential as a sociological treatment of law.

The evolution of punishment
In 'Two laws of penal evolution' Durkheim presents a self-contained analysis of the development of punishment. This discussion is significant both because of the intrinsic interest of the material, but also because of its relation to his discussion of law undertaken only seven years earlier in *Division of Labour*. While there are significant continuities there are also some obvious departures from earlier positions. What makes this more interesting is that there occurs no direct reference at all to the earlier work.

He sets out two 'laws' which he then seeks to substantiate and to provide a causal analysis for. One law is quantitative, the other qualitative. The first law is: 'The intensity of punishment is the greater the more closely societies approximate to a less developed type — and the more the central power assumes an absolute character.'[84] (It will be noted that he includes two variables: firstly the degree of social development on a simple-complex scale abandoning the mechanical-organic distinction relied on before; secondly the form of governmental power.)

The second law is concerned with qualitative changes in punishment. 'Deprivation of liberty, and of liberty alone, varying in time according to the seriousness of the crime, tends to become more and more the normal means of social control.'[85]

The two laws will be examined in turn. The first law posits a general relation between punishment and social development.

Punishments become less severe as one moves from the most primitive to the most advanced societies.[86]

The evidence he advances to support this contention shows that in simple or primitive societies an augmented death penalty is the supreme punishment; he lists in gruesome detail the variety of forms of augmentation. With the emergence of the 'city states' mutilation and other particularly harsh forms of treatment tend to decline and even disappear. The remainder of history is characterised in a rather cavalier fashion as 'Christian societies'. Within these societies there occurs a general decline in the severity of punishment. But again severity increases where monarchical power is absolute reaching its apex generally in the seventeenth century and declining again after the bourgeois revolutions.

It should be stressed that he does not posit the demise of punishment as such. It is not 'the sluggishness of the moral conscience' which gradually undermines social punishment; rather it is that the general process being described is a change in the *form* of punishment.

> There is not in reality, therefore a general weakening of the whole apparatus of repression; rather, one particular system weakens but it is replaced by another which, while being less violent and less harsh, does not cease to have its own severities, and is certainly not destined to an uninterrupted decline.[87]

His demonstration of the association between severity of punishment and simple societies suffers from the same deficiency as the equation of mechanical solidarity and repressive law. As Seagle has argued societies exhibiting especially harsh sanctions are those in which state structures concentrating extensive political, economic and military power are already in existence.[88] Without arguing the issue more fully we may nevertheless conclude that the 'First law' exhibits the same considerable empirical weakness which stems from the retention of the mechanical solidarity/repressive law couple.

Durkheim is however less concerned with empirical demonstration than he is with advancing causal analysis. His arguments exhibit a considerable force and his reader is taken along upon a syllogistic wave. He rejects any account premised upon a growing social horror of violence or on an increasing moral sensitivity. His starting point is consistent with his sociologistic methodology.

> Since punishment results from crime . . . it is in the evolution of crime that one must seek the cause determining the evolution of punishment.[89]

His primary objective is classically Durkheimian; whilst his immediate object of inquiry is punishment, punishment itself results from crime therefore it is in the evolution of crime itself that the evolution of punishment is to be pursued. In turn the evolution of crime links backwards to the development of the forms of social solidarity. The problem with this method of constructing the argument is that it assumes the very proposition, namely the paramount causal significance of social solidarity which the argument itself is intended to establish.[90]

He rests his analysis upon an analytical distinction between two types of crime. These are 'religious criminality' composed of acts 'which are directed against collective things' and 'human criminality', acts 'which only injure the individual'. These two types of criminality 'differ profoundly because the collective sentiments which they offend are not of the same type. As a result, repression cannot be the same for the one as for the other.'[91] Hence if a transition occurs from one type to the other there will be a transformation of the predominant type of punishment.

In the course of time, crime is reduced more and more to offences against persons alone, while religious forms of criminality decline, it is inevitable that punishment on the average should become weaker.[92]

Religious criminality produces very strong reactions against the offender since the offence is against the power that is the embodiment of collective existence which is superior to us and as a consequence the reaction evinced is one of horror leading to violent repression. This analysis is an application of his general theory of religion and is a substantially unchanged version of the account of repressive law found in *Division of Labour*.

Human criminality asserts itself with the decline of religious sentiment; there emerges a respect for humanity from a Kantian individualism based upon sympathy for humanity in general.[93] An offence by man against man does not arouse the same indignation as an offence against the supernatural. Hence there is a weakening of vengeance and therefore a change in the imposed punishment.

The great deficiency of this analysis is its failure to provide an adequate account of the process whereby acts come to be treated as offences against the collective. Acts which are intrinsically and exclusively offences against the supernatural, for example blasphemy or sacrilege, present little difficulty; while he shows that repressive sanctions were relied upon in particular societies he fails to show that they were exclusively reserved for religious offences. What he does not account for are the myriad offences which although intrinsically human offences, in the sense that the direct object of the act is a human person, come to be regarded as offences against the supernatural as the alienated embodiment of the collectivity.

What is new in the treatment in 'Two laws' provides a fruitful line of enquiry with respect to the interaction between the two types of criminality. He argues that where religious criminality is predominant human offences come to be treated as offences against the divinity. Likewise as human criminality comes to the fore it tends to assimilate religious criminality. However what is lacking in his discussion, but with which deviancy theory and sociology of law have recently been coming to grips, is the nature of the process whereby particular acts or types of acts come to be perceived, and hence classified, in a manner which is not dependent upon their intrinsic characteristics.

What is even more significant in this context is the complete absence of any discussion of perhaps the most persistent jurisprudential and sociological issue with respect to human criminality. The absence of any consideration of the social basis for this common duality of law is all the more surprising in the light of the central role that it plays in *Division of Labour*. It is possible to offer a tentative explanation for this significant anomaly. The major weakness of his treatment of law in *Division of Labour*, stemming from the dichotomous distinction between repressive and restitutive law, was the identification of repressive law as characteristic of simple societies and leading a somewhat residual existence in advanced societies. This proposition fitted uncomfortably with the very apparent persistence and vitality of repressive law in modern society. He therefore introduces a further classificatory distinction of repressive law into two types, religious and human. But in so doing whilst solving one of his problems he manages to abandon or overlook the sociologically and juristically more significant issue enshrined in the distinction between repressive and restitutive law. We have to ask why it is that some acts are treated as attacks upon the collective, irrespective of whether it be 'religious' or 'human' while others, being also acts causing injury to persons, do not partake, at least at the same level, in this collectivist character.

Durkheim succeeds in focusing our attention upon the fact that 'crime' is not a social invariant and provides some suggestive comments upon its development and transformation. Yet at one and the same time he, by omission rather than by design, draws back from what he had originally posited as his central concern, namely the study of the types of law in relation to types of social relations. This focus will necessarily be central to the general concerns of any sociology of law. Durkheim in 'Two laws' draws back and defines the field more narrowly, but disappointingly offers a solution to the transition between different forms of crime in terms of an overgeneralised conception of a transition from collectivism to individualism.

The first law, it will be recalled, contained a second causal variable namely the form of governmental power. Absolutist government is characterised by the reliance upon more repressive forms of punishment. It should be stressed that he is insistent that this is an independent variable and also that he attributes only secondary causal importance to it. Absolutism is not related to particular social types and is found in simple and complex societies alike. It 'depends on unique, transitory and contingent factors.'[94]

It must be frankly admitted that Durkheim's political sociology is undeniably weak. He insists on defining absolutism as the concentration of power in individual hands. His argument runs that the individual ruler comes to assume or acquire the attributes of a deity. Offences against the ruler come to have the character of religious offences and hence punishment tends to take the repressive form associated with religious criminality. There is such a complete absence of any serious discussion of state forms that it is difficult to say more than that he is wrong. He relies upon a constitutional theory that had its place in the eighteenth and nineteenth century but which offers little to an understanding of the relationship between law and the state. To separate one form of government from all others simply upon the formal criteria of the locus of power necessarily oversimplifies the question of law-state relations. This deficiency is compounded by the unacceptable causal autonomy that he insists on attributing to governmental forms. It can only be concluded that this second factor has a purely residual status which allows him to account for departures from the general law asserted for which his substantive theory is unable to account.[5]

While his treatment of state forms and their relation to law is weak it must be insisted that this area of discussion is central to the general concerns of sociology of law. The major advance that Weber's treatment makes over Durkheim in precisely his ability to grapple meaningfully with the relation between law, political relations and state forms.

The second law. of penal evolution seeks to explain the rise to predominance of imprisonment as the distinctive form of punishment found in advanced societies. He first seeks to demonstrate the factual emergence of 'pure' imprisonment. In simple societies imprisonment is unknown. Imprisonment served no function in primitive society since responsibility was collective; it made little difference if the offender was not available since the kin of the transgressor are available in substitution. We may note in passing that this is a thoroughly unsatisfactory treatment of collective responsibility which plays such an important part in the history of criminal law systems. It makes its appearances as a preventative measure to ensure that offenders do not evade judgment and punishment; A necessary condition for this stage is the existence of a sufficient extension of public authority as manifest in the availability of public buildings. He notes that the 'prison' as a specific institution is first found as an out-building of palaces, churches or other public buildings. This stage of development he associates with the growth of the city-states.

The next stage is that in which detention acquires a repressive function. The prison is made physically uncomfortable and unpleasant. Prisons often publicly exhibited the discomfort of the inmates and were close in character to other forms of punishment such as stocks and pillories which derive their character from the association of discomfort and humiliation. A related development is the shackling of prisoners and putting them to arduous labour.

Gradually, and often imperceptibly, the final or 'pure' form of imprisonment emerges in which its exclusive character is simply that of the deprivation of liberty. Although he does not make the point it is consistent with his position that when individualism is elevated then individual liberty of movement and activity is one of its major expressions. The removal of that liberty assumes a new import when it becomes the prevalent form of punishment. An important feature of pure imprisonment is its inherent potentiality for infinite gradation through the simple variation in the duration of imprisonment. As the maximum punishments of death and mutilation decline they are replaced by an ever flexible scale of imprisonment.

What he provides, without always fully developing it, is some valuable pointers towards a social history of punishment. The rise of individual responsibility flows from the decline of traditional family and kinship systems.

> These elementary groups lose their autonomy and become merged with the total mass, and responsibility becomes individual. [96]

However other than by assertion he provides no substantiation for this contention. But once the development of individual responsibility is established then the demonstration of the growth of imprisonment is easy. In order to prevent the flight of the transgressor detention is necessary. Hence imprisonment is born.

The subsequent transition from the inception of detention to 'pure' imprisonment is presented as a natural development. Firstly he argues that pre-trial detention passes into a form of punishment, but he does not advance any reason why this change should take place. Similarly he is less than convincing on the transition from repressive to pure imprisonment. The decline of the archaic repressive sanctions results in the need for substitute forms of punishment. What happens is that imprisonment as the new form of punishment invades the vacuum left. It should be observed that this is not an account of the 'pure' character of imprisonment with its distinctive character as deprivation of liberty alone. The association between individualism, individual responsibility and deprivation of liberty remains at a very tentative, philosophical level.

One rather surprising gap in his discussion of punishment is the omission of any consideration of the changing social goals of punishment. For example the major trend towards rehabilitation in modern penal policy produces no response from Durkheim. Punishment remains for him a simple expression of vengeance and hence a presumed single goal of punitive social action which merely becomes modified in form with the rise of individualism.

A comparison between Durkheim's analysis of punishment and that undertaken by Rusche and Kirchheimer reveals further problems and deficiencies in Durkheim's treatment. [97] Their analysis is located within a Marxist tradition with strong economic determinist characteristics which themselves give rise to a number of serious problems. If these are put to one side their approach points to what are, in the main, gaps or omissions in Durkheim's approach that stem from his general sociological position.

The central contrast is the absence in Durkheim of any concern with the impact of economic development on the forms of punishment. For example Rusche and Kirchheimer lay considerable emphasis on the transition from the 'productive' labour of prisoners in the pre-industrial period to the 'unproductive' employment of prisoners after the consolidation of industrial capitalism. Similarly they seek to account for the re-emergence of heightened repressiveness of criminal law and its sanctions at various stages in the development of capitalism; Durkheim's account presents only an evolutionist transition from collectivism to individualism. Like so much of Durkheim's sociology the significant of this work does not lie in that he succeeds in providing satisfactory solutions, but rather in the suggestive presentation. Without ever explicitly renouncing the central, legally relevant problematic of *Division of Labour* he turns from the schematic dichotomy between repressive and restitutive law to present a new focus on the transition in the forms of punishment.

Yet the contradictory character of Durkheim's work expresses itself in an analysis which in its generality is more compelling than that presented in *Division of Labour*. The evolution of repressive or criminal law in terms of a change in form of repressive law is more convincing than one which posits its general decline. Yet within that there remains the fundamental and significant deficiencies imposed by Durkheimian sociology itself. The root of those deficiencies lies in the absence, which is not accidental, but is a necessary consequence of his sociology. Absent are the theoretical means of grasping social phenomena, and specifically for our concerns, legal phenomena as located within a structure of economic and social relations. Economic and social structures are present in Durkheim only at the most generalised level (the division of labour) under the dominating influence of the central focus upon the ideological community ('conscience collective' and collective representations).

Contract

Durkheim returns on a number of occasions to the discussion of the nature and function of contract. In both *The Division of Labour* and in *Rules* his treatment is essentially polemical. His treatment is characteristically Durkheimian; he takes a phenomenon which as conventionally viewed seems to imply a fairly obvious and direct explanation, but he promptly seeks to demonstrate that a true understanding of the phenomenon is to be found in some diametrically opposed analysis. Contract bears all the characteristics of the pre-eminently individualist act as the expression of individual free will. But he is insistent that contracts are inherently social rather than individual in character.

In *Division of Labour* great importance is attached to contract because of the central role that it has played in the individualist, and particularly utilitarian, social theory. Indeed it is necessary to recognise the major role that the concept 'contract' played in nineteenth century thought, in economics, philosophy, sociology and in jurisprudence. His attacks are in particular directed against Spencer and, by implication, Maine.[98]

For Durkheim contract is essentially social.

A contract is not sufficient unto itself, but is possible only thanks to

the regulation of the contract which is originally social.[99]
Instead of the conventional two-party analysis he insists on a three-party
model with the third party, namely society, laying down in advance the
permitted framework of contractual activity. His insistence is upon the
social institution of contract, what he describes as 'the non-contractual
elements of contract'.

> If the contract has power to bind, it is society which gives this power
> to it . . . . Moreover it lends this obligatory force only to contracts
> which have in themselves a social value.[100]

So far his treatment of contract has not gone beyond his characteristic
assertion of the social character of the institution. He draws support for
this view from the extent to which the social character of contract is
winning wider recognition both in legal practice and in juristic thought in
particular through the growth of such concepts as duress and undue
influence and, of particular importance, the rapid advance of the doctrine
of 'public policy'.

His next step is also fairly unexceptional; he relates contract to the
advance of the division of labour.

> Contractual relations necessarily develop with the division of labour,
> since the latter is not possible without interchange and the contract
> is the juridical form of exchange.[101]

The more contentious aspect of his elaboration is to be found in
Professional Ethics. Here he is at his most challenging, if not necessarily at
his most convincing. He draws together apparently disparate elements of
social reality and spans the epochs of social evolution in order to produce
a very distinctive account of the historical evolution of contract. So crucial
a role has contract played in social thought that it appears today to exist
as a 'natural institution', a permanent and inevitable component of human
society. But he is anxious to show that it is a relatively recent innovation.
If its primary social function is as a means of acquisition of property, he
argues that the earliest form of such acquisition was through inheritance.
This he sees as giving way before the advance of contract. He is
particularly vehement against the institution of inheritance. His attack
upon it was his only enduring link with the socialists; its abolition he
demanded as a pre-condition of the realisation of a meritocratic society.

He posits the evolution of contract as passing through two distinct
stages. Using terminology very similar to that used by Maine he labels this
transition as the change from 'status-contract' to 'will-contract'.

> On the one hand we have relations in due form according to law,
> having as their origin the status of persons or of things, or of the
> modifications so far latent in this status; on the other, relations
> according to law having as their origin wills that are in agreement to
> modify their status.[102]

The earlier form of contract, based on status, is religious in origin, the
parties or the subject matter being endowed with a sacred character. It is

this sacredness which provides the basis of the obligatory nature of the undertaking. His central concern is to explain how the transition to 'will contract' takes place. The essence of the problem is to determine what it is that makes agreement between two wills binding. The crucial role is played by ritual.[103] Ritual may surround the parties to the contract, for example the sharing of a meal, shaking hands or drinking from the same cup, or it may surround the subject matter, for example the ritualistic character of transfer of realty in many societies. Such ritual gives a sacred character to the act of exchange. The decisive step is to endow the undertaking *itself* with a sacred and hence binding character. Thereby the declaration of will is given an exteriority; a ritual form of promise emerges, for example the universal appearance of the oath and other magico-sacred formulas. The undertaking is thus marked by 'sacred formalism'; the next step is for 'juridical formalism' to replace sacred formalism. Here the symbolic act becomes the substitute for the actual transference of property.

> The symbolism represents only a decadence that comes when the primary meaning of the custom is lost. Customs begin by being active causes, and not symbols, of social relations.[104]

The truly consensual contract arises only when the ritual and symbolic element declines in importance and finally disappears. He recognises that factors such as the quantitative increase in the number of transactions plays some part in his process, but it is significant that he explicitly resists a 'determinist' position.

> The mere fact that an institution is required does not mean it will appear at a given moment out of the void. There must be something to make it of, that is, current ideas must allow it to come about and existing institutions must not oppose it but, rather, supply the material needed to shape it. So it is not enough for the consensual contract to be demanded by the advance of economic life: the public mind, too, had to be ready to conceive it as possible.[105]

In order to assess his thesis it is necessary to recognise that the analysis fits fairly consistently with, for example, the historical development of contract in English law. However his overzealous efforts to avoid 'determinism' tends to leave the theory somewhat nebulous. A crucial feature for a consistent sociological theory of contract must start from the study of the type of exchange relations which have in fact manifested themselves as a consequence of the development of economic activity. An understanding of the economic form and content is a necessary pre-condition for an explanation of the role of ritual and formalism in the evolution of contract. Durkheim tends simply to presume that exchange is a natural and invariant consequence of the division of labour. Whereas in reality the transition from simple barter to developed capitalistic exchange spans major changes which necessarily had some impact upon the legal expression of these transactions.

The consensual contract, which Durkheim sees as reflecting a growing secularisation of society, rests no longer on the words used; the obligation becomes based on the intentions of the parties. The words as such are not formally binding; they are evidence of intention. The consensual contract amounts to a revolutionary innovation in the law.[106] So crucial a role has it played that a wide range of social relations have been subsumed under a contractual form. Of particular importance is the employer-employee relationship; to view such a relationship in purely contractual terms has major ideological implications and Durkheim stresses the unfree basis upon which this exercise of 'free will' is based.

The consensual contract did not mark the end of the evolution of contract; Durkheim posits a new stage, that of a 'contract of equity' which reflects an increasing awareness of social interest in not only the nature but the consequences of contractual activity. This process is reflected in the extension of the factors vitiating contracts, the emergence of the doctrine of public policy and the general movement towards increasing social intervention addressed towards the objective of 'just contracts'. Such a thesis has close resemblance to Pound's insistence upon the emergence of a new stage of the 'socialisation of law'.

Durkheim's model of the ideal society is of a system of socially just contracts as opposed to freewill contracts. This development he sees impeded by the pernicious institution of inheritance. This he sees as the cause although it is more correct to argue that it is a reflection of social inequality. Thus while rejecting the social doctrine of individualistic utilitarianism his projected society rests firmly upon contractual foundations, but with the proviso that such contracts must first pass the test of being socially just.

Property
Closely related to the discussion of contract is the analysis which Durkheim provides of the nature of property and property rights. His treatment is less fully developed than that concerning contract.[107] The treatment is predominantly philosophical rather than historical or evolutionary. The failure to treat the question developmentally is a major weakness and stems from his overriding ideological concerns.

In developing a theory of property Durkheim has two enemies to combat. One is the 'labour theory of property' which he attributes both to the classical political theorists, in particular to Locke, and to the socialists. His dismissal of this approach is somewhat cursory and rests on the proposition that since the market value of certain objects, for example works of art, cannot be accounted for in terms of the labour time embodied in their production it is therefore impossible to utilise the labour theory in accounting for the institution of property. Secondly he rejects the Kantian theory of property which attributes property rights to acts of individual will based upon a notion of 'first appropriation' which is unacceptable since it makes the whole theory rest upon the accidental or arbitrary event of 'first appropriation'.[108].

For Durkheim the allocation of property is an inherently social activity. 'It is the society that does the allocation of property.'[109] In order to provide an account that avoids the two rejected theories he characteristically locates the source of property relations in collective beliefs and values and in particular in religious values. It is 'the opinion of each society which makes certain objects susceptible to appropriation, and others not'.[110] The essence of religion is that it sets certain things, the sacred, aside as having particular attributes or qualities; once endowed the sacred object is shrouded with inviolability. Both the sacred and property have this common characteristic of inviolability and therefore he concludes must have a common origin.

> The origins of property are to be found in the nature of certain religious beliefs. Since the effects are identical, they can in all likelihood be attributed to similar causes.[111]

He is suggesting here that since they have a similar characteristic, consistent with his previously elaborated methodological position which has already been criticised, there must necessarily be a causal connection between the two phenomena.

In elaborating a theory of the religious origins of property he argues that initially sacredness is conferred upon special individuals, namely priests, and that they are able to transfer this inviolability to sacred objects. Gradually it is the object than the person who is regarded as sacred and hence inviolable.

> Human property is but sacred and divine property put into the hands of men by means of a number of ritual ceremonies.[112]

He finds support for his theory in the practical inalienability of property in many tribal and feudal societies and in the taboos that surround such things as marker stones demarcating property in land.

Durkheim's dualistic model of society, although he no longer uses the labels mechanical and organic, is reflected in his account of the transition from communal to individual property. The first step is the granting to certain individuals of a superior status manifested in the emergence of the patriarchal family. The sacred character is no longer invested in the land itself, but is placed in the hands of the head of the family. The second stage is the development of movable property which comes to have an increasingly important economic role and which is not endowed with the same sacred character as realty. Personalty is a 'weak reflection, an attenuated form'[113] of real property. Real property is historically primary and personal property is granted as a concession by the collectivity.

His theory of property has none of the power and persuasiveness of his analysis of the evolution of contract. His basic method is weak and no supporting evidence is produced. Stone correctly describes it as 'an exotic variation of the metaphysical theory of property'.[114] Any analysis of the evolution of property must have as its starting point a consideration of the economic function that various types of property play in the wider economic and social process. Attention must therefore be placed not only on the important role of land in early societies, but must take specific account of the particular forms of property in land related to the variety of forms of production that emerge under definite social and economic circumstances.

DURKHEIM : A SYSTEMATIC SOCIOLOGY OF LAW?

Durkheim was undoubtedly one of the 'founding fathers' of modern sociology; can the same claim be made for his contribution to the emergence of a sociology of law? Gurvitch for example speaks of him as having 'developed a systematic legal sociology'.[115] To assess this judgment it is not possible artificially to extract or lift Durkheim's 'sociology of law' from the totality of his sociological enterprise. It has been central to the argument developed in this chapter that his treatment of law flows directly from the total enterprise.

The fundamental significance of Durkheim's work is that he created the intellectual space within which modern sociology has developed. Starting from his critique of political economy and moral philosophy he carved out an area of intellectual enquiry which has become the preserve of a distinct form of intellectual activity that carries the label 'sociology'. It was Durkheim more than any other who prescribed the boundaries or parameter of sociology; he provided or designated the space which twentieth century sociology has occupied. This intellectual territory is to be sharply differentiated from that occupied by Marxist theory and it is the reason which first and foremost renders the current preoccupation of comparison between sociology and Marxism a largely misdirected activity.[116]

The territory of sociology is occupied for Durkheim by a central problematic of the individual – society relationship. It is specified in *Division of Labour*: 'This work has its origins in the question of the relations of the individual to social solidarity. Why does the individual, while becoming more autonomous, depend more upon society? How can he be at once more individual and more solidary?'[117] It is this central problematic which leads Durkheim to the concern with social integration and stamps the specific orientation upon his sociology which Parsons describes as 'This remarkable ability to see relations among fields usually treated as unconnected was possible only because Durkheim consistently kept in mind the fact that he was dealing with the problem of integration of a single system.'[118] The specific form which the social integration perspective takes, in terms both of Durkheim's analysis and his prescriptions, is with the normative process as the fundamental ingredient of social integration; it is a quest for the ideological community as the basis of the conception of what are taken to be the distinctive characteristics of modern Western society, namely industrial society and political democracy It is within this context that the contention strenuously advanced by Anthony Giddens that Durkheim should not be branded as a theorist of social order or of conservatism can be assessed. Giddens is correct in so far as he is reacting against a persistent vice of modern sociology to classify all sociological theory as either 'consensus' or 'conflict' theory.[119] However the counter-reaction cannot simply deny what has become the conventional wisdom. Were Durkheim simply a theorist of a non-problematic integrationist theory his influence on sociological thought would have rapidly faded. It is precisely because Durkheim presents the stability and integration of industrial society as problematic that gives stature and significance to his sociological theory. It is for this reason that his concept of anomie, and to a lesser extent that of the forced division of labour, is the medium through which the problematic character of contemporary society is conveyed. But, having made clear that Durkheim cannot be passed off as a pure integrationist, it needs to be insisted that his general perspective is precisely that of functional integration which operates primarily at the level of normative systems.

It is this dominant strand which directly informs his treatment of legal phenomena. His treatment of law rests upon an invariant and unquestioned assumption of law as a functionally integrative mechanism. It is central to the posited invariant relationship between law and social solidarity. Law is presented at one and the same time as the reflex and as an index of social solidarity. This orientation determines the specific character of his treatment of law. The spring of social cohesion rises from the collective sentiments, attitudes and values which are the product of social forces that operate upon individuals. Social cohesion is thus rooted in the normative system of society. Then law, along with morality, are presented both as embodiments of and as agents of social harmony.

This orientation has a number of quite specific consequences for his sociology of law. There is no space within his conceptual framework for a thorough analysis of social disharmony or conflict as an ever-present constituent of social relations. The nearest he can approach is either to regard conflict as pathological (forced division of labour) or as a consequence of social malfunction (anomie). As a result his sociology of law is marked by a number of important absences or gaps. Absent are the law-power relation, the law-domination relation and the law-state relation.

The direct relation posited between law and social solidarity amounts to a simple reductionism and as a consequence law whilst 'functional' can have no autonomy or even relative autonomy; it cannot be considered as an active causal force since the theoretical framework within which it is placed prescribes that it passively reflects transformations in the forms of sociality. Similarly the emphasis upon the normative as the central reality of human sociality expresses itself in concern for the normative content of law and as a consequence little or no attention is given to the institutional forms of legal systems.

The discussion of law in Durkheim's sociology arises in the first instance, as we have seen tangentially, as a methodological device for the analysis of the forms of social solidarity. This has generally lead commentators to attach little significance to his specific treatment of law.[120] But this ignores the extent to which law has an important location within his general sociology. Law is a major institutionalised expression, embodiment and vehicle of the ideological community. Its forms of existence and surrounding ideology are a veritable celebration of social cohesion at the level of the total society. In this form there is an important continuity with the social control perspective of law as a specialised form thereof encountered in Poundian sociological jurisprudence and American realism.

The central feature of Durkheim's sociology of law is contained in the focus upon the relationship between law and social solidarity. Extracting this from its specifically Durkheimian form it amounts to a definition of the object of the sociology of law as being that of the interrelation of law and the forms of social relations. This constitutes a necessary and persistent focus for sociological treatment of law, but it is little more than a minimum condition for a sociology of law. It does not constitute a specific direction or thrust of enquiry. Considered in conjunction with those elements which it has been argued are missing from Durkheim's treatment of law, it can be concluded that his work cannot be taken as constituting either the beginning or as a crucial point of development for the sociology of law. Yet the persistent sociologism of Durkheim ensures that his work will remain a significant point of reference, but this very characteristic requires that it is a position that must be encountered in the development of a sociology of law.

5 Max Weber's Sociology of Law

MAX WEBER LIVES

Max Weber occupies a central position in the development of sociology. His significance is not merely historical; he remains an ever-present force in contemporary sociology and in this respect he is to be differentiated from Durkheim whose historical importance is widely recognised but is less and less a point of reference in current discussions. Weber's presence insinuates itself into nearly every important debate and controversy within sociology. For this reason I want to argue that Weber is in a very real sense still alive. The questions that he poses remain the central subject matter not only of modern sociology, but also more widely of contemporary social and political thought. This prominence is reflected in the sustained treatment of Weberian sociology that occurs in contemporary sociology and social theory from widely divergent positions.[1]

Weber also has a special significance within the sociology of law. Durkheim arrived at his treatment of law and crime tangentially as a by-product of his pressing methodological concerns. Weber undertakes to develop a systematic sociology of law which is more rigorously developed than any other contribution to the subject. Perhaps of even greater significance is the fact that his sociology of law occupies a central position within his total sociological theory. The centrality of his sociology of law has not been widely enough recognised. Not only does it occupy an important place in his major text, *Wirtschaft und Gesselschaft*,[2] but it is also central to his preoccupation with the world historical importance of the 'uniqueness of the West', that is with European capitalist society. I will attempt to demonstrate this centrality of his sociology of law. But at the same time I want to argue that the most central and pressing problems for

the sociology of law are contained with Weber's work. However they are
not contained in a form which allows them simply to be extracted
ready-made from Weber; rather they must be liberated from Weberian
sociology, stripped from the impediment of the theoretical framework of
subjectivist sociology within which they are located. This approach
manifests both the strong pull or attraction of Weber and at the same time
a deeply critical, almost antagonistic, orientation to Weberian sociology.[3]
It will be from struggle with the legacy of Weber that the sociology of law
will be advanced; the failure of modern sociology of law which merely
gives polite recognition to Weber can be located in this failure to engage in
the theoretical terrain of Weber's sociology of law.

THE POLITICAL AND IDEOLOGICAL LOCATION OF WEBER

Biographical sketch
Weber's life spanned the crucial period in the development of modern
society from 1864 to 1920.[4] He was born into the German upper middle
class political environment. While his life was to be mainly centred in
intellectual activity he never lost the intense interest in politics which he
derived from the specific milieu of his background. 'I am a member of the
bourgeois classes, I feel myself as such and I am educated in its views and
ideals.'[5]

His academic training, like that of so many continental scholars, was in
law. He studied during he high water mark of German historical jurisprudence influenced by such men as Mommsen and Gierke. Although he
was to react sharply against this tradition his earliest work bore the very
characteristic stamp of the Historical School. His dissertations on medieval
trading companies,[6] and on Roman historical law were both part of this
tendency.[7] This early focus on the relation between legal development and
economic history was to remain.

His intellectual achievements were conditioned by a burning anxiety
about, and a very considerable involvement with, the major issues that
confronted German society and state. His concern was to be with the
overall characteristics of the development of 'Occidental society'. It was this
ever expanding field of interest that led him to the elaboration of
systematic social theory which is to be found in its most complete and
developed form in *Economy and Society*.[8]

Throughout his life Weber was passionately involved with politics. He
was never to become a figure of any major political importance, but there
is no doubt that he had considerable political ambition. He was first and
foremost a German nationalist.[9] He was deeply disturbed by the political
vacuum that remained at the end of Bismarck's era. He associated himself
with the *Verein für Sozialpolitik* (Association for Social Policy) and
collaborated with Freidrich Naumann in establishing the National Social

Party which had explicitly imperialist and expansionist aims designed to win the working party away from socialism and back to patriotism. He was an open and enthusiastic supporter of the German war effort between 1914 and 1918. After the War he came nearest to achieving political importance when he was involved in the drafting of the Weimar Constitution in particular with that section which gave extensive powers to the Reichpresident. After a hectic period of pol'tical and academic activity that followed the War he died leaving many of his major works unfinished.

It must be insisted that Weber's sociology can only be understood against the background of his political views and activity and therefore some attention will be given to this interrelation later in this chapter.[10]

Weber's ideological position

In Weber . . . the disenchantment of the world is completed.[11]

Likewise Horkeimer comments on the profound 'pessimism'[12] that permeated Weber's thought. He lacked the confident self-assertive faith in human progress of nineteenth and early twentieth century social thought. He reflected the declining self-assurance of the bourgeois order, confronted on the one hand with the submergence of its individualist values by the relentless advance of corporate industry, commerce and state, and on the other hand the threat of elimination at the hands of the increasingly threatening force of proletarian revolution. Yet the very penetration of social reality achieved by Weber is realised precisely because of the contradictions inherent in contemporary social development. Thus his standpoint was individualism yet he saw the individual being pushed by forces outside his control. He regarded himself as a liberal, yet his was an 'authoritarian liberalism'.[13] He was a defender of Western capitalism yet at the same time he pointed to some of its contradictory and potentially self-destructive characteristics. He was a powerful advocate of freedom yet was profoundly skeptical about popular democracy and never abandoned an attraction for authoritarian and despotic political leadership. History is the story of the advance of 'rationalism' yet at the same time man is trapped in 'an iron cage' stemming from the 'mechanised petrification' of industrial society.[14]

The construction of his thought is itself a product of the contradictory tendencies within nineteenth century social thought. Increasing recognition is now given to the need to understand his thought as a reaction against not only the political, but also the intellectual implications of Marxism. There has been a growing recognition that 'the debate with he ghost of Marx' is important to an understanding of Weber's sociology.[15]

The relationship between Weber and Marx is considerably more important and complex than is grasped by the widely used conception of a 'debate with Marx's ghost'. An examination of this relationship throws significant light on the Weberian project as a whole. It is important to stress that Weber rarely directly comments on 'historical materialism'; he never embarked on any detailed textual study of Marx's writings. Yet he explicitly subtitled his lecture programme on the sociology of religion 'A positive critique of the materialist conception of history'.[16] He certainly regarded Marx as a central focus of intellectual orientation; he is reported as saying: 'The honesty of a scholar today . . . can be measured by where he stands in relation to Nietzsche and Marx. Our intellectual world bears to a great extent the stamp of Marx and Nietzsche.'[17]

The problem is to specify the nature of the 'debate' with Marxism. If it was not a direct confrontation with Marx's work, one important dimension was a reaction against the Marxism current in the German working class movement. The most frequent objection that Weber raises against historical materialism is that it advances a mono-causal analysis and thus reduces sociological analysis to an economic determinism. This is not a debate with Marx but rather, as Colletti correctly argues, a debate with the Marxism of the Second International and of the German Social Democratic Party.[18]

It has become quite common to identify Weber as the 'bourgeois Marx'.[19] The correct element that is contained in this designation is in seeing Weberian sociology as the most systematic and influential non-Marxist social theory; in this sense it is available as an *alternative* to Marxism. But Weber was himself somewhat cautious in that he insisted that he was not intent on providing a simple negation of 'historical materialism' by substituting a cultural determinism for economic determinism. Thus it is possible to agree with those who note that Weber 'borrows' from Marx without being prepared to see any convergence between Marx and Weber.

Marx and Weber must be seen as at one and the same time addressing the same object of enquiry (capitalism) and addressing themselves to fundamentally divergent objects, Marx to the structure of social relations and Weber to the cultural science of inter-subjective relations.[20] Hence the opposition between them resides in the fundamentally different epistemological foundations on which their work rests. It is in the recognition of this that is to be found the reason why Weber never engaged in a direct or positive critique of 'historical materialism'.

At the other end of the intellectual spectrum, both philosophically and politically, from Marx was the powerful and academically predominant camp of German idealism. German academic activity, still marked by the all-embracing impact of Hegelian philosophy, found its most frequent expression in theories emphasising the role of a national spirit or Volksgeist. Nowhere was this tendency more apparent than in jurisprudence. As a consequence it was this particular facet of the idealist tradition that he first reacted against. He departed from both the 'Germanist' and the 'Romanist' camps of historical jurisprudence.

The major specific critiques that Weber made were directed precisely against the idealist tradition embodied for example in his critique of

Stammler.[21] It was on the basis of this reaction against the dominant intellectual tradition that Weber set about the task of specifying more rigorously a distinction between the natural and the cultural sciences. Thus it was precisely because he was in agreement with the dominant tradition in his rejection of the naturalism of Comte and Spencer that he embarked upon this project which provides the central intellectual framework of all his writing. It must be stressed that he never broke consistently with the idealist tradition. Nowhere is this more apparent than in his methodology with its insistence upon subjectivism and intuitive interpretation.[22]

Weber and German politics
His social theory must be placed in the context of the political position he adopted, not least because his self-conception stressed the connection between theoretical work and its practical bearing upon the political problems that confronted his country.

Germany entered the twentieth century already well advanced in the process of industrialisation, the speed and extent of which has only been repeated in contemporary Japan. Yet it did so on the basis of an archaic and traditionalist political order. For Weber the starting point was nationalism.

It is not our task to pass on to our descendants peace and human happiness, but the eternal struggle for the maintenance and enhancement of our national way. . . . The power and interests of the nation . . . are the last and decisive interests which economic policy has to serve.[23]

Thus he felt no anxiety about his chauvinist reaction to the First World War.

We can throw our weight on the scales of history, therefore we have the duty before posterity to throw ourselves against those two powers [England and Russia] which threaten to engulf the whole world. Our national *honour* ordered us to do it . . . and this war concerns *honour*, and not territorial changes or economic gain.[24]

What was central to his political concern was the means by which the German national interest was to be carried forward. He presented the problem in the following way:

The disturbing element in the situation which confronts us is that while the bourgeois classes as bearers of the power interests of the nation seem to be withering, there is no evidence that the working classes are in any sense qualified to replace them.[25]

This political vacuum lead him to a position in which attention was focused on the need for new and charismatic leadership. While we need not go as far as those who blame Weber for the path of German politics after his death there is a frighteningly prophetic element in his political perspective.

We [the Germans] have shown to the world 110 years ago that

we — and *we alone* — were able to be one of the great cultural peoples under foreign domination. *This* we shall demonstrate again! Then history, which has already given us — and us *alone* — a second youth will give us also a third one. I have no doubt about it.[26]
The authoritarian version of democracy which he expounded contained a cult of power for its own sake, adorned by metaphysical notions of German destiny. His position was implicitly Machiavellian stressing the concept of *Machstaat* (power-State). This relates very closely to the important role of the concepts 'power' and 'domination' in his sociological theory. It would therefore be wrong to treat Weber as the disinterested, 'above-the-struggle', 'pure' theorist. His work is fundamentally charged with major ideological and political implications.

WEBER'S SOCIOLOGICAL ENTERPRISE

Before turning to a closer examination of Weber's sociology of law it is necessary to situate it within his total sociological enterprise. Any comprehensive discussion of the whole of his work would be beyond the scope of this chapter; however it is necessary to isolate his major concerns and their relationship to the sociology of law and to explore the relationship between these and the methodology and epistemology with which they are approached.

The central focus of Weber's life work was his preoccupation with the uniqueness of 'the Occident'. The most distinctive feature of this epochal concern is the socioeconomic configuration of 'capitalism'; it is important to stress that he does not have a narrowly economic conception of capitalism. In this respect the parallel with Marx is of the greatest significance; what unites them, despite their fundamental differences of method, theory and political commitment, is this identification of capitalism as constituting the determinant characteristic of the modern world. It would not be necessary to lay such stress upon the centrality of capitalism in Weber's sociology were it not for the way in which his work has been received and disseminated in the English-speaking world. A key role in this process was played by Talcott Parsons, both through his part in translating and editing Weber's work and in his own presentation in *The Structure of Social Action*.[27] Parsons sought to harness Weber as a paradigm of general social theory of the abstracted and formalistic kind that characterised Parsons' own sociology. Weber's own concern with the elaboration of theoretical and methodological framework arose not because Weber saw this as a central characteristic of sociological activity but rather as a means of specifying his own separation from those intellectual positions against which he reacted. While his reaction against Marxism as suggested earlier plays a significant role in his orientation, it was the task of distinguishing himself from historical idealism on the one hand and sociological naturalism on the other that provide the key to his theoretical and methodological stances. In this sense Weber's enterprise is parallel to that of Durkheim in so far as it concerns the demarcation of the space or territory of sociology.

The central focus upon European capitalism provides the organising problematic through which the disparate strands of Weber's substantive work can be seen as constituting a totality. The 'uniqueness of the West' leads into two fields of work. On the one hand the historical and comparative studies of major world civilisations, the major thrust of which is concerned to determine the absence of capitalistic development and which in general distinguishes these societies from those of Western Europe.[28]

The second element was what may be described as the internal development of Occidental society. This embraces the identification of the characteristics that constitute the uniqueness of the West, one aspect of which is the pervading process of 'rationalism' which occupies such a central position within his sociology and specifically within his sociology of law. The other is the historical studies of the specific conditions of capitalist development which range from the general studies of economic history to his work on the city and on the *Protestant Ethic*.[29] Inter-related with this study of the specific conditions of capitalism is Weber's sociology of law. Weber posits a relatively high degree of autonomy for the political sphere, but at the same time argues for the causal significance of the political forms of the state in the transition to capitalism. Specifically with reference to the development of legal systems it will be seen that he places considerable emphasis upon he causal interrelationship between bureaucratic monarchies and bourgeois legal interests in the development of modern legal systems.

The nature of Weber's substantive sociology is determined in both the form of its development and presentation, as well as in its content, by the methodological and epistemological stance which he adopts. The root of his theoretical position stems from his insistence on the distinction between the natural and cultural sciences; in this he is reacting against the sociological naturalism of Comte and Spencer and reworking the neo-Kantianism of Dilthey. The two most important consequences that stem from this position are that he adopts a stance of methodological subjec-tivism which lies at the heart of his 'interpretive sociology'; the other element is the insistence on the fact/value distinction which manifests itself in the assertion of value neutrality as a necessary condition of social scientific activity. These two related aspects can now be briefly con-sidered.

Weber's definition of the subject matter of sociology takes its starting point as 'The specific action of *individual* human beings since only these actions are for us the understandable embodiment of meaningfully orientated conduct.'[30] His position is that of 'methodological indi-

vidualism', but it must not be taken to imply a general 'individualism' in
the sense of an attempt to explain social facts solely by reference to the
behaviour of individuals. Perhaps a more accurate designation of his
position is 'methodological subjectivism' for this embraces not only
individuals as the starting point or subjects of sociological enquiry, but
also lays emphasis upon the key concept 'meaningful'. Weber's sociology is
'couched in terms of the subjective point of view, that is of the meaning of
persons, things, ideas, normative patterns, and notions from the point of
view of the persons whose action is being studied.'[31]

Weber asserts that social action can only be understood by reference to
its 'meaning', 'purpose' or 'intention' for the individual. Thus he describes
his sociology as 'interpretative sociology' characterised by the method of
Verstehen.

He treats 'ends' and 'values' as given but as not being amenable to
rational or scientific assessment. This reflects itself in the concentration in
his sociology upon the 'means' selected by individuals to realise their ends.
The 'ends' that are pursued are not themselves evaluated; hence rational
action may consist in the pursuit of any end so long as the means are
'rational' with respect to the chosen end.

The radical separation of 'ends' and 'means' leads him to insist upon the
necessity of a 'value free sociology'. It is 'value free' in the sense that while
recognising the importance of values in social action it refuses to make any
evaluation of those values. Such an approach to the nature and preconditions of the social sciences raises fundamental problems.[32] Irrespective of any decision we may make about the 'desirability' of such an
approach, it must be insisted that Weber failed in any case to realise it. It
amounts, as Marcuse correctly points out, to 'an attempt to make science
'free' is to accept obligatory valuations that are imposed on it from
outside.'[33] It results in the acceptance of, and finally the apology for, the
world as it is. Thus the assertion of value freedom becomes a 'fiction' in
Weber's work.[34] In fact his whole conceptual framework is value
loaded.[35] Thus for example such an important concept of 'rationality' is
profoundly value oriented. The concept is counterposed by Weber against
'irrationality'; the implicit evaluation that the rational is 'higher than',
'more advanced' is never denied by Weber. Hence when one type of action
is classified as rational and another as irrational what is effected is more
than a classification, it is at the same time an evaluation. Since rationality
seeks to deal merely with the means of social action it leads to an
acceptance of the existing social configurations. The pursuit of the most
outlandish objectives may remain rational as long as efficient means are
utilised in pursuit of that end. There is an inherent ambiguity in the
concept, 'ambiguous precisely because at one and the same time it gives
expression to the specific accomplishments of the modern world and to
the whole questionableness of this accomplishment.'[36] Thus occidental
'reason' becomes nothing more than the acceptance of the logic or 'reason'

of modern capitalism. The 'rational' becomes the defence of the irrational.³⁷ Since for Weber no scientific choice between ends can be made, social action is rendered arbitrary; it becomes a matter of commitment, of vocation, an 'act of will'.³⁸ The value content of his concept 'rationality' is compounded by a considerable ambiguity in its application; he in fact uses it in a number of quite distinct ways. For example it sometimes refers to the internal logic of a system or set of ideas, at others it means 'efficient', 'predictable' or even 'purposive'. It is a significant defect in his sociology that such a central concept should be surrounded by such lack of precision.

A distinctive characteristic of his methodology is his use of 'ideal types'. The ideal type is a heuristic device which is 'drawn' from reality by means of an accentuation of selected features, but which does not purport to describe reality; it is held up as a hypothesis against which the empirical world may be explored. Such a method stems from his subjectivist theory of knowledge, that there can be no 'real' knowledge, there is only that which is gained through experience. Hence social science cannot advance hypotheses in the same way or of the same type as the natural sciences. The ideal type is applied as a means of bringing order to experience. Thus when we consider his typology of legal systems we will not be considering what purports to be an empirically derived model of legal evolution. Yet it may fairly be insisted that Weber does quite frequently slip from the limitations which he himself places upon the ideal type method; he does slip into the habit of treating them as evolutionary descriptive models. This is particularly marked with respect to the elaboration of the typology of legal systems.

Weber's methodology is an expression of his general theoretical and ideological orientation. He rejected both the naturalist identification of the natural and social sciences by the sociological positivists and also the dominant idealist tradition in German academic life. He sought to 'insert' himself between these two antithetical positions through the adoption of a neo-Kantian epistemology which on the one hand allowed him to approach social reality as inter-subjective experience and on the other to assert the possibility of scientific knowledge within the social sciences. It is this location of this thought which as much as anything else has ensured that Weber has been a significant point of reference for the diverse tendencies within modern sociology. The essence of his position is a neo-Kantian positivism, but within it the positivism provides a methodo-logical gloss to a pronounced idealist stance.³⁹

The implications of the epistemological critique of Weber require comment. While such a critique serves the important function of locating the distinctive features of his *method* of thought they do not directly provide a critique of his substantive sociology. The rejection of his epistemology does not lead to a necessary rejection of the whole corpus of his work. This position is radically different from that adopted by Paul

Hirst in his epistemological demolition of Weber.[40] The inference that Hirst draws is that Weber can be disposed of by means of a critique of his method and of the epistemological foundation of his major sociological categories. Weber's general sociology and his sociology of law contains a relevance and power which cannot be negated at the level of epistemological critique. His treatment of the uniqueness of the West, his analysis of domination and of the relation between law and rationality persist as relevant, indeed as crucial foci, for contemporary debate despite the epistemological framework in which they are developed. Weberian sociology 'survives', rather in the same way that Marx has done despite the succession of definitive and 'final' critiques, because of the centrality of the substantive concerns to the intellectual, social and political problems of the modern world.

THE SOCIOLOGY OF LAW

Introduction
Weber was the first of the important figures in modern sociology to attempt a comprehensive sociological treatment of law. He had of course very considerable advantages. His early legal studies provided him with an intimate knowledge of the legal tradition, in particular of legal history and with the necessary source materials. As Roth remarks 'his ability to write the sociology of law as a legal historian makes this the most difficult chapter to the legal layman and the mere sociologist.'[41] A similar point is made by Freund when he notes that his sociology of law 'is better evidence of his encylopedic learning than any of his other sociological studies.'[42]

His sociology of law not only constitutes a self-contained whole, but it is intimately related to the main themes of his sociological enterprise. Law constitutes a major facet of his study of domination; and the existence of rational legal order is a central feature of his analysis of modern capitalist society. Parsons, who has done more than anyone else to disseminate Weber's work, insists 'In my opinion, the great extent to which the core of Weber's substantive sociological work, both theoretical and empirical, lay in the sociology of law has not been adequately appreciated.'[43] Elsewhere he goes even further and argues 'I should like strongly to suggest that the core of Weber's substantive sociology lies neither in his treatment of economic and political problems nor in his sociology of religion, but in his sociology of law.'[44] Yet despite the high importance which Parsons attaches to his sociology of law, it is of the greatest significance that it remains the area of his sociology that has received the least attention from sociologists and jurists alike. His contribution to the sociology of religion, of politics or bureaucracy has received extensive attention from friends and enemies alike. His sociology of law receives in general reviews of his work either a few paragraphs or at best a short chapter.[45] Only two jurists, Clarence Morris[46] and Stoljar,[47] have devoted any sustained attention to it; elsewhere works on sociological jurisprudence or the sociology of law usually contain only passing references to Weber's work.[48] It is only very recently within the sociology of law that any detailed re-examination of his contribution has been undertaken.[49]

The scope of Weber's sociology of law is such that some indication should be given of the method of exposition to be adopted. After some preliminary matters the heart of his sociology of law is approached through he formal typology of the 'internal' modes of legal thought. This typology exercises a determining influence upon his substantive analysis of the development of legal systems and of their relation to economic and political systems which provide the predominant themes of his sociology of law. In addition the 'internal' typology is central because it is constructed around the concept 'rationality' which is Weber's key to the uniqueness of the West.

A note on sources
Weber's exposition of his sociology of law finds its main expression in his major work *Economy and Society* in which one complete section is entitled 'Sociology of law'. In addition other sections of this same work also contain extensive discussion of law.[50] The main and subsidiary sections, along with selections from the introductory chapter on conceptual frameworks, were translated by Edward Shils and appeared as *Law in Economy and Society* under the editorship of Max Rheinstein in 1954. In the main this earlier translation has been relied upon. But some quotations are made from the later translation of the complete work *Economy and Society*. There are some significant differences between the various translations. In particular attention is drawn to the translation of the concept *Herrschaft* which Fischoff translates as 'domination', Henderson and Parsons as 'imperative control' and Shils as 'authority'; its translation as 'domination' is preferred, 'imperative control' is adequate although unnecessarily positivistic, but its rendering as 'authority' is positively misleading.

The definition of law
Weber's analytical procedure generally starts with the setting out of a rigorous definition of his subject matter. His sociology of law commences with a formal definition of law:

> an order will be called *law* if it is externally guaranteed by the probability that coercion (physical or psychological), to bring about conformity or avenge violation, will be applied by a *staff* of people holding themselves specially ready for that purpose.[51]

The most striking feature of this definition is the extent to which it resembles more traditional 'imperative' definitions. Skoljar notes 'Weber arrives at what is clearly a positivist, a semi-Austinian conception of law.'[52]

Although he rejects the equating of 'law' with 'state law' he does not go as far, for example, as Ehrlich in elevating the law of voluntary associations as the causal determinant of state law. Indeed he strenuously attacks Ehrlich's thesis that law equals adopted custom.[53] For Weber each type of law has its autonomous existence, but he demonstrates, particularly in his study of medieval trading companies, how rules adopted and developed in voluntary associations may pass over and be adopted in state law.

His definition of law constitutes a substantial acceptance of the conventional 'law as a system of rules' definition. Lasswell notes that this element is taken over without amendment from the prevailing German jurisprudence, from the 'jurisprudence of concepts' so forcefully criticised by Jhering.[54]

The 'new' feature of his definition is his emphasis upon the existence of a 'staff' as a necessary condition fr the existence of law. He stresses that his concept of 'staff' is broad and includes non-professional roles and even situations in which individuals merely play a socially recognised 'legal' role (for example a tribal chief who puts on a symbolic garment or headdress before commencing 'legal' adjudication).

Weber thus starts with an unashamedly positivistic definition of law. However caution should be adopted before attributing too great a significance to the positivism of his starting point. In the context of his subsequent treatment it provides a relatively neutral starting point, one that remains acceptable to jurists and sociologists alike. Its most significant consequence is that it reinforced his marked concern with what I shall argue are the 'internal' characteristics of law. Martin Albrow is wrong in placing the emphasis that he does on Weber's positivist definition of law; it is not sufficient grounds for labelling him a 'legal positivist'.[55]

The internal typology of law

Weber advances a typology of law which has the distinctive characteristic of being constructed upon the basis of differentiation in the method or type of legal thought. It focuses upon the way in which legal materials in the form of substantive rules are developed and the way in which they are applied in arriving at decisions. It is for this reason that it may be identified as an 'internal' typology; for although he derives from it characteristics of total legal systems its basis of construction is narrowly delineated. Its mode of construction is an example of his ideal type method; it is conceived as a hypothetical construct not drawn directly from empirical reality, but against which empirical material may be evaluated and tested.

Weber's persistent concern with the search for the distinguishing features of Occidental society leads him to posit the advance of 'rationality' as the key. It is this concept which he uses as the basis for the construction of his typology of law. He presents one major typology which is an 'internal' typology, but in addition to this he gives us two other substantive models, closely related to the former. His major typology is constructed around two axes. First he distinguishes between 'formal' and 'substantive' systems. The essence of this distinction lies in the extent to which the system is internally self-sufficient where all the rules and procedures necessary for decision-making are available within the system. Substantive systems are characterised by their reference to external criteria, in particular to religious, ethical or political values. Such substantive systems may either be 'empirical' in that they represent reactions to individual cases, or they may be 'effectual', that is reactions based upon emotion or faith.

The second set of variables are the polar types 'rational' and 'irrational' which relate to the manner in which the materials of the system, its rules and procedures, are utilised; thus in expounding his typology he concentrates upon the internal features of legal systems, that is on the forms of legal thinking. He presents the following typology:
(1) Irrational
    (a) Formal irrationality,
    (b) Substantive irrationality,
(2) Rational
    (a) Substantive rationality,
    (b) Formal rationality.[56]
This typology may also be presented in terms of a paradigm:

	FORMAL	*SUBSTANTIVE*
IRRATIONAL	Formal Irrationality	Substantive Irrationality
RATIONAL	Formal Rationality	Substantive Rationality

Before discussing his elaboration of this typology some general features should be noted. It is significant that both the axes (formal/substantive, rational/irrational) refer to essentially 'internal' procedures or characteristics of legal thought rather than to their content. This is apparent in his analysis of actual legal systems in which considerable attention is focused upon procedural features while little or no attention is given to substantive law. Further his usages of the concept 'rationality' carries with it, as has been noted above, the implied value judgment that systems which are designated as 'rational' are thereby 'higher' or 'more advanced' than those which are designated 'irrational'. The notion of Weberian rationality as applied to legal systems reproduces the fiction of all analytical jurisprudential theories namely the myth of the possibility of realising a logical, systematic and gapless system. Thus he defines the highest stage of rationality as being characterised by the 'integration of all analytically derived legal propositions in such a way as to constitute a logically clear, internally gapless system of rules, under which, it is implied, all conceivable fact situations must be capable of being logically subsumed.'[57]

There is a degree of controversy surrounding the interpretation of this typology. Parsons believes that he is positing a law of advancing rationalisation, that is of presenting a picture of legal evolution as passing through the various stages of the typology. Parsons goes as far as comparing Weber's 'law of advancing rationalisation' with the second law of thermodynamics. Eldridge and Freund both reject this 'determinist' and strictly evolutionary interpretation of Weber.[58] Instead they argue that Weber was much more concerned to stress that legal development is a product of dynamic interaction of various facets of legal systems. In particular both Eldridge and Freund insist that he was conscious of the tension between formal and substantive rationality in the process of legal evolution. Weber was quite explicit when he talks about 'the insoluble conflict between formal and substantive principles of justice.'[59] He recognised that a reaction against formalism is inevitable 'a 'lawyers' law' has never been and never will be brought into conformity with lay expectations unless it totally renounces that formal character that is immanent in it.'[60] Yet it is important to note that Weber sharply attacked those trends in juristic thought, for example the 'free law' movement, which sought to give a greater scope to substantive justice as constituting a retreat towards 'irrational law-finding'.[61] Hence they conclude that the objective of a formal rational law that is logically consistent and gapless which Weber sees as the highest stage of development does not blind him to the ever-present counter-pressure for a law that is seen, with reference to extra-legal values, to be 'just'.

In coming to Weber's defence both Freund and Eldridge are in fact guilty of imputing their own ideas to Weber. He may be consistently understood by recognising that his philosophical and methodological position does lead him to advance a 'law of advancing rationalisation', but at the same time he has sufficient insight to realise the ambiguities and tensions involved in this process. This awareness is at the root of his pessimism; he sees the realisation of formal rational law inhibited by the demand for substantive justice. He holds a sociological variant of an 'original sin' doctrine; humanity necessarily holds itself back from the realisation of a purely rational ordering of its relations.

When Weber turns his attention to the concrete process of legal development he advances a typology which, while bearing close resemblance to the internal typology discussed above, is constructed around (i) the mode of creation of law (ii) the formal qualities of the law so produced and (iii) the type of justice realised.

From a theoretical point of view, the general development of law and procedure may be viewed as passing through the following stages: first, charismatic legal revelation through 'law prophets'; second, empirical creation and finding of law by legal *honoratiores*, i.e. law creation through cautelary jurisprudence and adherence to precedent; third, imposition of law by secular or theocratic powers; fourth and finally, systematized elaboration of law and professionalized administration of justice by persons who have received their legal training in a learned and formally logically manner.[62]
This developmental model may be represented as follows:

Mode of creation	Formal qualities	Types of justice
Charismatic	magical formalism + irrationality	charismatic justice
Empirical	reliance on *honoratiores*	khadi justice
Secular theocratic	theocratic substantive rationality	empirical justice
Professionalised	logical sublimantion	rational justice

It will be noted that this developmental typology conforms fairly closely to the ideal type paradigm set out previously. Yet it is noticeable that the four stages of justice do not completely coincide with the four stages of the 'mode of creation' in that the rather anomalous result is that the 'empirical' mode of creation does not coincide with 'empirical justice'. Too much significance should not be attached to this anomaly; he insists that his typologies are not intended to be descriptive historical models and that in studying the empirical evolution of legal systems one should not attempt to 'force' the material to 'fit' a theoretically constructed model.

The rationalisation of law
His primary concern is not with the analysis of the general course of legal development, but rather with the more specific problem of tracing the factors which contribute to the process of the rationalisation of law. As a consequence he does not devote a great deal of attention to the 'lower stages' of legal development. This significant contrast with Durkheim's approach may be noted. Where he does deal with these earlier stages it is usually in connection with the studies of the various societies that failed to develop occidental rationalism.
    He classifies primitive law as 'formal irrational law'. The validity of such law rests upon the sacredness of the law-giver and is marked by a heavy reliance on magic, the significant characteristic of magic being its inherent formalism, its reliance upon detailed prescriptions concerning the procedures whereby legal rules are to be developed and applied.

Law has always developed first through legal oracles, precedents, responses of charismatically qualified bearers of legal wisdom.[63] The charismatic character of primitive law manifests itself in the lack of any consistent elaboration of substantive law. The formalism associated with this stage may contribute to such a system enduring for long periods of time. He points to the heavily formalistic character of the early stages in the development of English common law. Morris suggests that the emphasis upon the irrational roots of law constitutes a useful corrective to the more conventional association of law and reason.[64] While we can associate with Morris's rejection of a simplistic equation of law and reason, Weber's concept of 'irrational' law is not without problems. It implies, or rather imposes as Parsons recognises, an artificial antithesis between the 'rational' and the 'irrational' in law. Weber's use of 'irrational' is weighed down with perjorative value judgments.

'Substantive irrational law' exists where decisions are influenced by the concrete facts of particular cases as evaluated upon an ethical, emotional or political basis rather than by the application of general norms to the facts. This corresponds to what is termed 'empirical justice' in his systematic theory, but which in his developmental exposition he more frequently refers to as 'khadi justice' (or elsewhere as 'Solomonian justice'). The term 'khadi justice' is not used merely to describe the specific Islamic institution, but is used in a more general sense to apply to any system in which individuals submit to the authority of an official who is free to find the law not being bound by any extensive framework of legal rules, but who may arrive at decisions within the framework of general ethical principles. Thus charismatic law is 'informal judgment rendered in terms of concrete ethical or other practical valuations.'[65] Thus for example he characterises the traditional Chinese patrimonial judge as dispensing 'khadi justice'.[66]

Weber notes that the irrational stages are never completely superseded by the advance of rational law. This insistence flows directly from his ideal type methodology with its rejection of unilinear models of social development. Many characteristics of modern legal systems may exhibit features of formal or substantive irrationality; this comes out clearly in his treatment of English law which is to be considered separately.[67]

He devotes the majority of his attention to the emergence of rational law and in particular to the higher form of 'formal rational law', namely 'logically rational law'. The second sub-type of formal rationality, which we may identify as 'extrinsically rational law', is only most loosely indicated by Weber himself. Extrinsic rationality refers to ritualistic reliance on legal formalism as embodied in the use of prescribed forms of words and documentation. He suggests that this form of legal thought leads to casuistry, but never returns to further elaboration. Thus in practice his discussion of 'formally rational law' is confined to its sub-type logically rational law'.[68]

Before proceeding to a detailed examination of his conception of rational law it is important to stress its connection with his wider theoretical position. His radical distinction between ends and means necessarily leads to attention being concentrated upon the means since the ends themselves are taken as given and are not themselves amenable to sociological evaluation. Hence his conception of rationality is concerned with the selection of appropriate means. As Keat and Urry observe 'judgment of rationality are limited to an assessment of the relations between means and ends.'[69] Hence it follows that a rational society or a rational legal system is one in which the most effective means are selected for realising the values or ends that are treated by Weber as given.

His general view of the rationalisation of law is of a transition from 'substantively rational law' to 'formally rational law'; such a legal system being characterised as one in which 'the legally relevant characteristics of the facts are disclosed through logical analysis of meaning and where . . . definite fixed legal concepts in the form of highly abstract rules are formulated.'[70] His ideal type thus corresponds closely to Kelsenite 'pure law'; the legal system is conceived as operating like a 'technically rational machine.'[71]

His attention is focused on the means whereby this process of rationalisation takes place. Because of his theoretical insistence on multi-causal analysis problems are encountered in unravelling his views on the development of rational legal systems. He presents on the one hand very detailed analyses of the relation between particular political forms and the corresponding legal developments based on specific historical examples and on the other hand he advances a number of more generalised expositions of the relation between law and a number of potential causal variables. He is insistent that the study of the general features of the process cannot be allowed to replace the analysis of concrete historical examples. The difficulty is often in determining the amount of causal weight he attributes to the variables which he isolates.

Rational law is a product of,

the specific and peculiar rationalism of Western culture[72]

Only the Occident knows the state in the modern sense, with a professional administration, specialized officialdom, and law based on the concept of citizenship . . . . Only the Occident knows rational law, made by jurists and rationally interpreted and applied.[73]

Our modern occidental rationalization of law has been the product of two forces operating side by side. On the one hand, capitalism interested in strictly formal law and legal procedure . . . . On the other hand, the rationalism of officialdom in absolutist states led to the interest in codified systems and in homogeneous law . . . . No modern law has emerged when one of these two forces was lacking.[74]

This last formulation of the problem is of vital importance for his subsequent analysis. Rationalisation is seen as a result of the coincidence of two sets of interests, firstly developing bourgeois interest and secondly the interests of absolutist states, 'the immanent needs of patrimonial monarchical administration'; the total process is characterised as 'the alliance of monarchical and bourgeois interests.'[75]

In this analysis he rejects any specifically 'economic' causation. He frequently points to the example of England to refute the thesis that modern law is simply a result of the needs of the bourgeois class. However it is not that economic imperatives are unimportant; he attaches considerable significance for example to the development of medieval towns and in particular to 'special urban law' which is seen as playing an important catalytic role in the development of rational law.

Weber, like others trained in the traditions of the Historical School, was well grounded in Roman law. In his search for the causes of rationalisation of law he came sharply into conflict with the Romanists who argued that the development of capitalism in Europe was made possible by the reception of Roman law since this provided the rational basis for entrepreneurial activity. While recognising the rationality of Roman law and devoting considerable attention to the analysis thereof he is insistent that it did not play any substantial causal role in the development of capitalism.

> All legal institutions specific to modern capitalism are alien to Roman law and are medieval in origin.[76]

The development of political institutions saw the emergence of national states, with a wide variety of forms but sharing the common characteristic of having to cope with expanding administrative tasks which give rise to the creation of a 'bureaucracy'.[77] Bureaucratic organisation under the pressure of its own internal needs tends to produce rational means of administration (although the extent of its rationalisation may be inhibited by tightly formalistic methods of work) and as a consequence will come to recognise the need for rational law.

> Only bureaucracy has established the foundation for the administration of a rational law conceptually systematised.[78]

Within such forms of social organisation there is a general tendency towards codification. He argues with respect to England that codification failed to develop because of the resistance of the highly organised and autonomous legal profession. Codification is seen as a general precondition for the existence of formal rational law.

He is anxious to stress that the alliance between bourgeois and monarchical interests was not necessarily one of conscious cooperation, but was rather an objective coincidence of interests.

Factors, other than political and economic ones, are seen as playing an important role in the process of rationalisation. Particular stress is laid upon the role played by the specialist bearers of legal traditions, the legal professionals. Two main lines of development of the legal profession are contrasted. In the first the emergence of a legal profession centred around the training in law as a craft with the entrant undergoing an apprenticeship; the purest example of this pattern is the English 'guild' method. This method of training gives rise to 'cautelary jurisprudence' which manifests highly developed skills in the adaptation, utilisation, innovation of substantive law and of procedures by practitioners in their clients' interests.[79] About such organisational principles he draws rather pessimistic conclusions 'from such practices and attitudes no rational system of law could emerge.'[80]

The second course of development of the legal profession was characterised by the dominant role of 'legal education', as opposed to 'training', based upon legal theory and science which was undertaken in special schools or universities separated from the practice of law.

> Modern legal education in the universities represents the purest type of the second way of legal training.[81]

Such a method emphasises conceptual and abstract features of law thereby elevating the rational and logical propensities of legal systems.

Thus the type of legal education is presented as being closely linked to the organisation of the legal profession. He goes as far as to say that in accounting for the rationalisation of law 'the prevailing type of legal education, i.e. the mode of training of the practitioners of the law, has been more important than any other factor.'[82] He contrasts the rational character of Roman law as in part being the product of the limited extent to which the system relied upon specialised law officers. The ability of the jurisconsults to articulate a rigorously abstract scheme of juristic concepts is explained by their relative remoteness from actual legal business.[83] On the other hand the guild organisation of the English legal profession resulted in the acquisition of a monopolistic position under which they came to have a vested pecuniary interest in the retention of archaic and formalistic features and thereby constituted the major impediment to the rationalisation of the English law. English lawyers impeded not only rationalisation, but also codification and rational legal education.

Supplementing the analysis of the factors contributing to the rationalisation process stress is also placed upon the causal importance of legal procedure and technique. The development of a rational superstructure of legal thought cannot take place without a similar process affecting procedure and technique. As has been observed previously his definition of law itself has a tendency to focus upon the internal characteristics of law in which attention to procedure and technique play an important part. The level of technical development of a legal system determines the extent to which it can respond to and allow new legal developments or innovations, stemming from the pressure of social and economic interest. He observes that 'the peculiar kinds of techniques used in a legal system ... are of far greater significance for the likelihood that a certain legal institution will be invented in its context than is ordinarily believed.'[84]

An additional causal factor in the analysis of rationalisation is the significance attached to 'natural law'.[85] His concern is not with its philosophical or juristic characteristics, but with its 'sociologically relevant' facets. 'They [theories of natural law] become sociologically relevant only when practical legal life is materially affected.'[86] Natural law is defined as 'the sum total of all those norms which are valid independently of, and superior to, any positive law and which owe their dignity not to arbitrary enactment but, on the contrary provide the very legitimation for the binding force of positive law.'[87] He suggests that its general role is to provide a legitimation of legal change and as such is a necessary factor in the rationalisation of law. 'The invocation of natural law has repeatedly been the method by which classes in revolt against the existing order have legitimated their aspirations.'[88] He sees natural law resulting from 'the tension between formal law and substantive justice'.[89]

The causal significance attached to natural law is brought out clearly in his account of the failure of Chinese law to undergo a rationalisation process. One important factor was the non-emergence of a natural law which had it developed would have imposed pressure towards a rationalisation of law and would have legitimated any consequent change.[90] Similarly one of the characteristics of Judaic law was the failure of the Jewish prophets to articulate a natural law. Even at the stage when Yahwe was portrayed as the helper of the oppressed no natural law critique of the positive order was advanced. Again the absence of a natural law was therefore a factor in the failure of Judaic law to advance far along the road to rationalisation.

Weber's analysis of the causes of rationalisation of law reveals his pluralistic or sociological determinism. It also demonstrates the way in which he seeks to advance causal explanations by means of the parallel harnessing of his abstract concepts, 'the ideal types', alongside a very detailed historical and comparative study of empirical material. Yet he can be legitimately accused of elevating multi-causal theory to a new dogmatism. With this reservation stated it must be conceded that his ability to bring together disparate facets of the process of legal development results in his typology of legal development being much more compelling and flexible than the more common unilinear theory of 'stages' of legal development.

Law and Domination
Our comprehension of Weber's sociology of law is assisted if we are able to distinguish between the respective statuses of the different typologies which he makes use of in the course of his exposition. The typology of modes of legal thought discussed above is essentially internal in that its subject matter is the modes of thought that take place within legal processes; this is his sociology *in* law and as such has pronounced jurisprudential characteristics. But, as has been previously suggested, his interest in legal phenomena exists at a more general level determined by

his central problematic of the characterisation of Occidental society. At this level he enters into a different range of theory construction which revolves around the relationship between 'law' and 'domination'; its concern is with the relationship between law and other components of social systems and is therefore more concerned with a sociology *of* law as opposed to a sociology *in* law. It must be borne in mind that his discussion passes unannounced between these two conceptually distinct levels. Thus in his discussion of the types of legal justice we encounter the direct interplay between these two levels.

Herrschaft is a central concept in Weber's sociology; it is a relational concept in that it is concerned with the impact of one person upon another in so far as the behaviour of the one may be analysed as having been determined by the other. His concept is consistent with his subjectivist orientation since 'domination' designates an inter-subjective relation as distinguished for example from Marx's concept of the structure of social relations. In his substantive discussion he devotes almost exclusive attention to particular types of domination and this has led some to see 'domination' as synonomous with 'authority'. He is however careful to situate the discussion of those forms that he regards as having special importance. 'Domination constitutes a special case of power.'[91] 'Power' has a very positivistic content for Weber; it is simply the fact of behaviour determination. His concern is with the meaning of this relationship, in particular with the bases of obedience.

> The motives of obedience to commands ... can rest on considerations varying over a wide range from case to case; all the way from simple habituation to the most purely rational calculation of advantage.[92]

Broadly he identifies two sources of domination.

> In addition to numerous other possible types, there are two diametrically contrasting types of domination, viz., domination by virtue of a position of monopoly and domination by virtue of authority, i.e. power to command and duty to obey.[93]

The majority of his consideration is devoted to 'domination by virtue of authority' or, as he more generally refers to it, 'legitimate domination'; the qualification frequently slips away entirely and he speaks, in this more limited sense, of 'domination'. It is on this basis that he introduces his well known threefold classification of domination which is thus strictly concerned with forms of legitimate domination, namely traditional, charismatic and rational legal domination. These types are distinguished by the form of legitimacy on which the system's claim to exercise authority is based.

Thus his typology of domination is not concerned primarily with the form or mechanism of particular types of domination.[94] Their basic characteristic is the content of the claim to legitimacy which the particular forms articulate. In essence therefore his typology is concerned with the ideological form of the modes of domination rather than with the modes of domination themselves. This major distinction becomes obscured because it is hidden in the extent to which his discussion of domination takes the form of a discussion of 'legitimate domination', one of the significant consequences being that, although he deals with the claim of authority of the system of domination, he provides little or no analyses directed at explaining why particular claims to legitimacy are accorded legitimate status by those subject to them.

The persistence of his debate with Marx is evident with respect to his treatment of domination. Marx presented the different forms of class society as being characterised by different modes of domination. He argued that the forms of domination arose not out of the intentions of people, nor out of particular claims to authority, but rather that they arose from the types and structures of social relationships that exist in various forms of class society. Thus the variety of forms of consciousness associated with them and the types of authority claimed while not being unimportant were for Marx logically secondary characteristics. Weber reverses this treatment; he does not deny the existence of 'factual power'[95] but his central concern is with the forms of legitimation of power, namely the types of legitimate domination. Upon this basis he constructs his substantive political sociology rooted in the concern with the historical uniqueness of Occidental capitalism. It is on the basis of the three types of legitimation that he proceeds to the discussion of the concrete forms of his pure types.

From the standpoint of the sociology of law the paramount feature of the discussion of legitimate domination is that it is 'legal domination' that constitutes the basis of the pure type of political order of modern Occidental society. Sociology of law in this sense is not concerned primarily with the internal characteristics of the legal order, but rather it is concerned with the relationship between law and the other major structural components of social systems. Law for Weber is therefore central to his total social theory in a way which supersedes the sub-disciplinary status of the 'sociology of law'. Both traditional and charismatic domination have associated with them certain types of legal system. It is however with respect to 'legal domination' that the form of law is not merely a characteristic of a particular type of political order, but is its central and determining feature.

One feature of the typology of forms of domination which deserves elaboration is the relationship between legal domination and the other two forms. Little attention needs to be devoted to the discussion of the characterisation of the forms themselves; these have been extensively discussed by Weber himself and by his major commentators.[96] Both traditional and charismatic domination have as the source of their claim to legitimacy a specific relationship between ruler and subject. In the case of charismatic domination the specifically personal relation between leader and subject is paramount; in the case of traditional domination the duty of obedience owed to the particular holder of the leadership role is personal and at the same time rooted in the past legitimacy of that role. Thus while varying in form and degree both charismatic and traditional domination are founded upon personal authority.

Legal domination on the other hand is to be distinguished by the fact that the source of its legitimacy is *impersonal*; thus 'obedience is owed to the legally established impersonal order.'[97] The legitimacy claimed rests 'on a belief in the legality of enacted rules and the right of those elevated to authority under such rules to issue commands.'[98] Thus although the command will emanate from a particular office-holder the basis of their authority lies in the principle and rules enshrined in that office and not in its occupant for the time being. The obligation is very simply to 'the law'. He tends to make the leap from this generalised notion of law to identify 'legal domination' with the 'formal rational law' of his internal typology. The danger in so doing is that it obscures the relationship between the two different theoretical constructs which then tend to be used interchangeably.

It must be insisted that Weber's theory building does not constitute a totally integrated structure. The typology of the forms of legal thought[99] must be distinguished from his typology of forms of domination. Thus his amalgamation of these two produces his developmental model of law[100] which does not produce, from the standpoint of formal theory building, the neatest of typologies. The main thrust of his heuristic endeavour is to bring the concept of legal domination into a close association with that of formal rational law.

This type of theory building results in a presentation of the characteristics of legal domination in a one-sided way. The concept of legality necessarily has a circularity about it. Laws are 'valid' or legitimate if they have been enacted where this enactment has taken place in accordance with rules laid down for the legislative process. Now, although such a process *may* take the form indicated by Weber in his elaboration of formal rationality in law, such a model of legality is also applicable to traditional domination for under it, given the initial act of force which created the particular content of the political order, the subsequent life of that social order may well correspond to the ideal of legality given the procedural definition thereof which he shares in common with analytical jurisprudence.

If the source of legitimacy under legal domination is seen as residing in an impersonal order of logically derived and structured rules then it produces a reified view of law. The reification of law marries neatly with the purported value neutrality of Weberian sociology, but it does so by advancing a false antithesis between personal and impersonal order. A system or order which does not come to rest at the feet of a particular law-giver may none the less serve the substantive social interests of groups or classes within society. In reality it is merely the *form* which is impersonal, but the ideal type of legal rationality obscures the quest for the social basis of legal order.

The reified impersonal model of legal domination reveals the proximity between Weber and Hegel. The embodiment of society in the state or legal order has a definite historical location in the rise of the nation state as the major form of the bourgeois social revolution of the eighteenth and nineteenth centuries. The posited impersonality, impersonal only in contrast to the personified monarchical system, in fact incorporates and at the same time legitimises the domination of the market system.

The reification of law inherent in his association of legal domination with formal rational law is especially manifest in the stress which he lays upon the institutional form taken by legal domination. With respect to both traditional and charismatic domination he clearly indicates that a range of institutional forms of these modes of domination have occurred; whereas he suggests that legal domination takes only one pure form, that of bureaucratic organisation whose functioning is predicated upon adherence to a formal rationality in the decision-making process.

> Only the Occident knows the state in the modern sense, with a professional administration, specialized officialdom, and law based on the concept of citizenship . . . . Only the Occident knows rational law, made by jurists and rationally interpreted and applied.[101]

Legal domination is characterised by a continuous rule-bound conduct of official business, a jurisdiction defining spheres of competence, a hierarchical organisation of offices staffed by those trained for their roles. Those filling offices are separated from ownership of both the means of production and of administration and cannot appropriate the posts that they occupy. This model of bureaucratic administration is itself subject to and also applies rational rules. Thus its internal organisation and its social output are an embodiment of a system of legal domination; those subject to its decisions accord it legitimacy specifically because of its rule-bound conduct of its affairs. It is presented as the embodiment of an impersonal system of order.

Not only is his conception of rational law itself reified, but so also is the form of administration that is associated with it. Bureaucratic administration implies a high degree of separation of powers and one which renders not only the rules applied but also the machinery which applies them deserving of obedience in their own right as a system that stands apart having an internal and self-sustaining validity. Such a position has significant ideological implications. The legal bureaucratic administration stands outside and beyond the economic and social contests that permeate society.[102] Thus the concept of the state almost disappears from his political sociology of capitalist society; it is replaced by the rationality of administration. The Hegelian state is replaced by abstracted rationality embodied in legal bureaucratic administration.

It is the conception of legal institutions as reified rule dispensing mechanisms which is common to the general tradition of Anglo-American jurisprudence and also to modern sociology of law. But there always remains an ambiguity and uncertainty in Weber. It is contained within the ideal type methodology which allows him both to point to the ideal of legal bureaucracy but at the same time to recognise empirical departures from it. Thus as Bendix expresses it he sees the development of rational legal domination as 'the hope of a precarious chance of human freedom.'[103] Behind the purity of the ideal type there remains a recognition of the precariousness of the projection of his political ideals. Theoretically his position is untenable in that empirical departures from the ideal typical are analysed in a quite arbitrary manner that leads to both historicism and eclecticism. Yet this uncertainty of Weber has been largely absent amongst modern sociologists of law who have taken his ideal type as a sufficient account of contemporary legal systems.

Thus his treatment of legal domination must be understood in its wider ideological implications and once so placed it loses its apparent formalism. At the same time it stands out as a very partial treatment of the social phenomena of power and domination. Yet despite this it is contended that Weber performs a service that makes his contribution stand out above that of other contributions to the sociological movement. His sociology of law is 'systematic' not so much because of the formal qualities of his theory building, but because it provides a model which embraces both he internal and external dimensions of law as a social phenomena. His specific contribution is to stress the latter as a substantive area of enquiry. Through the exploration of the relationship between law and the political forms of social order he, by that act alone, renders a service in positing that question for it is a question which is largely absent from the sociological movement in law taken as a whole.

His contribution goes further than merely asserting the importance of the relationship between the legal and the political order. By restricting his attention to the forms of legitimate domination he frustrates the realisation of an integrated treatment of domination, but nevertheless he draws attention to the major historical role of the process of 'voluntary submission' as a central ingredient of the modern bourgeois society.[104] It is the focus on what may be identified as sociological domination[105] that provides a potentially fruitful line of enquiry for the sociology of law and which will ensure that he will retain a central importance for the sociology of law.

The feature of his discussion of the forms of domination that has been concentrated upon is that of the form of legitimacy claimed and the associated basis of obedience. Weber himself, in developing his substantive political sociology, devotes his major attention to the forms of administration associated with the types of domination. While his theory of bureaucracy has played an important role in the development of sociological theory its impact upon the sociology of law has been relatively limited.[106]

We may conclude this section by trying to link the different levels of Weber's sociology of law encountered so far. The presentation (see opposite page) sets out a typology which seeks to link the general types of legitimate domination to the particular forms of law and legal administration. It will be noted that an attempt is made to relate the earlier typologies discussed. The major substantive point to emerge is the absence of a direct parallel between the developmental typology of forms of domination with the typology of the forms of legal thought. This emphasises the formal and non-developmental character of the latter. It will therefore be noted that the major stages indicated contain within them different types of legal thought. It is only with reference to the pure type of legal domination that Weber posits a direct congruence with a specific form of legal thought, namely logical formal rationality.

Law and capitalism

The focus on the relationship between the economic system and the wider social system is central to Weber's sociology and it also plays an important part in his sociology of law. This concern manifests itself in two themes: first the causal importance of 'rational law' in the development of the distinctive features of modern capitalism; this theme underlies the whole discussion in he earlier section on the rationalisation of law. The second theme concerns the extent to which economic factors *determine* law, that is whether or not any decisive causal role may be attributed to economic factors in accounting for the development of legal systems. Both of these themes are manifestations of the wider debate with Marxism.

His position may be summarised as the explicit repudiation of any attempt to explain law as the *direct* product of economic forces. Law, it is insisted, constitutes a sphere of autonomous social reality which, while influenced in its development by economic forces, in turn also influences the economic (and indeed other) processes within society. This autonomy is thus relative rather than absolute. He rejects the view that the development of any particular aspect of a legal system can be explained as a response to economic need.

> The absence of an economic need is by no means the only explanation of the lack of certain legal institutions in the past. Like the technological methods of industry the rational patterns of legal technique to which the law is to give its guarantee must first be 'invented' before they can serve an existing economic interest. . . . Economic situations do not automatically give birth to new legal forms; they merely provide the opportunity for the spread of a legal technique if it is invented.[107]

From this assertion of the relative autonomy of law he arrives at the conclusion 'generally it appears, however, that the development of the

	LEGITIMATION: form of legitimation	ADMINISTRATION: associated form of administration	BASIC OF OBEDIENCE owed by subject	FORM OF JUDICIAL PROCESS	FORM OF JUSTICE	TYPE OF LEGAL THOUGHT
FORM OF TRADITIONAL	TRADITIONAL personal authority of King/Prince; belief in the sanctity of immemorial tradition.	PATRIMONIAL – hereditary principles major factor in determining structure and content	TRADITIONAL duty to individual incumbent (e.g. King or Prince) as holder of traditionally legitimated office or role. Strong individual flavour or duty to 'King's person'.	Combines a number of elements: (i) empirical and/or (ii) substantive justice, and/ or (iii) personal (Khadi)	(Secular or theocratic) empirical justice	Formal irrationality/ substantive rationality
FORM OF CHARISMATIC DOMINATION	CHARISMATIC AUTHORITY of leader(s). 'Personal devotion to the specific and exceptional sanctity, heroism or exemplary character of an individual person'.	In pure ideal type NO ADMINISTRATION; but where form persists process of 'routinisation of charisma' takes place.	Response to social-psychological characteristics of individual charismatic leader i.e. to qualities of individual personality.	Revelation: empirical justice; strong emphasis upon formalism in association with purely intuitive authority of charismatic leader.	Charismatic justice	Formal irrationality/ substantive irrationality
RATIONAL DOMINATION	RATIONAL LEGAL: authority derived from reified system of law, rationally and consciously enacted.	BUREAUCRATIC – professional	Duty of obedience impersonal, owed not to individuals, nor even to office but to 'the system'.	Rational: cases decided by application of rational, abstract rules to cases by professional staff.	Rational justice	Formal rationality – in particular logical formal rationality.

legal structure of organizations has by no means been predominantly determined by economic factors.'[108]

The form of relationship which does subsist between law and economics finds its nexus in the concepts of 'calculability' and 'predictability'.

The modern capitalist enterprise rests primarily on *calculation* and presupposes a legal and administrative system, whose functioning can be rationally predicted, at least in principle by virtue of its fixed general norms.[109]

But the association of law and economic activity does not imply that one can be regarded as the causal determinant of the other.

Modern rational capitalism has need, not only of the technical means of production, but of a calculable legal system. . . . We must hence inquire where that law came from. Among other circumstances, capitalistic interests have in turn undoubtedly helped, but by no means alone nor even principally, to prepare for the predominance in law and administration of a class of jurists specially trained in rational law. But these interests did not themselves create that law.[110]

Law then is perceived as crucially related to, rather than determined by, economic forces; it is thus an autonomous force in social development. For proof of the non-determinant role of economic factors Weber relies heavily on the example of England which was the first country to produce modern capitalism, but within the framework of a legal system which had not yet become rationalised; while on the other hand a law 'suitable' to capitalist development had first been developed in the economically more backward continental Europe.

Although he rejects a general causal determination of law by economic forces he frequently stresses the particular role that they play with respect to specific aspects of legal development. In his analysis of the development of corporate personality he insists that the different forms which have been recognised within legal systems are to be explained by variations in the economic purposes pursued. Thus for example economic activities with large capital requirements produce corporate entities with closed membership and formally defined objects; while those characterised by low reliance on capital input give rise to corporate forms with loose membership and wider objects.[111]

The function of law is conceived as being a means of guaranteeing economic activity. Thus for example the act of exchange relies upon he probability that parties will fulfil their mutual undertakings; yet underlying the mutuality of the transaction is the presence of legal institutions ready to guarantee that transaction. The granting of legal 'rights' is simply a means of giving durability and certainty to the pre-existing power of factual control. Law is recognised as being 'directly at the service of economic interests.[112] An analysis of the extent to which law serves economic interests cannot be gleaned merely from an examination of substantive law. Such an analysis must take into account the general distribution of access to economic interests and to the means of coercion. Discussing the concept of 'freedom of contract' he observes that contract law has the social consequence of being 'accessible only to the owners of property and thus in effect supports their very autonomy and power positions.'[113] Thus he recognised that law lends itself to particular class interests. He notes in general that 'it is precisely this abstract character which constitutes the decisive merit of formal justice to those who wield economic power.'[114]

> Formal justice guarantees the maximum freedom for the interested parties to represent their formal legal interests. But because of the unequal distribution of economic power, which the system of formal justice legalizes, this very freedom must time and again produce consequences which are contrary to religious ethics or political expediency. Furthermore, the development of the trial into a peaceful contest of conflicting interest can contribute to the further concentration of economic and social power.[115]

With specific reference to English common law he remarks that it exhibits the dual characteristics 'of formal adjudication within the upper class, combined with arbitrariness or *de facto* denigration of justice for the economically weak.'[116] These passages make clear that it is quite wrong to regard Weber as an apologist for bourgeois economic interests or that he denies the significance of economic interests in general.

Weber sees the extent to which the legal order is directly subservient to economic interests as being determined by the relative strength of private economic interests as compared with the interests promoting general conformity to the rules of law. With a touch of realism, and perhaps cynicism, he remarks 'the inclination to forego economic opportunity simply in order to act legally is obviously slight.'[117] However he qualifies a position which appears to be moving towards positing the 'dependence' of law by arguing that law, and in particular he singles out the internal structure of legal thought, has 'exercised a strong influence on economic organisation'.[118] For example he argues that economic development has been influenced by the legal restrictions placed upon exchange and competition, by means of price regulation, or by the limitation of the acquisition or exchange of rights of control.[119]

The treatment of the relationship between law and economics is significant because of its presence in his sociology of law rather than because of the actual position he develops. Its importance lies in the fact that the sociological movement has had relatively little to say on the relation between law and the economy.[120] The fact that he moves it into the field of discussion is in itself a major contribution. The great weakness of his substantive treatment is that the positions he adopts are essentially reactive in that he has a clear perception of what he labels the deterministic Marxist position and sets out to avoid its taint. Thus while he suggests some interesting leads on specific topics his overall position is eclectic — no general position that goes beyond the rather unsatisfactory assertion of partial dependence and partial autonomy between the two spheres.

The 'England problem'

Weber's general theoretical position on the relationship between law and capitalism can be summarised as follows: capitalism consists of rational economic conduct oriented to the market; such rational conduct is facilitated by a legal system that maximises certainty and predictability. Logical formal rationality in law results in certainty and predictability. The existence of logically formal rational law is a *necessary*, but not it must be stressed a *sufficient* condition for the emergence of capitalism.

The 'England problem' arises from the empirical fact that England underwent the first major historical development of capitalism, but did so with a legal system which could not be subsumed under the category of formal rationality.[121] A number of questions are therefore thrown into relief: is his general theoretical position on the relationship between law and capitalism invalidated? Is the English case merely an exception? If it is an exception, how is the exception to be explained? A subsidiary strand of this set of problems may also be isolated: if English law failed to undergo the rationalisation process why did it not do so? It is apparent that the debate about the 'English problem' involves a number of the major components of Weberian sociology of law; its exploration may lead towards further conclusions concerning the status and merit of his general theory. The method of procedure will be to examine what he had to say about English law.[122] It will then be possible to draw some conclusion and in particular to consider the significance of the 'England problem' for his sociology of law as a whole.

The English legal system, particularly as manifest in the common law, has exhibited a very striking durability; Weber comments that the common law had been able 'to preserve a highly archaic character and survive the greatest economic transformations without formal change.'[123] It was a prime example of his thesis that different stages of legal development could exist side by side within a single socio-economic system. The common law enshrined a veritable conglomeration of stages of legal development.

He points to the retention of facets of inherently irrational archaic law and also argues that subsequent developments were influenced by he archaic origins from which they sprang. Thus the early development of the common law exhibited 'magico-formalism' in its adoption of irrational modes of proof, manifested in such situations as ordeal and trial by battle. The use of oaths is an example of the retention of formally irrational modes of procedure. The important institution of jury trial, associated with the growth in importance of the royal courts, was seen by him as the retention of oracular methods.

Weber also subjects the whole basis of trial procedure at common law to close scrutiny. The 'adversary procedure' of English law is a product of a formalistic stage of development which is itself an outgrowth of oracle and ordeal, which in turn may be traced to an initial conception of law constituting a formalised and restraining force upon the feudal system. With the growth of legal formalism there developed the legal profession. The advocates are the champions of their clients waging battle within the framework of complex procedural rules. He is particularly interested in the effect of adversary procedure upon the position of the judge. Here he makes more explicit the comparison with the continental inquisitorial trial which imposes a more activist and interventionist role upon the judge. Within an 'adversary' system the judge is bound by its inherent formalism; he has to wait upon the motions and evidence advanced by the parties; thus his ability to pursue evidence on his own initiative is severely limited. It is a procedure of 'relative truth' in that facts not alleged or proved or undisclosed must be excluded. While this system of formal justice allows maximum freedom to the parties in the conduct of actions, as has been previously noted, he recognised that this formalism could operate to the advantage of the economically powerful.

Weber saw the system of lay magistracy, which has played such an important part in the administration of criminal law, as a 'highly irrational'[124] element having many of the characteristics of khadi justice in that the magistrates are not bound by the same degree of formalism as the higher courts. The consequence of this informal justice is to leave much greater scope for class-oriented ethical evaluations to determine the decisions that are handed down. In particular he stressed that it reflected the dualism of the English law; it constituted an inferior and less rational law that was imposed on the economically weaker classes. His picture of the development of the common law is of a gradual stripping away of the irrational elements and their replacement by legal formalism which does not in itself rid the system of its irrationality.

The precedent system as a distinctive feature of the common law receives considerable attention. He deals with it not only because of its important part in the common law but also because it provides him with a good example of his category 'empirical justice' which corresponds to the classification of 'substantive irrationality' in his general typology of legal thought. He defines empirical justice as 'formal judgements rendered, not by subsumption under rational concepts, but by drawing on 'analogies' and depending on and 'interpreting' concrete 'precedents' '[125] Such a system of law is necessarily irrational, 'empirical justice of the pure type does not (give any) reasons which in our sense can be called rational.'[126] The irrationality of the precedent system derives from its combination of syllogistic and inductive method. The syllogistic method has as its major premiss solely empirical propositions derived from the particular facts while the general norm or principle is relegated to the status of minor premiss. The essentially inductive method allows, in his view, the importation not only if irrelevancies, but also of extra-legal factors into the judicial process because of the overriding emphasis that the system places upon the fact situation at the expense of the general principles of law.

However it should not be thought that his treatment of the common law simply dispatched it to the netherworld of substantive irrationality. He can be interpreted as advancing an implicit thesis that a process of 'internal rationalisation' takes place within the common law. A major step occurs when the case law method becomes subject to the demand for a rational statement of the grounds upon which the decision in a case is based. This constitutes a retreat from purely empirical justice where the analogy applied in the instant case is the *fact* situation of the precedent case. Once rational grounds come to be widely expected there is a greatly accelerated development of general rules and principles. The consequence of this evolution is that there comes into existence a system of general and abstract legal rules and principles, and the precedent system in its operation becomes less immediately bound by the fact situations of instant and precedent cases, but focuses upon the principles of law and their relevance to the instant case. Weber has fixed upon a feature of considerable importance in the development of the precedent system, that it has undergone a transformation sufficient to have effectively transformed its very nature. So great has been this process of internal rationalisation that English jurists in the modern period have been able to conceive of English law in terms of 'pure law', of it consisting of a gapless, rigorously deductive system of abstract rules which Weber would have considered possible only in a codified system.

However a word of qualification is necessary. While it is undoubtedly true that this internal rationalisation of the precedent system has occurred we must avoid a simple acceptance of the proposition that it has now become a fully rational system. Rheinstein makes the perceptive observation that one of the most attractive features of the precedent system 'is its special aptness to hide behind a screen of verbal formulae of apparent logically formal rationality, those considerations of substantive rationality, that is, of social policy, by which the decision has been actually motivated but which judges are reluctant to reveal to the public and, often enough, to themselves.'[127]

Such a warning must be the legacy of the realist tradition of Anglo-American jurisprudence. Contemporary legal development has accredited a formally recognised role to such concepts as 'public policy'. It is significant that in Weber's view the reliance upon such legal techniques advocated by Pound as part of the 'socialisation of law', mark a movement from logical formal rationality towards substantive rationality.[128]

Weber returns time and again to emphasise the 'durability' and 'elasticity' of the English legal system and places considerable stress upon

the fact that the system has not undergone the same systematic rationalisation process as did Continental law. English law emerged from its feudal
origins without having decisively cast off those features. Property law
for example is most sharply influenced by the retention of feudal
concepts; he suggests that this had substantial effect upon the subsequent
distribution of property.[129] The common law passed over into the
modern world as a result of the internal collapse of feudalism whereas on
the continent modern legal systems were a product of the deeper and more
thoroughgoing bourgeois revolutions of the late eighteenth and early
nineteenth century; during the course of this development a decisive break
between the pre-existing law and the codified systems was the result.

Weber keeps returning to the problem of the development of English
law because of the central issue involved in the 'England problem': the
relationship between the development of capitalism and the evolution of
legal systems. He states his general position in the following way: 'It must
indeed be said that England achieved capitalistic supremacy among the
nations *not because of but rather in spite of its judicial system.*'[130]

The development of capitalism in England would therefore appear to
present a refutation of Weber's general theory of the interrelationship
between law and capitalism. However he seeks to turn this apparent
contradiction to the advantage of his general theoretical position.[131] His
commitment to a pluralistic or multi-causal analysis of history allows him
with apparent consistency to set out general ideal-typical relations of
which that between capitalism and rational law is but one example and at
the same time to be prepared to explain empirical departures from these
posited general relationships by reference to specific conjuctures of other
causal variables. Thus from Weber's standpoint the 'England problem' is a
less serious threat to his overall theoretical position than it at first appears
to be.

He goes further and argues that capitalist development took place in
England not merely 'despite' its legal system, but advances what may be
described as a theory of the 'advantages of backwardness'. He points to the
example of the late development of concepts of corporate personality and
suggests that this resulted in the advantage of producing a range of
practical forms of corporate organisation advantageous to economic
developments.[132]

> These very elements of 'backwardness' in the logical and govern-
> mental aspects of legal development enabled business to produce a
> far greater wealth of practically useful legal devices than had been
> available under the more logical and technically more highly ration-
> alised Roman law.[133]

In seeking to explain the uniqueness of the English law system he
emphasises two key factors. These were the key role of the English legal
profession and secondly the political framework within which the common law developed. Reference has already been made to his emphasis on

the 'two paths' of development of legal professions.[134]

In England, the reason for the failure of all efforts at rational codification of law, as well as the failure to 'receive' the Roman law, was due to the successful resistance against such rationalization offered by the great and centrally organised lawyers' guilds, a monopolistic stratum of notables from whose midst the judges of the high courts of the realm were recruited. They retained in their hands juristic training as an apprenticeship transmitting an empirical and highly developed technology, and they successfully fought all moves towards rational law.[135]

The great success of the English legal profession was its inventiveness. They were able to create suitable forms, even if this meant the extensive use of fictions, for the transaction of business in the service of their capitalist clients.[136] The outstanding example of this 'inventiveness' is the history of the evolution of the trust mechanism.

The dominant role of the legal profession manifests itself in the emergence of 'cautelary jurisprudence' which is marked by a highly 'practical' orientation to law with an associated instrumentalism in the utilisation of technical skills to advance the interests of clients. The legal profession comes to have a pecuniary interest in the preservation of its technical skills, which results in these interests becoming an obstacle to the rationalisation of law. Thus while his general thesis is to see legal professions as a *means* towards the rationalisation of law he regards the English legal profession as actually *inhibiting* such developments.

Roman law triumphed wherever there did not exist a legal profession with a nation-wide organization.[137]

The second causal factor that accounts for the uniqueness of English law is the political framework in which it developed. The English common law developed at the same time as, and was in many respects a product of, the very early development of a centralised state, and in particular of the early development of the centralised Royal courts.[138] The subsequent legal development is therefore always influenced by the intervention of the central political authority ('imperium').

The intrusion of the imperium, especially the monarch, into the legal system, has contributed to the unification and systematization of the law.[139]

Common law, as it developed under Henry II and Edward II, was increasingly rationalised particularly with respect to the mode of·proof and trial and saw the elimination of much of the magical formalism and folk-justice of Anglo-Saxon law. Yet this very process of overcoming magical formalism resulted in the consolidation of a new and more rigid type of formalism, especially evident in the writ system. The role of the state also had important consequences for the development of substantive law. The law of landlord and tenant was influenced by the authoritarian relations instituted within English feudalism.[140] Continental notions of corporate personality were a product of legal recognition of *de facto* autonomous economic units developed within the medieval city. English concepts of corporate personality on the other hand are essentially a law of 'privileges' because of the extent to which their development was dependent on royal grant or patronage.

This discussion of the interaction of political forms and legal development has been taken further by Little's attempt to test Weber's *Protestant Ethic* thesis.[141] He sought to bring within a common approach a detailed analysis of religious developments and a similar detailed historical treatment of legal development during the same period. He starts by noting the alliance that had developed between the Puritans and the common lawyers.[142] This alliance was of an indirect character, a 'marriage of convenience', in that both groups found themselves opposed to monarchical power. Little proceeded by means of a detailed examination of work of Sir Edward Coke, in particular with reference to his treatment of corporation cases.

Little presents an interpretation generally favourable to the Weberian position. The theological conflicts of seventeenth century England embodied a conflict between the values of traditionalism and legal rationality. Likewise the legal developments, embodied in the judgments of Coke, contain the same conflict; the judgments are seen as full of internal contradictions as Coke strives to discover authority in antiquity while his judgments in opposition to royal monopoly were facilitating the development of new economic forces. Thus in significant respects he sees the common lawyers as taking up positions close to the traditional, authority-orientated theology of the Anglican supporters of the monarchical order. What Little fails to come to grips with is something which Weber had himself pointed out namely that the majority of social movements had sought some traditional ideological support for positions whose objective content was socially progressive.

The lesson of Weber's treatment of the 'England problem' is not that it presents a direct refutation of his general thesis; rather it exposes a real weakness in his substantive, as opposed to his conceptual, sociology. He fails to advance any coherent solution to the problem which he himself presents. He resorts to an eclectic method that lapses into an historicism which seeks to account for the phenomenon in terms of discrete and historically specific causes which bear no direct relationship to his conceptual sociology. He therefore leaves revealed a major area of enquiry that confronts the sociology of law concerning the relationship between economic and legal development; it is an area that has not received any consistent attention in modern sociology of law.[143]

As has been argued previously the significant contribution that Weber makes has not been the solutions that he offers, but rather it lies in the fact that he isolates the major problems upon which the sociology of law must concentrate its attention. Thus his consideration of the relationship

between legal and economic development not only brings out that
relationship as a central question, but at the same time links it directly
with the discussion of the forms of domination nd their relationship to the
legal order.

Contract

Weber devotes a complete chapter to the consideration of the institution
of contract.[144] Apart from his continuing interest in the development of
corporate institutions it constitutes his only extended examination of
substantive law.

Recognised legal rights, advanced in 'legal propositions', represent the
most basic relationship between law and economic life. Legal rights are not
merely the reflection of social relations of power, but have a creative role
in delinating the scope and nature of that power. His treatment of the
evolution of contract is very markedly 'economic' and this constitutes the
major difference betwéen his treatment and Durkheim's who failed to
situate his discussion in an economic context.

In a society where self-sufficiency prevails, and hence exchange is
limited, the law will necessarily be more restricted than that which
emerges in societies in which exchange plays a central role.

> There exists, of course, an intimate connection between the expan-
> sion of the market and the expanding measure of contractual
> freedom.[145]

The development of the market results in a quantitative increase of
transactions and it also gives rise to important interest groups who have
'market interests'; the pressures that they generate come to have increasing
importance. 'Their influence predominates in determining which legal
transactions the law should regulate.'[146]

The distinctive feature of his thesis is that he is not merely concerned
with the simple quantitative expansion of contract, but with stressing a
fundamental change in the type of contract that emerges. His thesis is that
a transition takes place from 'status contracts' to 'purposive contracts'. He
is here implicitly rejecting the sharp conceptual separation between 'status'
and 'contract' posited by Maine; rather he insists that what has occurred is
a change in the *type* of contract.

> The present day significance of contract is primarily the result of the
> high degree to which our economic system is market orientated and
> of the role played by money.[147]

Thus he insists that 'contract' as such plays an important part in early law
particularly with respect to 'landlord-tenant' relations and family relations.
What he seeks to emphasise is the significance of the modern market-
oriented 'purposive contracts'. He traces the transition from transactions
based on 'barter' to those based on 'obligation'. The fundamental turning
point being occasioned by the growth of a money economy; it rendered
transactions quantifiable, abstract and thus perceived as neutral. The early

stages of contract were strongly influenced by religion and magic, the subsequent development is not so much concerned with purely consensual activity, but is characterised by the elimination of magical and religious elements and is a manifestation of the 'secularisation of law'. The development of purposive contract is associated with distinct changes in legal thought; earlier forms stress 'composition', the buying off of vengeance, whereas notions of payment of 'compensation' arise, that is payment for quantifiable loss occasioned.

Weber enters into the discussion of the extent of contractual freedom and the relationship between freedom and coercion. He differentiates himself sharply from individualistic theories which posit an even expansion of 'free contractual activity'. He insists that modern societies impose limitations on contractual activity; these limitations arise both from the interests of the state and of market-oriented groups themselves. He therefore rejects the simplistic view that associates the advance of contract with an increase in the sphere of freedom and a decrease in coercion.

The root determinant of freedom lies in the distribution of social and economic power.

> The exact extent to which the total amount of 'freedom' within a given legal community is actually increased depends entirely upon the concrete economic order and especially upon the property distribution.[148]

He cuts through a purely formal analysis of the substantive law and draws attention to the power relations of society. The factual development of social relations may actually result in an expansion of 'free contract' resulting in an increase in the domination over others.

> The result of contractual freedom, then, is in the first place the opening of the opportunity to use, by the clever utilization of property ownership in the market, these resources without legal restraints as a means for the achievement of power over others.[149]

In particular he stresses that in viewing the contract of employment it is necessary to cut through the element of purely formal freedom enshrined therein in order to perceive the inherent inequality and the factual lack of freedom.

> The more powerful party in the market, i.e. normally the employer, has the possibility to set the terms, to offer the job 'take it or leave it', and, given the normally more pressing economic need of the worker, to impose his terms upon him.[150]

This exposition of his treatment of contractual relationships is valuable in pointing to its marked contrast to the weaknesses that have been pointed to in Durkheim's treatment and is valuable in cutting through the ideological connotations that surround the identification of contract and freedom in juristic and political thought. He grounds his discussion of the emergence of substantive law in the context of the historical development of exchange relations. Such an approach provides a useful model for the general investigation of substantive law. It is interesting to note that in this discussion he makes relatively little use of his theoretical treatment of the internal evolution of the modes of legal thought. It may therefore be concluded that while it has an intrinsic value his treatment of contract is divorced from the mainstream of his sociology of law.

CONCLUSION

Weber's sociology of law is the most important and substantial contribution to the sociological movement in law. It constitutes a significant advance, both in terms of its systematic elaboration and its substantive content, over the contributions of both sociological jurisprudence and of Durkheimian sociology. In important respects it achieves a higher level of development than that realised within the sociology of law that succeeded it. The limitations of post-War sociology of law stem from the extent to which this trend has been locked within its sub-disciplinary status and dominated by perspectives and problematics which remain restricted by an essentially jurisprudential frame of reference.[151]

Modern sociology of law has until very recently restricted itself to deferential references to Weber's sociology of law; no systematic effort has been made to take up or to develop his major themes and to explore the central arenas of enquiry that are marked out in Weber's sociology of law. Talcott Parsons comes closest to providing an exception to this characterisation of modern sociology of law, but his attempt to make use of Weberian approached results in their transformation into defences of ideological significant doctrines characteristic of Anglo-American legal systems in particular of the doctrine of the separation of powers.[152]

The explanation for the failure of modern sociology of law to take up Weber's potential contribution to the field helps to account for recent revival of interest in Weber.[153] These works represent a trend towards a more explicit concern with theory in reaction against the atheoreticism of American sociology of law. The dominant trend in the institutionalisation of sociology of law operated, and indeed continues to operate, with an unproblematic conception of the field of sociology of law seen as the application of the methods and resource of 'sociology' to a distinct and definite object namely 'law'. The sociology of law is thus seen as involving problems of the method of applying social science perspectives and as a corollary as not requiring the development of a substantive theoretical base. A reaction has developed to the absence of explicit theoretical concern within the field and the revival of interest in Weber can be seen as a facet of this development.

The importance that I attach to Weber, both with respect to his sociology of law and incidentally with reference to the wider debates within sociology should not imply an acceptance or support for either his general theoretical position or his substantive analysis of law. Rather I wish to argue that Weber provides the central point for theoretical encounter within the tradition of the sociological movement in law. It is through engaging with Weberian sociology of law that advances are possible both theoretically and in the direction of empirical enquiry. This centrality of Weber for the concerns of the sociology of law stems not so much from his role as 'grand master' of the sociological traditions, but rather from the major directions or problematics posed in his sociology of law. The problematics designated by Weber are not to be accepted in the form presented by Weber but rather require to be transformed or reconstituted.

The central problematics which Weber poses for the sociology of law are threefold, but they are not ones which are necessarily integrated within Weber's own work; rather they are three pointers or directions as to what constitute the major issue confronting the sociology of law. The first problematic in Weber's sociology of law is relationship between law and domination. His treatment of this relationship is both restricted and distorted by his reduction of domination to the inter-subjective relationship between ruler and ruled. He distinguishes domination from 'economic action', which is a product of factual power, whereas domination is a product of the specific forms of legitimacy claimed. By adopting this inter-subjective perspective he in fact takes the ideological form of the legal order, manifest in the specific form of its claim to legitimacy and obedience, as the real form of legal or political relations. If the law and domination relationship is to be made use of, it must be liberated from this inter-subjective and idealistic orientation. The process of domination must be located within the structure of social relations within which context the ideological forms taken by law and legal relations can be examined, but not as the only focus as if the ideological form constitutes the real relation.

The isolation of the process of domination as a central problematic for the sociology of law stands in marked contrast to the social control orientation that has been paramount in both sociological jurisprudence and Durkheimian sociology. The major differentiation between the social control and domination perspectives results from the fact that the social control perspective presents the determination of social reality as stemming from the fact of human sociality itself. The social person is subject to the determination of social forces which are universal in that they are pervasive, containing people in the fact of social life.

In Weber's sociology of law the process of domination characteristic of capitalist society places and legal system at the centre of that process. It is not necessary to accept this centrality of law which he asserts; it is sufficient to stress the significance of the fact that it provides the basis for insisting that the sociology of law must focus upon law in the context of the processes of social domination. The nature of these processes of social domination, freed from the inter-subjective restrictions imposed by Weber, form a central problem upon which the sociology of law must work and which provides a major link with the wider concerns of social theory.

The second problematic present in Weber's sociology of law is provided by the relation between law and the political structure and specifically the relation between the law and the state. Weber's own treatment of political forms is very much restricted by his almost exclusive concern with the forms of legitimacy claimed by specific state forms. His treatment of the modern state, characterised by bureaucratic forms of administration, makes the relation between law and state a central focus of his sociology of law. Again while it is necessary to be critical of his specific treatment of the state, distorted as it is by the nature of his concern with legitimacy, the posing of the law-state relation as a central concern must be defended against its almost total absence from the main tradition of sociological jurisprudence and sociology of law. The sociological movement in law has almost universally adopted the constitutional doctrine of the separation of powers as socio-political reality and has, as a consequence, not posed the relation between law and the state as a problem for the attention of the sociology of law. The prominence of this question in Weber immediately outweighs the criticisms of his specific treatment of the relation.

The third major problematic advanced by Weber is the relationship between law and the economic system. Durkheim's universalistic theory of the division of labour does not as such raise the law-economy relation as a field of enquiry since he asserted their identity in he form of a reflection theory. This relationship has been absent as a focus of investigation or discussion in the sociological movement in law. Weber's merit is that he reinstates it, albeit within the unsatisfactory context of a sociological pluralism, which renders his position unambiguously empiricist.

This treatment is unashamedly 'opportunist in that it quite consciously seeks to harness the general prestige which surrounds Weber to a critique of what are regarded as major deficiencies and absences in the sociological movement in law. The presence of the problematics relating to domination, the state and the economy in Weber's work makes his sociology of law a central point of reference in a way which, despite the deferential forelock-touching of modern sociology of law, it has not been to date. It is suggested that a critical engagement with Weber's treatment of these central questions is a necessary point of departure for the sociology of law.

This engagement with Weber's legacy must confront not only his general sociological position but also the specific direction that this imposes on his sociology of law, in particular the predominant tendency which led him to concentrate upon an internal analysis of the forms of legal thought. It needs to be stressed that range of specific questions addressed within the framework of any specific problematic are not exclusively designated by the statement of the problematic itself, but are determined by the general theoretical and methodological position within which they are developed. Thus to applaud Weber's sociology of law does not imply any endorsement of the particular areas of enquiry into which he was led nor of their substantive treatment.

Weber was not self-consciously a part of the 'sociological movement in law' in the way that Pound and the Realists were. Yet he represents a major peak of achievement of that movement on two counts. First he succeeded in articulating in general sociology of law rooted firmly within an elaborated theoretical context; second, and it is here that he stands out from other contributors to the movement, in his decisive identification of the central theoretical questions that confront the further development of that movement albeit questions distorted by his specific theoretical and ideological orientation.

6 The Sociological Movement: Results and Prospects

A conclusion is rarely simply a conclusion. It is therefore perhaps useful to indicate at the outset what the specific issues are with which this chapter is concerned. The method of exposition has been to study the writings of selected individuals and groups who have contributed to the sociological movement in law, but the conclusion is not significantly concerned with making final pronouncements upon individuals. The explicit motivation has been a concern with the contemporary situation of the movement. It has however been necessary to insist that the intellectual roots and preoccupations of that movement be explored since its contemporary exponents frequently have little understanding of the historical process of which they constitute a part.

This chapter therefore concerns itself with advancing an assessment of the sociological movement, drawing out and attempting to account for the relatively underdeveloped state of contemporary sociology of law. It seeks to locate the source and the character of the continuity which has been manifest in both the jurisprudential and the sociological phases of the movement. In moving towards a discussion of the prospects for the sociological movement an effort has been made to indicate the major orientations that have provided the motivating energy and which link them to the founders of the movement and finally to locate them in the historical context within which they developed.

The sociological movement in law arose in its most persistent expression from within the general context of Anglo-American jurisprudence. Its emergence was paralleled by a similar development in the legal thought in Europe which, though different in many respects, embodied problems common to legal systems in rapidly developing capitalist societies. Sociological jurisprudence expressed an attempt to

break out from formal legal individualism and to provide a more compelling and coherent account of the social context of the legal system
within capitalist society. This new attempt to provide an account of, and a
justification for, law was 'sociological' in the sense that such an orientation
signified the elevation of the 'social' within the frame of reference. It was
facilitated by the rapidly developing intellectual hegemony of the social
sciences. Sociology provided a means of intellectual transition from the
traditional individualistic assumptions of nineteenth century jurisprudence.

Sociological jurisprudence was a reflex in the realm of legal thought of
a particular stage of capitalist development which is in particular marked
by a more extensive role of the state in economic and social life. But the
adoption of a 'social calculus' did not resolve the problem with which it
sought to grapple. The central problematic of juristic theory has been to
provide a socially persuasive — that is relevant to a particular socio-
historical situation — account of the grounds of legitimacy of the existing
legal order and through that of the existing social order.

Analytical jurisprudence had rested upon an implicitly Hobbesian
assumption that the social imperative of adherence to law was located in
an individualistic view of human nature as needing to be brought under
control if social life is to be possible. Yet the extended period of the
bourgeois democratic revolution, in its later period expressing itself
concretely in the reform agitation that dominated English political life
throughout the majority of the nineteenth century, was characterised by a
changing social problematic. No longer was it sufficient to demonstrate
that law was the command of the sovereign; the question had now
become, who was to be the sovereign? That is, it posed the issue of the
source of the legitimacy of the political order. The transition that occurred
within analytical jurisprudence was expressed in a utilitarianism which
asserted that legitimacy resided in the extent to which the system was
capable of satisfying the disparate and competing claims of citizens. Yet its
inherent individualism made its equation of justice with the satisfaction of
the maximum of individual claims unconvincing. Its conjunction with
laissez-faire economic ideology imported an assumption of the individual
as entrepreneur motivated by a market orientation. The entry more
centrally upon the social and political stage of non-entrepreneurial classes,
in particular the working class, made the individualistic utilitarianism less
relevant and persuasive.

Sociological jurisprudence had as its implicit concern the provision of
an account that carries conviction as a basis for the legitimation of law in
mass political democracies. The solution that it posited was at no stage
concerned to question the legitimacy of the capitalist social order itself. Its
proffered solution posited an assumption of a potentially infinite multiplicity of interests and claims, that is social pluralism. It therefore argued
for a calculus in which the individual and group (social) claims could be

expressed and thus weighed and valued; its form was the Poundian 'social interests' conceived as social universals. The universal social interests provide the standard against which the legitimacy of the legal order could be assessed. All citizens are deemed to have an interest in for, example, the preservation of social institutions or the security of acquisitions. Hence it was argued that in so far as the legal order functions to preserve such universal interests it is deserving of obedience. The universal social interests protect the 'reasonable' claims of capitalist and worker, of farmer and town-dweller, of shopkeeper and consumer. In functioning to balance and satisfy these claims in terms of a higher order of 'social' valuation the legal system is presented as providing a unity within the framework of a core of 'national' interests. It sought to provide a coherence within which the conflicts between groups and classes could be resolved.

In a sense sociological jurisprudence marked the close of the development of Western jurisprudence. What came after sociological jurisprudence has been concerned to find new ways of expressing this same 'solution' to the legitimacy of the legal and social order. What is distinctive about modern jurisprudence is the extent to which the value problem is more consciously to the fore; this tendency had become pronounced as the jurists, particularly in the United States, have grappled with the very apparent decline in the legitimacy of the legal order.[1]

Sociological jurisprudence attempted to provide a coherent account of the basis of the legitimacy of the legal order in class society within the framework of an unquestioned assumption of the reconcilability of class interests. It is the juristic adjunct of political pluralism. Sociological jurisprudence, and in particular American Realism, having advanced the social utilitarian calculus, became increasingly concerned with the means of furthering and perfecting the performance of the legal system. In Pound this manifests itself in an extensive elaboration and classification of the system of interests. Another manifestation was the recognition of the fallibility of the legal order. With the legal system being conceived as not simply a rule-applying mechanism, but as having a substantive evaluatory role, then the focus increasingly shifted to attempts to assess the extent to which these tasks are fulfilled. This led to an increasing emphasis upon a narrow reformatory frame of reference rooted in pragmatic philosophy. Its most direct and important expression being the concern with the judicial process and the movement towards empirical study of the functioning of the various institutions of the legal system.

It is this transition from the jurisprudential problematic to the focus on the means of its realisation through an instrumental orientation that determined the general characteristics of sociological jurisprudence. It provides its reforming concerns and accounts for its 'radicalism'; this was a radicalism not in terms of its theoretical content, but rather of a reformist character that is necessarily confined within the existing institutional and procedural framework. Further this more pronounced concern with the instrumentality of law explains what may be described as the defeat of sociological jurisprudence at the very time when its triumph appeared assured. The general orientation of sociological jurisprudence has achieved widespread if not universal acceptance, but at the same time its concern with instrumentalism has kept alive the narrow and technical concerns of legal thought and practice. Nowhere is this more apparent than with respect to American realism; the radical debunkers of traditionalism came to devote their efforts to a reworking of the most traditional juristic problems, epitomised in their almost obsessive concern with the judicial function.

The rise of sociology of law upon the terrain of sociological jurisprudence embodies both the victory and the defeat of the latter. This stage, notwithstanding its claim to autonomy, has its roots firmly in the law schools, despite the seminal influence of major sociologists in particular of Durkheim and Weber. Without the ascendancy of sociological jurisprudence such a development would not have been possible, but the emergence of sociology of law marks the defeat of sociological jurisprudence in the sense that it expresses a frustration with the extent to which the path that sociological jurisprudence took led to its reabsorption in the mainstream of jurisprudence.

Sociology of law is the second phase of the sociological movement in law; it has assumed the proportions of a movement in its own right. Durkheim and Weber, through their central role in the development of sociology, are not so much 'founders' of the sociology of law, but rather should be regarded as key points of reference for the field that was to achieve a generalised presence only in the post-war period. It has subsequently achieved institutional expression in the form of courses, departments, programmes, conferences and the other criteria that mark the process of academic institutionalisation. Its potentialities have been proclaimed, its enthusiasm has been considerable. Yet at root the contemporary status of sociology of law is marked precisely by a lack of clarity as to its nature, purpose and direction; it is a hot-house plant, the forced offspring of the deficiencies of sociological jurisprudence and the jurisprudential tradition in general.

The sociology of law was born of the failure of sociological jurisprudence to provide an adequate and lasting solution to the jurisprudential problematic. The post-war period in which it has developed has witnessed a sharpening crisis not only of the wider social system, but specifically of legal systems themselves. The reaction of academic movements to the social contexts in which they are situated rarely fully grasp and understand that context; as a result the academic movements often lack homogeneity and uniformity of purpose. This is certainly the case with the sociology of law and it manifests itself in an apparent diversity of both ends and means. One response has been a self-conscious concern to grapple with the general jurisprudential problematic;[2] and has resulted in a trend which amounts to a restatement, albeit in more fully fashioned sociological guise, of the social utilitarian position of sociological jurisprudence. This trend constitutes the harnessing of sociology in order to breathe fresh life into the bourgeois democratic model of legal democracy; the key expressions are the repeated emphasis upon the separation of powers and the due process doctrine.

The alternative response has been one which has sought to retreat from the value problem and to present the sociology of law in a narrowly positivistic form as a technical or servicing function. This response has also varied in its expression; on the one hand some have welcomed and accepted the servicing function to the craft needs of the legal profession, on the other hand it has denied that the value problem has any role within the domain of the sociology of law. There is also a discernible middle position which recognises the value problem, but expresses a pessimism about the possibility of an adequate solution in the short-run and which therefore directs itself towards the alleviation of some of its symptoms in the present; it is this strand which has the most direct continuities with the Realists.

The momentum which produced the transition from sociological jurisprudence to sociology of law has not, as yet, produced any development which constitutes a significant theoretical advance that might have provided either a focus of unity or alternatively constituted a focus of theoretical controversy as a stimulant to clarification and further advance for the field. There has been no theoretical contribution which matches the comprehensiveness or systematisation of Weber's sociology of law or which provides such a powerful identification of the central questions to which that study must address itself. Just as structural functionalism has within sociology been a restricted and barren truncation of Weberian sociology, so within the sociology of law the dominant trend has retreated from Weber's contribution; this weakness ensures that Weber's contribution will for some time to come need to remain a central point of reference.

The intellectual roots of the sociological movement arose most immediately from the jurisprudential tradition, but this jurisprudential influence is reinforced by the lack of attention that has until the more recent period been devoted to the phenomenon of law by the mainstream of sociology. More recently there has been a shift of interest which involves a general concern with public regulatory activity. This development has been paralleled by the rise of the sociology of deviance and of the 'new criminology'. Both of these trends have tended to subject questions concerning law, crime and legal regulation to a closer scrutiny. Despite these developments the general picture has been one in which the interests and concerns of academic sociology have resulted in law not being regarded as an appropriate or substantial focus of interest. This situation is all the more significant in view of the demonstration made in previous chapters of the extent to which the two most influential figures in sociology, Durkheim and Weber, placed law very much within their major concerns. It is therefore necessary to enquire why it has been that law has received such minimal consideration from academic sociology.

A number of explanations have been advanced to account for this neglect of law, but it is suggested that to a greater or lesser extent they are inadequate. The most widely held explanation is one which points to the 'craft mysticism' that surrounds law and thus renders it relatively impenetrable to the sociologist. This view has been advanced amongst others by Aubert, Schur and Sawer.[3] There is no dispute about the extent to which lawyers have developed and protected their craft mysticism, but this does not make it inevitable that this should inhibit the sociologists. Sociology has long sustained interest in other fields in which similar technical problems are encountered, for example in the sociologies of medicine and science. Although the sociologist in venturing into the legal arena may not meet with a warm reception from its present incumbents this in itself cannot account for the relative neglect of law.

A second line of argument has suggested that law has been shunned by the sociologists because of the normative character of law.[4] Such an objection reveals an ultra-positivistic conception of sociology. It is simply inaccurate to suggest that sociology has avoided the normative sphere; rather the whole history of Western sociology is a demonstration of the opposite — that concern with the relationship between social values and social actions and institutions has occupied the centre of the sociological stage. This is true of Durkheimian positivism, Weberian subjectivism, structural functionalism and more recently of interactionism and ethno-methodology.

A more adequate, but by no means sufficient, explanation draws attention to the process of academic institutionalisation and notes a tendency for sociology, as a late arrival on the academic scene, to adopt as its primary concern areas of enquiry not already covered by established disciplines. The most important example is the extent to which academic sociology has largely ignored the field of economics. This factor can be regarded as having played some part in accounting for the lack of attention devoted by sociologists to the established academic discipline of law.

None of these explanations of sociology's neglect of law provide a sufficient account. The concerns of sociology naturally tend to focus upon what the philosophical and ideological orientations of its exponents perceive as the primary determinants of social reality. Sociologists have tended not to regard law as falling within this category; especially within American sociology, which British sociology has largely reflected, there has been a predominant concern with the informal, non-institutional areas of social life. The search has been for the most universal components of social reality. These universal features have been seen in what are regarded as the most 'basic' aspects of social life which have tended to be perceived as being manifest in the most informal, face-to-face social relations and activities. The greatest attention has been devoted to non-institutionalised forms of human activity. Law has suffered from what may be described as the paradox of institutionalisation. The very institutionalised character of law which because of its visibility commends it on the one hand as a subject of social investigation, on the other the belief that non-institutionalised forms are more 'basic' has resulted in law receiving only limited attention; the latter response has formed the dominant tradition.

The reason which underlies this persisting concern with informal social action is in itself important, but it is the more so for the light that it throws upon the backwardness of the sociology of law. Sociology despite its commitment to scientific status and value neutrality has, like all other social sciences, been subject to powerful ideological influences. One of the strongest of these is a tendency that is rarely articulated to present a particular social order as 'natural', that is as the self-evident, logical or universal form of social life. This tendency has been particularly pronounced in Western sociology where it is reinforced by an implicit adherence to the superiority of the prevailing form of society.

The attempt to demonstrate the 'naturalness' of a particular social order takes the form of a search for its origins in the simplest constituents of social life that can be presented as universal characteristics of human existence. Perhaps the most extreme example of this approach is the attempt within traditional economic theory to derive a universal market orientation from the analogy of Robinson Crusoe. In sociological thought the basis of the social system is presented as founded upon primary face-to-face and small group relations which are invested with a social universality; it is upon this foundation that the edifice of structures and institutions is constructed. The basic processes that constitute the root of social order are seen as being a spontaneous consequence of the very fact of sociality; hence not only these processes, but the total society itself, comes to be seen a 'natural'.

The generalised commitment of the American academic tradition to liberal capitalist ideals, coupled with a persistent philosophical individualism, has resulted in the dominant focus of attention being placed upon the informal, non-institutionalised forms of social activity. The more directly organised and organising, let alone coercive features of the social system, have tended to suffer relative neglect. This orientation goes hand-in-hand with the tendency to emphasise the stability of the social system and to ignore those features that manifest conflict and point towards persistent structural tensions in society. The consequence has been that law as such has suffered neglect and at the same time the treatment of it that has occurred has tended to focus upon its value integrative features.

The tendency of American sociology to neglect the treatment of law has the following major consequence. Not only was the sociology of law born of the jurisprudential tradition and thus, understandably, has been concerned with jurisprudential issues, but the fact that law has received only limited attention from academic sociology further reinforces the dominance of the jurisprudential problematic.

Detailed attention has been devoted to what have been isolated as two main strands within the sociological movement in law. These has been grouped under the labels 'sociological jurisprudence' and 'sociology of law'. From their diverse locations those figures that have been examined in the preceding chapters have been concerned to demarcate the field into conceptually discrete compartments. While the particular differentiations differ widely they have all rested upon a distinction between a jurisprudential and a sociological approach to law. The predominant tendency within modern sociology of law has been to insist upon the necessity of maintaining a separation from jurisprudence. This feature is most explicit in those who adhere to a positivistic or empiricist position and who present the distinction between the two stands as that between the speculative and the scientific. While there has been a pursuit of a differentiation from jurisprudence, the only level at which they can be said to have succeeded is in the adoption of a narrowly empiricist position which simply ignores, and thereby abolishes, jurisprudential problems; but to ignore certain questions does not in itself constitute a realisation of the objective of differentiation between sociology and jurisprudence.

The relationship between the jurisprudential and the sociological strands within the movement goes far beyond a particular intellectual heritage, that of Realism, which provided the immediate stimulus to modern American sociology of law. There exists a fundamental continuity between the two strands.

This common core can be identified as a consistent adherence to a shared set of domain assumptions.[5] The domain assumptions which have permeated the sociological movement in law may be designated as a set of interrelated ideas which constitute 'bourgeois legal ideology'. Before considering the content of the domain assumptions it is important to stress that these positions never appear in a pure or complete form in the writings of particular individuals; they will frequently be combined with other positions which may to a greater or lesser extent be in conflict with the domain assumptions. It will also generally be the case that individual expressions will tend to emphasise different facets of the totality. It is a necessary qualification to stress that ideology should not be treated as a monolithic self-sustaining entity. Edward Thompson, in another context, expresses it well:

> No ideology is wholly absorbed by its adherents: it breaks down in practice in a thousand ways under the criticism of impulse and of experience.'[6]

It is now necessary to consider the content of bourgeois legal ideology. Its central feature is an adherence to the 'inevitability' or 'naturalness of law'. Law is seen as a necessary consequence of social life itself. In accounts of the origin and evolution of law it is presumed that the transition from non-law to law is a necessary response to the growing size and complexity of society. Such a position is predicated upon an acceptance of classical political philosophy, particularly the Hobbesian solution to the problem of order, which gives rise to social contract theories in which the emergence of law and government is seen as marking the subjugation of primitivism and the rise of civilisation. Such a view incorporates the conventional wisdom that associates the absence of law, in anything other than the idyllic 'simple society', with anarchy.

Once law is deemed to be natural and inevitable it is a short step to an insistence upon the rationality and efficiency of law. Law is not merely regarded as an inevitability, but it is viewed as a rational means of social organisation in that authoritative rules are regarded as being necessary and desirable; Weber provides the strongest and most explicit example of this position. Such a view rests on a games analogy; every game requires explicit rules that are known to the players. So also must society have rules; their absence it is assumed would necessarily result in a higher level of social conflict. What is particularly significant is that the existence of rules *per se* is regarded as important. The content of the rules themselves is a subsidiary matter; although their substantive content effects their efficiency, their primary function is simply that of being rules for the guidance of social conduct — hence the primacy of social order for its own sake is implicit. This is particularly pronounced in the juristic concern with the ideal of legal certainty; even where, for example among the Realists, doubts are expressed about its realisation, the ideal itself remains intact.

It is a common presumption that not only is it desirable to have a system of authoritative rules, but that a civilised or democratic society is one characterised by the subjection of all, rulers and ruled, to a common set of rules. The 'rule of law' doctrine thus forms not merely a constitutional dogma, but constitutes a major element of the general legal ideology. Such a view incorporates the 'universalism' which is embodied in Western political and legal theory and is encapsulated in the concept of citizenship. The concept of citizenship abstracts each individual from their social and economic relations in society and raises or lowers them, as the case may be, to a position of formal equality with fellow citizens. In front of the ballot-box every citizen is a unit, but such a perception, whether applied to the political or the legal process, hides from view the real divergencies and inequalities in social and economic power.

The incorporation of the rule of law within bourgeois legal ideology is very closely connected with a common adherence to a view of the state and of the legal system as neutral institutions embodying the necessary collective interests of the society. Departures from the ideal of neutrality may be detected and deplored, but especially within pluralistic perspectives the ideal is retained. This leads back into legal ideology, particularly in the Anglo-American context, with a widespread implicit incorporation of variants of the separation of powers doctrine. The general consequence is seen in a tendency to ignore or to give only superficial attention to the relationship between the law and the state and the more general issue of the distribution of power in society. It is for this reason that it has been suggested that Weber's contribution to the sociology of law offers a fruitful point of reference for, despite his tendency to deflect from a full treatment of the law-state relationship because in his treatment of rational legal domination the notion of the state is virtually superseded by that of bureaucratic administration, he does place these questions at the heart of his sociology of law.

The consequence of positing the inevitability and rationality of law is to assert a presumption that adherence to law is natural. A generalised imperative of adherence to law is the product of a utilitarian calculus which perceives the satisfaction of both individual and collective ends facilitated by rule adherence. What is significant is that the imperative of rule adherence makes no reference to the substantive content of the rules to be obeyed. Whether or not rule adherence is rational must depend upon the content of the rules. It is rational and natural for those whose interests they advance or protect; it is far from self-evident where the reverse is the case. A direct corollary of the assumption that adherence to law is normal and rational is that rule violation is deemed to be deviant and inherently irrational. It is this assumption and its consequences that has provided the starting point for the critique of criminology that has been developed within the sociology of deviance.

The commentary upon the major figures of the sociological movement is given coherence when it is recognised that the set of domain assumptions that has been designated as bourgeois legal ideology has provided a persistent background, sometimes remaining unarticulated and sometimes emerging as central themes. The adherence to bourgeois legal ideology has the effect of circumscribing the range of meaningful and significant questions about law by an acceptance of the naturalness and rationality of the legal order and by a tendency to stress the positive or integrative functions of law. This circumscription of the problematic of the sociology of law is reinforced by the sociological theory that has been the most influential. These have been the more conservative forms of social theory, conservative social theory being that which tends to perceive the existing social order as a natural or inevitable form of social organisation and which tends to emphasise its degree of stability. Hence the sociological theories that have been taken up by the legal sociologists have been varieties that are founded upon a consensus model of society which gives rise to an emphasis upon the functional integration of society.

These choices in the field of theory are themselves intimately linked to one of the other main areas of 'choice' that confronts social enquiry, namely the problem of methodology. The acceptance of conservative social theory and adherence to bourgeois legal ideology lends itself to a positivistic view of social science thus embodying the circumscribed range of pertinent questions. Such a stance readily manifests itself in the espousal of an empiricist method of enquiry. A narrow empiricism has been the dominant trend during the great quantitative expansion of sociology of law during the last decade.

The sociological movement in law takes as its shared object of enquiry the 'law-society relationship'; this constitutes an extremely under-developed problematic in the sense that it provides little explicit direction to work within the field. The 'law and society' focus encourages a certain atheoreticism for its apparent neutrality fails to provide a focus or direction, or to specify the problems within the field. Its very lack of specificity encourages an eclecticism which is associated with a pluralistic theory of causation in which a variety of causal factors determine the interrelationship between 'law' and 'society'. Within the 'law and society' perspective there are two distinct but related theoretical frameworks, the sociological jurisprudential problematic and the 'law as social control' perspective. It will be through an examination of these alternative problematics that a characterisation of the major trends within the sociological movement in law can be arrived at. Further their elucidation will facilitate an assessment of their impact upon modern sociology of law.

It is necessary to stress that the two problematics to be discussed are pure types; pure not in the sense that they are not to be found in the real world, but in the sense that they do not appear complete and uncontaminated by the elements of other positions. They are present in combination with other elements and in this form constitute the specific and distinctive characteristics of the individual contributors to the sociological movement.

The first problematic is the 'sociological jurisprudential problematic'. It is expressed with particular clarity in Julius Stone's definition of sociological jurisprudence.

> Sociological jurisprudence, and any study which seeks to bring social science knowledge to serve legal problems, address address themselves to the influences of social, economic, psychological and other non-legal factors on the process of change in the concrete content of legal propositions.[7]

First we should note the explicitly servicing function attributed to sociological jurisprudence; its object is specified as being 'to serve legal problems'. The central reality of law is posited as being its normative content, the substantive rules of law and the changes to which they are subject. The second and most important implication of this conception is that law is seen as being subject to external forces (social, economic, etc.) which act upon it and whose action results in internal changes. What is significant about this conceptualisation of law is that it enshrines a simple and unquestioned assumption of the centrality of law. For the jurist, as for the practitioner, the law *is*, and is therefore self-evidently important. This provides a causal explanation for the general contention advanced in the earlier discussion of sociological jurisprudence that, despite their efforts and protestations, the sociological jurists did not succeed in making any significant break from the jurisprudential tradition. What the sociological jurisprudential position provided was the assertion that law does not exist and cannot be studied in a vacuum. It is subject to the influence of external forces, but at the same time the central focus remained the action of social forces upon law in so far as it was determinant of the internal dynamic of the legal order itself. Such a perspective gives rise to an eclecticism in the methods of study within a pluralistic theory of causation for, in so far as the factors impinging on the legal system are regarded as independent variables, then these factors can be viewed independently and in isolation from each other. It manifests itself in the predominant tendency to see the field of 'law and society', or socio-legal studies as they are frequently described, as being multi-disciplinary activities in which the social scientists subserve the interests of the jurist who is, if not the leader of the team, its link-pin. As Colin Campbell comments the lawyers define the role of the sociologists 'as intellectual sub-contractors, who are *hired* by the lawyers for their technical skills.'[8]

There is a subsidiary variant of this sociological jurisprudential problematic which not only focuses upon the social factors that impinge upon law but also includes within its implicit statement of the problematic a concern with the 'social consequences of law'. In other words the law remains very much in its assumed centrality subject to social forces that act upon it, but itself reacting back upon the wider social system. This model retains the implicit assumption not only of the centrality of law, but also perpetuates the same eclecticism of method. This variant manifests itself in its purest form in the behaviouralist tendencies in American realism, and has been carried forward by judicial behaviouralism.[9]

The general form of the sociological jurisprudential model is one which is common to both Poundian and Realist jurisprudence. Pound's version of this position is more developed in so far as it tackles the question of the form in which social forces act upon law, namely in the form of claims pressed upon the system which embody 'interests'. The Realists, in so far as they are to be differentiated from Pound, tended to a greater eclecticism in that social pressures upon law were not treated as being subsumed under a general form, but remained a multiplicity of forces acting upon law. The sociological jurisprudential problematic is the one which motivates many studies that are conventionally treated as part of the sociology of law, in particular providing the general orientation for emergence studies and impact studies.

The second major problematic develped within the sociological movement in law is one that may be identified as the 'law as a means of social control' problematic. The major change of emphasis involved is that the 'importance' of law is not derived from something intrinsic to law itself, but rather stems from its classification or identification as part of a wider social process. Law then is not significant in and of itself, but as one of the forms of the societal processes of social control. The situation of the examination of law thereupon proceeds upon the basis of a consideration its relationship firstly to the social control process as a whole and secondly to the other forms of social control.

The 'law as social control' perspective is significant in that it has provided a central focus for both wings of the sociological movement. It is one which contains the potentiality of breaking from the hallmark of the jurisprudential tradition in that it avoids the assertion of the centrality of law. However it should be stressed that this potential has not generally been realised in the application that has been made of the perspective. Thus for example within Pound's jurisprudence it provided a major definitional role yet it remained subordinate to the sociological juris-prudential problematic, whereas in Durkheim the social control perspec-tive is dominant, expressed in terms of his overriding concern with social solidarity in which law is treated as a form of its exemplification. The social control perspective has also played a significant role in American sociology of law being regarded as a means of breaking out from the jurisprudential tradition.

The law as social control perspective has undoubtedly been a unifying theme within the sociological movement, but because of its somewhat self-evident character there has been insufficient attention given to the implications that flow from its adoption. It is therefore necessary to devote some attention to these consequences for the sociology of law.

Underlying the discussion of social control is a pervasive concern with a question which has been fundamental in the history of sociology, social philosophy and jurisprudence, namely the problem of order.[10] How is it that the complexity of the actions of individuals and groups allows us to speak of 'society' as an entity, as an 'organic community'? The social control perspective has provided a particular way of posing the problem of order. The existence of society gives rise to certain social forces which act upon society in the form of mechanisms of social control, which are social facts in the Durkheimian sense, in that they impose themselves upon members of society. Social control operates in a sense despite the individuals who constitute society; it is a product of the totality itself, never willed or wished or planned by its members but which emerges as a necessary consequence of the existence of society itself whose preservation is a consequence of these social forces spontaneously gene-rated.

This position manifests elements of a reified conception of society perceived as an autonomous social relation, independent of those who form it, giving rise to social forces that act upon, control and determine the conduct of its constituents. Society, through the mechanisms of social control, is perceived as 'acting upon' and 'controlling' its members. The adoption of this perspective has determined certain characteristics of the sociological movement in law. Since the process of social control is perceived as a necessary consequence of social life itself it is located in primary social activities and in particular is presented as a product of the normative process. Hence the process of social control is seen mainly in terms of the socialisation process operating through the internalisation of values. The means of social control that receive attention are the value embodying processes variously identified as custom, mores, folk-ways and morality.

If primacy is accorded to the informal, non-institutionalised mechanisms of social control then a certain model of the social control process is developed. This model may be schematically depicted in the following terms: social activity and interaction gives rise to social values expressed as expectations of others which constitute norms; adherence to normative expectations is induced by a range of socially available sanctions that are applied as a response to norm violation in the course of primary social activity within the primary social units of 'group', 'family' and 'kinship'. The constraint of society flows naturally from the primary constituents of social life itself; it is exercised through the informal mechanisms of social control. As a consequence it is seen as being essentially a process of self-regulation endemic in the postulation of social life itself.

Now if law is regarded as one of the *forms* of social control there is implied a view that they form a continuum ranged along a spectrum from informal to institutionalised forms of social control with law being located as the most institutionalised or 'specialised' form.[11] To treat law as one of the forms of social control carries with it the implication that it partakes of the characteristics of the other forms. This association has tended to enhance a view of law which stresses its normative character and lays emphasis upon the relationship between societal values and the value content of legal rules. Hence an apparently self-evident truth is imported into the identificaiton of the rules of law as embodying the most widely diffused and shared social values.

Further the general non-institutionalised character of the forms of social control with which law is compared tends to result in an assumption that law shares with these other agencies a reliance upon enforcement through widely diffused social consensus. The most extreme variant of this is Durkheim's identification of law as the direct embodiment of the 'conscience collective'. Such an emphasis accounts for the tendency for the sociological movement in law to ignore the coercive character of law.

It is however important to stress that a plea for greater attention to the attention to the coercive character of law should not be read as implying a reductionist position in which law is reduced to coercion. It is a platitude that law does not operate exclusively through coercion; that legal systems depend upon their being invested with legitimacy is also a commonplace. What is neglected is the relationship between coercion and legitimacy. The merit of Weber's sociology of law with its emphasis on the relationship between law and domination is precisely that it permits the exploration, without ignoring the problem of legitimacy, of the coercive character of legal systems. Weber's own predominant concern however with rational legal domination and his tendency to regard coercive forms of domination as being residual categories detracts from the possibility of a full treatment of law as a form of domination. It is however suggested that Weber, despite the criticisms that have been made of his general theoretical orientation and of his specific treatment of dominantion which flows from the former, offers a valuable point of reference and one whose potential has not been taken up within the sociology of law as it has proceeded subsequently.

The sociological movement in law has, I have argued, been a response to a new set of questions concerning law which have emerged during the course of the century. Western jurisprudence and sociology have for well over a century been situated in he context of capitalist societies that have undergone unprecedented development both in the economic and social fields. Particularly in the period since the Second World War this development of the major capitalist societies has been at a high rate of expansion and has taken place under conditions of relative stability, which has not only been economic but also political. Yet the stability has always been relative. Despite the high level of material production capitalist society has persistently under-achieved with respect to its major ideological goals. The expression of this under-achievement has been the failure to realise the general goals of 'freedom' and 'equality'; in the political arena there has been the failure of the property-owning democracy and of the Great Society. The self-evident perpetuation of inequality and social injustice has not always disturbed the political calm, but it has never been far below the surface. This must be set in the context of a rapidly changing international context with its self-conscious confrontation, waged both militarily and ideologically, between contending social systems.

If in the context of this brief sketch of relatively stable capitalist society we turn our attention to the place of law within the social system the same persistent failure to realise major legal ideals is evident. The social ideals of freedom and equality find their reflex in the ideal of justice; while the ideal remains buoyant there is persistent under-achievement in its operation. The manifestation of this failure has taken varied forms; at the general level there has been a failure to achieve the ideal of equality both in the access to and in the application of law, and in individual fields of law, whether it be race relations, consumer protection, or industrial relations, varying degrees of failure are widely recognised. The consequence has been a generalised crisis of the legal order. This crisis has been compounded by the extent to which the traditional distinction between the public and the private realms of law has been blurred as a consequence of the increasing ramifications of state activity. The form of state intervention is increasingly legislative and as a consequence social, economic and political conflict comes to involve conflict with respect to the content and the application of law. Legislation frequently exhibits, to adopt Gusfield's distinction,[12] a symbolic rather than an instrumental social function. As a result law becomes directly implicated in the dynamic of social change. As a consequence the perception of law as external to social conflict and integrative in its function is constantly in question. The legal system moves always closer to the vortex of social conflict.[13]

The protracted and simmering nature of the crisis of the legal order has induced a re-evaluation of the legal ideals themselves. At the same time reformist attitudes that focus upon particular operational failures and weaknesses within the legal system have not waned, but have taken their place alongside a more general critique. It is in this context that there is the need for a fresh examination of the theory that informs the contemporary discussion of the legal system. It is not a call for a theoretical revolution from above but rather a response to an urgently felt need. This urgency has already found expression in the upsurge of sharply polemical interventions from critical and radical trends.[14]

Despite the general nature of the social and legal crisis through which capitalist societies are passing and the growth of radical critiques it is still very much the case that 'the system' lives; it may be more tarnished but it is not in any imminent danger of collapse or overthrow. It is in his sense that the emphasis has been laid upon the stability and persistence of capitalist social order and of the associated legal orders. Implicit is the view that the legal system plays a significant, and possibly an increasingly important role in the maintenance of this precarious stability; it is this which makes law an increasingly important object for sociological enquiry.

The strategy of this book has been to start from a thorough immersion in the key contributors to the sociological movement in law. While this leads to an approach which necessarily emphasises the historical development of intellectual thought an effort has been made to relate this to the social , economic and political context in which the sociological movement in law has developed. Upon this basis of the detailed studies undertaken an analysis of the sociological movement has been advanced. The major conclusion is that in spite of its division into two different strands, with different intellectual roots, there has been a fundamental coherence and continuity; it has only been through the analysis of both wings of the movement that its basic unity has been demonstrated in contrast to other studies within the field which have focused on one strand or the other and have consequently failed to grasp the character of the movement as a whole.

The unity of the movement rests upon its adherence to bourgeois legal ideology. The extent to which this perspective manifests itself has varied in intensity but its continuing presence accounts for the inability of the movement to effect a breach with the dominant jurisprudential tradition.

The consequence of the adherence to bourgeois legal ideology has been to stamp a number of characteristics upon the movement. Firstly there has been a common tendency, more pronounced in the jurisprudential wing but present also in the sociological, to subservience to 'legal problems'. This particularly expresses itself in the generalised pragmatic orientation and the adoption of reformist or melioristic goals. This has been particularly pronounced in American jurisprudence of the twentieth century and in modern sociology of law. Secondly, flowing from the previous consideration, there has been a marked lack of concern with the elaboration of a theoretical foundation upon which the movement could achieve an autonomous problematic. Thirdly the orientation towards legal problems has determined the type of sociological theory that has been incorporated into the sociological movement; its major expression has been the predominant influence of social control theory.

In studying the sociological movement through a selective sample of its major figures it has been possible to examine their work in some depth; this would not have been possible had an attempt been made to embrace all those who have contributed to the development of the field. That significant, possibly major, figures have not received attention does not detract from their role; but the opportunity offered by the method adopted has allowed an approach to a number of key figures that has certain advantages. Each study is to some extent self-contained, but at the same time they have been studies undertaken from the perspective of the movement as a whole. Through this it has been possible to see in a more integrated way than would otherwise have been possible not only the individual works but at the same time to place them in the context of the wider movement. It has been possible to concentrate upon the way in which persisting questions have been treated and therefore to see in perspective the dominant themes and tendencies.

The treatment of first Pound and then of the Realists, not in terms of their generic category as jurists but from the standpoint of their contribution to the sociological movement, has shown them unable, and to some extent unwilling, to free themselves from the positivitistic tradition of Anglo-American jurisprudence. As a consequence the extent to which they could utilise the sociological perspective that they attempted to embrace was restricted. In particular it has been stressed that this attempt was no fortuitous part of intellectual history, but was directly rooted in the social and economic conditions of early twentieth century America. It has also been possible to bring out the very substantial continuity that exists between the Realists and modern American sociology of law.

The work of Durkheim and Weber has been shown to have a more general significance. Their work, while rooted in a particular historical period, has achieved a generalised role as a point of reference for social theory which gives to their contributions a contemporary relevance which distinguishes them from other early contributors to the sociological movement. In so far as they epitomise general theoretical stances their impact stands apart from their specific substantive sociologies of law; in this respect very different assessments of their significance have been advanced.

Durkheim's overt functionalism led him to a rather narrow and mechanical assertion of the integrative role of law. Even within the mainstream of American sociology of law, developing as it has in a period when functionalism had a powerful impact on academic sociology, Durkheim has had few followers in Anglo-American sociology of law. But on the other hand he is the most consistent and developed exponent of the law and social control perspective and as such has had a pervasive influence as a generalised point of reference for the sociology of law. Weber, on the other hand, stands out as having made a contribution that confronts a set of problems that are central to the development of the sociology of law. They are questions which it is significant to note have not in any consistent manner been taken up or pursued in modern sociology of law. The point also needs to be made that they are posed by Weber in a form that is conditioned by his general theoretical position which, as has been argued, is one from which they need to be disentangled or freed. Hence it is not suggested that Weber's texts offer adequate solutions, but it is necessary to recognise that he provides a focal point for theoretical engagement. He provides a focus for the sociology of law around certain key concepts and relations: the law and the political order, law and domination, power and authority and law and the economic order. It will be in the context of a continuing debate with the legacy of Weber that the sociology of law will develop.

The plea for the sociology of law is not for a sociology of law conceived of as a specialist subdivision within sociology; rather it has been the intention to demonstrate that questions about law involve major questions that confront contemporary society. As such law presents itself as an important area of inquiry for social theory and sociology in general. This central importance of law revolves around its contribution to a participation in the social processes whereby modern capitalist society is sustained. These processes are constituted through complex interaction of the state and political structures of capitalist society. It is these questions to which the general and pervasive tradition of the sociological movement in law has failed to address itself.

Abbreviations

The following abbreviation of periodical and journal titles have been used:

American Behavioral Scientist	— A. B. S.
American Bar Association Journal	— American B. A. J.
American Journal of Sociology	— A. J. S.
American Law Review	— American L. R.
American Law School Review	— Am. Law School R.
American Political Science Review	— Am. Pol. Sci. R.
American Sociological Review	— A. S. R.
Berkely Journal of Sociology	— Berkeley J. S.
Bristish Journal of Law and Society	— B. J. L. S.
British Journal of Sociology	— B. J. S.
Columbia Law Review	— Columbia L. R.
Fordham Law Review	— Fordham L. R.
Harvard Law Review	— Harvard L. R.
Journal of Legal Education	— J. L. E.
Law and Society Review	— L. and S. R.
Modern Law Review	— M. L. R.
New York University Law Review	— New York Univ. L. R.
Stanford Law Review	— Stanford L. R.
Sydney Law Review	— Sydney L. R.
University of Chicago Law Review	— U. Chicago L. R.
University of Pennsylvania Law Review	— U. Penn. L. R.
University of Toronto Law Journal	— U. Toronto L. J.
Vanderbilt Law Review	— Vanderbilt L. R.
Wisconsin Law Review	— Wisconsin L. R.
Yale Law Journal	— Yale L. J.

Notes

NOTES TO CHAPTER 1

1. The overstatement of legal exclusivism should be avoided; never have lawyers had a complete monopoly of discussion and analysis of law. The intellectual ascendancy of analytical jurisprudence in the nineteenth century and its persistence as the dominant trend during the twentieth century has had the effect of greatly restricting the extent to which law and legal systems have been a significant or substantial focus of inquiry for non-lawyers.
2. Mills, C. W., *Sociology and Pragmatism: The Higher Learning in America* (New York, 1966).
3. In the United States *Law and Society Review*, in Britain *British Journal of Law and Society*.
4. Hunt, Alan, 'Perspectives in the sociology of law' in Carlen, P. (ed.) *The Sociology of Law* (Keele, 1976).
5. Hunt, Alan, *ibid* (1976).
6. Llewellyn and the Realists were the exceptions to this general situation having a specific orientation to Pound's sociological jurisprudence and also some contact with Weber's work.
7. For an account of the relation between historical jurisprudence and the sociological movement see Stone, Julius *Social Dimensions of Law and Justice* (London, 1966).
8. See in particular Stone, Julius, *ibid*.
9. Ehrlich, Eugen, *Fundamental Principles of the Sociology of Law* (first published 1913) (New York, 1962), foreword.
10. Gurvitch, Georges, *Sociology of Law* (London, 1973); Timasheff, N. S., *An Introduction to the Sociology of Law* (Cambridge, Mass., 1939).
11. For a discussion of the sociologies of law of Gurvitch and Timasheff, see Hunt, Alan, 'The sociological movement in law', Ph.D. thesis, Leeds University 1974, chapter 6.
12. See for an account of the development of the sociology of law in different national contexts Treves, R. and Van Loon, G., *Norms and Actions: National Reports on Sociology of Law* (Hague, 1968).
13. See Hunt, Alan, 'Law, state and class struggle', *Marxism Today* 178—87 (June

1976), and in 'Perspectives in the sociology of law' *op. cit*; and a book currently in preparation, in conjunction with Maureen Cain, *Marx and Engels on Law*, forthcoming, Martin Robertson.

NOTES TO CHAPTER 2

1. The extent of Pound's intellectual 'productivity' is revealed in Setaro, F. C., *Bibliography of the Writings of Roscoe Pound* (New Haven, 1942).
2. Pound, *Jurisprudence* in 5 volumes (St. Paul, 1959).
3. Pound, *Outlines of Lectures in Jurisprudence* (New Haven, 1903) hereafter referred to as *Outlines*.
4. See below pp. 17—18.
5. In particular see Pound, *Jurisprudence* (1959), *Interpretations of Legal History* (New York, 1923) hereafter *Interpretations*; 591—619 (1911) 'The scope and purpose of sociological jurisprudence' 24 *Harvard L. R.* and 25 *Harvard L. R.* 140—68 and 489—516 (1911—12), hereafter 'Scope and purpose'; 'Fifty years of jurisprudence' 50 *Harvard L. R.* 557—82 (1937) and 51 *Harvard L. R.* 444—72 and 777—812 (1937—8).
6. Grossman, W. L., 'The legal philosophy of Roscoe Pound' 44 *Yale L. J.* 605—18 (1935).
7. Morris, H., 'Dean Pound's jurisprudence' 13 *Stamford L. R.* 185—210 (1960).
8. Pound, 'Philosophy of law and comparative law' 100 *Pennsylvania L. R.* 17—18 (1951).
9. A similar point is made by Cohen, Felix 'Field theory and judicial logic' 59 *Yale L. J.* 238 (1950).
10. See, for example, Amos, M. S., 'Roscoe Pound' in *Modern Theories of Law* (London, 1933); Goodhart, A. L., 'Roscoe Pound' 78 *Harvard L. R.* 23—37 (1964); Grossman, *op. cit*.
11. Simpson, S. P., 'Roscoe Pound and interpretations of modern legal philosophies' 23 *New York Univ. L. Q. R.* 410 (1948).
12. Pound stresses this himself in *Spirit of the Common Law* (Boston, 1921), hereafter referred to as *Spirit*.
13. A very similar process is taking place in England between 1900 and the outbreak of the First World War.
14. Pound, 40 *American L. R.* 729 (1906).
15. Simpson, S. P., *op. cit.*, p. 410.
16. See in particular Pound, 'Law in books and law in action' 44 *American L. R.* 12—36 (1910); 'Mechanical jurisprudence' 8 *Columbia L. R.* 605 (1908).
17. Pound, *Introduction to the Philosophy of Law* (New Haven, 1922) 140—1, hereafter *Introduction*.
18. Pound, 'The call for a Realist jurisprudence' 44 *Harvard L. R.* 697 (1931).
19. Rumble, W. E., *American Legal Realism* (New York, 1968) p. 89.
20. Pound, 'Liberty of contract' 18 *Yale L. J.* 464 (1909).
21. Cohen, Morris, *Law and the Social Order* (New York, 1933).
22. Pound, 'Sociology of law and sociological jurisprudence', 5 *Toronto L. J.* 20 (1943).
23. *Ibid.* p. 20.
24. Pound, *Spirit op. cit.*, p. 212.
25. Pound, 'Law in books and law in action' 44 *American L. R.* 12—36 (1910).
26. Pound, 'Philosophy of law and comparative law' 100 *Pennsylvania L. R.* 17 (1951).
27. Pound, 'A survey of social interests' 57 *Harvard L. R.* 1, 15 (1943).
28. Pound, *ibid.*, p. 17.
29. Friedmann, W., Review, 4 *Journal of Legal Education* 506 (1952).

30. Reuschlin, H. G., *Jurisprudence — It's American Prophets* (Indianapolis, 1951).
31. Pound, (Claremont, 1940) pp. 32—3.
32. Kohler, J., *The Philosophy of Law* (New York, 1928).
33. Pound, *Jurisprudence* I, 363.
34. Pound, *ibid.* I, p. 364.
35. Grossman, *op. cit.*, p. 607.
36. Stammler, R., *The Theory of Justice* (New York, 1925).
37. Pound, *Interpretations*, p. 149.
38. See in particular, Pound and Frankfurter, F. (eds), *Criminal Justice in Cleveland* (New Jersey, 1922).
39. Lepaulle, P., 'The function of comparative law with a critique of sociological jurisprudence' 35 *Harvard L. R.* 838—58 (1922).
40. For example, see Pound's criticism of economic determinism in *Interpretations*.
41. Pound, *Jurisprudence* I, p. 428.
42. Llewellyn, K. N., 'A realistic jurisprudence — the next step' 30 *Columbia L. R.* 341, 435 (1930).
43. Ross, E. A., *Social Control: A Survey of the Foundations of Order* (New York, 1901).
44. Ross, *ibid.*, p. 106. It is interesting to note that it was to Pound that Ross dedicated his *Principles of Sociology* in 1921.
45. Sumner, W. G., *Folkways* (1906).
46. Cooley, C. H., *Human Nature and Legal Order* (1902) *Social Organisation* (1909).
47. Small, A., *Origins of Sociology* (1924).
48. Hart, H. L. A., *The Concept of Law* (Oxford, 1961).
49. Pound, *Social Control*, p. 41.
50. Llewellyn, K. N., *op. cit.*, p. 435.
51. See in particular Pound 'Sociology of law' in Gurvitch and Moore (eds), *Twentieth Century Sociology* (New York, 1945).
52. Pound, *ibid., pp. 306—8; Jurisprudence* I, p. 333.
53. Pound, *Sociology of Law op. cit.*, pp. 309—10; *Jurisprudence* I pp. 314—18.
54. Pound, *Jurisprudence* I, p. 310.
55. Pound, *'Law and Morals'* (Chapel Hill, 1924) p. 115.
56. Pound, 'Scope and purpose', pp. 514—16.
57. Pound, 'Sociology of law', *op. cit.*, pp. 311—13.
58. Pound, *Social Control*, p. 49.
59. Lepaulle, *op. cit.*, p. 845.
60. Pound, *Social Control*, p. 66.
61. Pound, 'A survey of social interests' 57 *Harvard L. R.* 1 (1943).
62. Pound, *Jurisprudence* III, p. 16.
63. Pound, *ibid.* III, p. 7.
64. Pound, *ibid.* III, p. 17; *Spirit* p. 196.
65. Cohen, Felix, *Ethical Systems and Legal Ideals* (New York, 1959).
66. Cohen, *ibid.* 89.
67. James, W., *The Will to Believe* (1897), p. 205.
68. Pound, 'The role of will in law' 68 *Harvard L. R.* 19 (1954).
69. Pound, *Jurisprudence* III, p. 23.
70. Pound, 'Survey of social interests', *op. cit.*, p. 2.
71. Pound, *Jurisprudence* III, p. 23.
72. Patterson, E. W., 'Pound's theory of social interests' in Sayre, P. (ed.), *Interpretations of Modern Legal Philosophies* 558—73 (1947) and 'Roscoe Pound on jurisprudence' 60 *Columbia L. R.* 1124—32 (1960).
73. Stone, J., 'The golden age of Roscoe Pound' 4 *Sydney L. R.* 1—27 (1962); 'Roscoe Pound and sociological jurisprudence' 78 *Harvard L. R.* 1578—94 (1965); *Human Law and Human Justice* (London, 1965) chapter IX; and *The*

Province and Function of Law (London, 1947) chapter XV.

74. Pound, 'A survey of public interests' 58 *Harvard L. R.* 900–929 (1945).
75. Stone, 'The golden age of Roscoe Pound' 4 *Sydney L. R.* 1–27 (1962).
76. Pound, *Jurisprudence* III, p. 328.
77. Braybrooke, E. K., 'The sociological jurisprudence of Roscoe Pound' in Sawyer, G. (ed.), *Studies in the Sociology of Law* (Canberra, 1961) appears to support Patterson's interpretation.
78. Pound, *Spirit*, p. 203.
79. Pound, *Introduction, op. cit.*, p. 46.
80. Patterson, E. W. in Sayre (ed.), *op. cit.*, p. 566.
81. Pound, *Jurisprudence* III, p. 332.
82. Pound, *Jurisprudence* III, p. 23.
83. Pound, 'Fifty years of jurisprudence' 51 *Harvard L. R.* 810–11 (1938).
84. Pound, *Contemporary Juristic Theory, op. cit.*, p. 82.
85. Pound, 'The role of will in law' 68 *Harvard L. R.* 19 (1954).
86. Pound, 'Survey of social interests', *op. cit.*, p. 39.
87. Llewellyn, K. N., *op. cit.*, p. 435.
88. Pound, *Jurisprudence* III, p. 8.
89. Pound, *Interpretations*, p. 148.
90. Pound, *Social Control*, pp. 133–4.
91. Pound, *Jurisprudence* III, p. 8.
92. Pound, *Introduction to American Law* (1919).
93. Pound, *Social Control* (1942).
94. Stone, J., *Human Law and Human Justice*, chapter 9; *The Province and Function of Law*, chapter 15.
95. Stone, J., *Human Law and Human Justice*, pp. 264–5.
96. This typology appears in its most developed form in two papers: 'The end of law as developed in legal rules and doctrines' 27 *Harvard L. R.* 195–234 (1914); 'The end of law as developed in juristic thought' 27 *Harvard L. R.* 605–28 and 30 *Harvard L. R.* 201–25 (1914 and 1917); and also in *Jurisprudence* I, chapters 5 and 6.
97. See in particular *Jurisprudence* I, chapters 1–5; *Interpretations*; 'Fifty years of jurisprudence'; 'The Scope and Purpose of Sociological Jurisprudence'; and *Spirit*.
98. This typology is based upon a similarly constructed table that appears in *Jurisprudence*. The table on the following page differs in that the stage of 'socialisation of law' has been added, its characteristics have been abstracted from Pound's general discussion of the current stage which he believed his sociological jurisprudence reflected.
99. See in particular, Pound, *Interpretations*, pp. 141–51.
100. Pound, *Introduction*, p. 40.
101. Pound, *Interpretations*, p. 1, opening line.
102. For example, Pound characterises the Historical school as a 'reaction from the active, creative juristic thought', *Interpretations*, p. 12.
103. Pound, 'Fifty years of jurisprudence' 51 *Harvard L. R.* 471–2 (1938).
104. Maine, *Ancient Law* (1st ed. 1961), (London, 1905), p. 141.
105. Pound, 'Scope and purpose', *op. cit.*, p. 143.
106. See for example, Pound, 'Law in the service-state – freedom versus equality', 36 *American B. A. J.* 977 (1950).
107. Pound, 'Scope and purpose', *op. cit.*
108. Patterson, E. W., *Jurisprudence: Men and Ideas of the Law* (Brooklyn, 1953)
109. Pound, *Introduction*, pp. 140–1.
110. For an interesting discussion of the origins of the theoretical weaknesses of sociological jurisprudence see Schiff, David 'Socio-legal theory: social structure and law' 39 *Modern L. R.*, pp. 295–7 (1976).

NOTES TO CHAPTER 3

1. See, for example, the polemic between Pound and Llewellyn, Llewellyn, K. N., 'A realistic jurisprudence – the next step' 30 *Columbia L. R.* 431 (1930); Pound, R., 'The call for a realist jurisprudence' 44 *Harvard L. R.* 697 (1931); Llewellyn, 'Some realism about realism' 44 *Harvard L. R.* 1222 (1931); and also between Lon Fuller and the Realists, Fuller, Lon L., 'American legal realism' 82 *U. Penn. L. R.* 429—62 (1934); McDougal, M. S., 'Fuller v. the American legal realists: an intervention' 50 *Yale L. J.* 827—40 (1941).
2. Cahill, Fred V., *Judicial Legislation: A Study in American Legal Theory* (New York, 1952), p. 97.
3. A task that is adequately covered by the work of: Rumble, W. E., *American Legal Realism; Skepticism, Reform and the Judicial Process* (New York, 1968); Garlan, Edwin, *Legal Realism and Justice* (New York, 1941); Twining, William, *Karl Llewellyn and the Realist Movement* (London, 1973).
4. There has been a tendency to use these labels rather too simply; in general classification seems to be based on the radicalism of their literary style; hence Frank is widely, but probably erroneously, identified as the 'left' of the realist movement.
5. It is necessary to speak of 'membership' of the realist movement with considerable caution since relatively few individuals used the term by way of self-description. Further a number who show a close connection consciously apply alternative designation; for example, Felix Cohen describes his position as 'functional jurisprudence'; even Jerome Frank is anxious to renounce the crown of 'realism' and prefers 'constructive skepticism' or 'experimentalism'.
6. Twining, W., *Karl Llewellyn and The Realist Movement* (London, 1973), chapter 5.
7. Llewellyn, K. N., 'On philosophy in American law' 82 *U. Penn. L. R.* 205—12 (1934), p. 211.
8. The insistence of the importance of 'social change' is a common characteristic of the realist movement.
9. See, Hofstadter, Richard, *The American Political Tradition* (London, 1962).
10. Gilmore, Grant, 'Legal realism: its cause and cure' 70 *Yale L. J.* 1037 (1961).
11. Amongst others Thurman Arnold (Securities and Exchange Commission), Felix Cohen (Department of the Interior), Jerome Frank (Securities and Exchange Commission), Herman Oliphant (Department of Treasury), William Douglas (Securities and Exchange Commission) all became involved in the administration of the New Deal. For further details see Schlesinger, Arthur, *The Age of Roosevelt: The Coming of the New Deal* (Boston, 1959), pp. 16 ff and Leuchtenburg, W., *Franklin D. Roosevelt and the New Deal* (New York, 1963). pp. 259 ff.
12. The only English figure reflecting a similar influence was Harold Laski who had an association with many of the figures of the realist movement during his stay in the United States, particularly at Yale. His writings of that period are an interesting mixture of realist and Marxist influences.
13. See for example Llewellyn, K. N., '*A united front on the court*' 144 *Nation* 289 (1937).
14. For example, Bodenheimer, H., describes as 'a radical wing of the sociological school of law' *Jurisprudence* (Cambridge, Mass., 1968) p. 116; Paton, George W. describes as 'the left-wing of the functional school' in *A Textbook of Jurisprudence* (3rd edition, Oxford, 1964), p. 22.
15. Llewellyn describes the basis of traditionalism in the legal profession in the following terms:
    Dominated by bourgeois, business, serving and knowing only, as specialised offices counsel, the interests of the 'ins', they had no ears for words that

betoken change in an existing order. One still meets gentlemen who still voice their profound conviction that such conservative men as Holmes, or Brandeis or Pound are dangerous.
Llewellyn, K. N. 'On philosophy in American law' (note 7 above) pp. 211—12.

16. Pound was not without his followers; amongst his contemporaries, both Dickinson and Patterson were very much 'sociological jurisprudes'. Pound had had a continuing direct impact upon the work of for example Julius Stone and Wolgang Friedmann.

17. For example upon legal education, changing judicial attitudes and approaches.

18. Pound, R. *et al.*, *Criminal Justice in Cleveland* (directed and edited by Pound and Felix Frankfurter), Cleveland Foundation (1922).

19. Frank, Jerome, 'Are judges human?' 80 *U. Penn. L. R.* 18 (1931).

20. Oliphant, Herman, 'Parallels in the development of legal and medical education' 167 *Annals of the Am. Acad. of Pol. and Soc. Sci.* 162 (1933).

21. See Mills, C. Wright, *Sociology and Pragmatism: The Higher Learning in America* (New York, 1966) and White, Morton, *Social Thought in America: The Revolt Against Formalism* (Boston, 1957).

22. O. W. Holmes was appointed to the Supreme Court by Theodore Roosevelt in 1902.

23. Mills, C. W., *Sociology and Pragmatism* (see note 21).

24. *Lochner v. New York* 198 US. 76 (1905).

25. Holmes, O. W., *The Common Law* (London, 1968) p. 5.

26. The Realists have been accused of ignoring or denying the role of values and ideals in law. This criticism has come from diverse source, for example Pound, Morris Cohen, Fuller and others. This criticism is largely tangential to our present concerns, but it may be observed that it rests on an erroneous interpretation of Realism; far from denying the role of values, their general call for a recognition of the policy issues inherent in the legal process gives values a central part in their jurisprudence, but within the confines of their general positivistic orientation.

27. Shuman, Samuel I., *Legal Positivism: Its Scope and Limitations* (Detroit, 1963) pp. 4—5.

28. Holmes, O. W., 'The path of law' 10 *Harvard L. R.* 457—78 (1897) at 461.

29. For example, Llewellyn: 'What officials do about disputes is, to my mind, the law itself' (*The Bramble Bush: On Our Law and its Study* (New York, 1930) p. 3; and Frank, 'the law with respect to any particular set of facts, is a decision of a court with respect to those facts as that decision affects that particular person' Frank, J., *Law and the Modern Mind* (New York, 1930) p. 46.

30. Frank, J., 'Preface' to sixth printing of *Law and the Modern Mind* (1948); Llewellyn, K. N., 'The normative, the legal and the law-jobs: the problem of juristic method' 49 *Yale L. J.* 1355—1400 (1940).

31. A number of the Realists were considerably influenced by the developments in linguistic philosophy. The realisation of the imprecision of language and of its cultural and contextual meaning provided ammunition in their attack on formal syllogistic logic and the 'jurisprudence of concepts' generally.

32. Moore, Underhill and Callahan, Charles C., 'Law and learning theory: a study in legal control' 53 *Yale L. J.* 1—143 (1943).

33. Frank, J., *Law and the Modern Mind* p. 244.

34. Frank, J., 'Are judges human?' (note 19) p. 246.

35. This is of course the underlying theme of Llewellyn *The Common Law Tradition — Deciding Appeals* (Boston, 1961), hereafter *The Common Law Tradition*.

36. The existence of a 'frozen record from below' is one of the steadying factors which he enumerates in *The Common Law Tradition*.

37. *The Common Law Tradition*, p. 510.

38. See further upon methodology of Realists, pp. 55—8.
39. For example, Bingham, J. W., 'What is the law?' 11 *Michigan L. R.* 1 and 109 (1912) which has been described as the first realist work.
40. See for example the highly unconventional and polemical style of Llewellyn in *The Bramble Bush* (see note 29), and Frank in *Law and the Modern Mind* and *Courts on Trial — Myth and Reality in American Justice* (Princeton, N.J., 1950).
41. Allen, C. K., *Law in the Making* (7th ed. London, 1964), p. 46.
42. In particular in the following: Llewellyn, K. N. and Hoebel, E. A., *The Cheyenne Way: Conflict and Case Law in Primitive Jurisprudence* (Norman, 1941), hereafter referred to as *The Cheyenne Way*; Llewellyn, 'Law and the social sciences — especially sociology' 14 *A. S. R.* 451—62 (1949) also 62 *Harvard L. R.* 1286 (1949), and in Llewellyn, *Jurisprudence: Realism in Theory and Practice* (Chicago, 1962) pp. 352—71 hereafter *Jurisprudence*; and 'The normative, the legal and the law-jobs' (note 30).
43. Cook, W. W., 'The logical and legal basis of the conflict of laws' 33 *Yale L. J.* 475 (1924).
44. See discussion on legal realism and behaviouralism, pp. 53—5.
45. Llewellyn, 'Some realism about realism' (note 1), p. 43.
46. Llewellyn, 'A realistic jurisprudence — the next step' (note 1), p. 23.
47. Llewellyn, 'Some realism about realism' (note 1), p. 69 in *Jurisprudence*.
48. Perhaps its clearest articulation is in Llewellyn and Hoebel, *The Cheyenne Way* chapter 10 'Claims and law-ways'.
49. Llewellyn, 'The effects of legal institutions upon economics' 15 *Am. Econ. R.*, p. 666 (1925).
50. For discussion of legal Realism and functionalism see pp. 48—53.
51. See in particular Hofstadter, Richard, *Social Darwinism in American Thought* (Boston, 1955).
52. Llewellyn, 'Law and the social sciences' (note 42), quoted from *Jurisprudence*, p. 358.
53. A number of them for example Thurman Arnold and Fred Rodell, had few illusions about the social system and frequently attacked it stridently, but rarely went outside its confines for solutions or remedies.
54. Mulkay, M. J., *Functionalism, Exchange Theory and Theoretical Strategy* (London, 1971).
55. Llewellyn, 'Some realism about realism' (note 1).
56. *Bramble Bush* (1960), p. 22.
57. Llewellyn, 'A realistic jurisprudence — the next step' quoted *Jurisprudence*, p. 39.
58. Malinowski, Bronislaw, *Crime and Custom in Savage Society* (London, 1928).
59. Llewellyn and Hoebel, *The Cheyenne Way* (See note 42).
60. Llewellyn contributed only 10 days' field work; see for full account Twining, *Karl Llewellyn and the Realist Movement* (note 3).
61. Twining, William, 'Two works of Karl Llewellyn' 30 *Modern L. R.* 514 (1967) and 31 *Modern L. R.* 165 (1968) at p. 167.
62. The 'trouble case' method represents a continuum of the 'cases and materials' approach to legal education that Llewellyn developed and applied in his *Cases nd Materials in the Law of Sales* (Chicago, 1930); it manifests a general concern with what the law does, what actually happens in practice whether it be in commerce or among American Indian tribes.
63. Gluckman, Max, *The Judicial Process Among the Barotse of Northern Rhodesia* (Manchester, 1955).
64. Bohannan, P., *Justice and Judgement Among the Tiv* (London, 1957).
65. The 'law-jobs theory' is developed in Part III of *The Cheyenne Way*, this part being almost exclusively Llewellyn's work.

66. Llewellyn and Hoebel, *The Cheyenne Way*, p. 291.
67. Llewellyn, 'The normative . . .' (see note 30), p. 1373.
68. Llewellyn, *ibid.*, p. 1357.
69. Llewellyn, *ibid.*, p. 1358.
70. See note 42 above.
71. Llewellyn and Hoebel, *The Cheyenne Way* and also in 'The normative, the legal and the law-jobs' (see note 30).
72. Llewellyn, 'Law and the social sciences' (note 42) at p. 355 in *Jurisprudence*.
73. Llewellyn, *Law in our Society*, p. 112 — unpublished manuscript quoted extensively by Twining, W. in *Karl Llewellyn and the Realist Movement* (note 3), he characterises this work as representing Llewellyn's 'last attempt to articulate a general theory' as the basis of a sociological treatment of law.
74. Twining, *Karl Llewellyn* (note 3) pp. 171 ff.
75. For detailed account of Llewellyn's involvement, see Twining, *ibid.*, Chapter 11.
76. Quoted above at p. 47.
77. Llewellyn, 'A realistic jurisprudence — the next step' (note 1) p. 40. See also very similar formulations in *ibid.*, p. 16; 'The conditions for and aims and methods of legal research' 6 *Am. Law School R.*, p. 672 and 674; 'The normative . . .' (note 30), p. 1356.
78. Yntema, Hessel, 'American legal realism in retrospect' 9 *Vanderbilt L. R.* 317 and 318 (1960).
79. Oliphant, Herman, 'A return to stare decisis' 14 *American B. A. J.* p. 159 (1928).
80. For detailed account see Twining, *Karl Llewellyn* Chapters 3 and 4.
81. Moore, U. and Callahan, (note 32).
82. In particular of Watson and Clark Hull.
83. Moore, U. and Callahan, *ibid.*, p. 3.
84. For more detailed consideration see pp. 55—8.
85. Ingersoll, David, 'Karl Llewellyn, American legal realism and contemporary legal behaviouralism' 76(4) *Ethics* p. 253; a similar argument is also advanced by Rumble, *American Legal Realism* (note 3) and by Becker, Theodore L., *Political Behavioralism and Modern Jurisprudence: A Working Theory and Study in Judicial Decision-Making* (Chicago, 1964).
86. Mills, C. W., *Sociology and Pragmatism* (note 21) chapter 5, on the relationship between pragmatism and prediction.
87. Llewellyn, K. N., 'Realism, the genesis of this book' which appears as an appendix to *Common Law Tradition* p. 510.
88. Llewellyn, *ibid.*, p. 510.
89. Yntema, Hessel, 'Legal science and reform' 34 *Columbia L. R.* 207 (1934).
90. For detail upon the work of the Johns Hopkins Institute see: Twining, *Karl Llewellyn* Chapter 4; Rehbinder, Manfred, 'The development and present state of fact research in the United States' 24 (5) *J. L. E.* pp. 572—5 (1972) and Rumble, *American Legal Realism* (note 3) pp. 15—20.
91. A full bibliography of the work of the Institute appears at the end of Gehlke, Charles E., *Criminal Actions in the Common Pleas of Ohio* (1936); and extensive details of publication appear in Rehbinder (note 90).
92. Douglas, W. and Thomas, D., 'The business failures project — a problem of methodology' 39 *Yale L. J.* 1013 (1930); Clark, Charles E. *et al. A Study of Law Administration in Connecticut* (1937).
93. Friedmann comments that Realism's
      clearest achievement so far has been the use of statistics as an auxiliary instrument to test the working and effects of law.
    Friedmann, W., *Legal Theory* (London, 1966), p. 299.
94. Llewellyn, K. N., 'Behind the law of divorce' 32 *Columbia L. R.* 1281—1308

(1932), and 33 *Columbia L. R.* 249—294 (1933).

95. Twining, *Karl Llewellyn* p. 188 (note 3).
96. He is referring here to concept formation nd definition — *Common Law Tradition*, p. 338.
97. Llewellyn, *ibid.*, p. 516.
98. Llewellyn and Hoebel, *Cheyenne Way*, p. 29.
99. Llewellyn, 'A realistic jurisprudence' (note 1) p. 7 in *Jurisprudence*.
100. See in particular his definition of 'law-government' concept quoted at p. 51.
101. Llewellyn and Hoebel *Cheyenne Way*, p. 286. Twining, *Karl Llewellyn* notes that on his visits to Germany in 1928—9 and 1931 he undertook extensive reading of Weber.
102. Llewellyn, K. N., 'Frank's *'Law and the modern mind'* ' 31 *Columbia L. R.* **82** (1931); also in *Jurisprudence*, p. 103.
103. See the elaboration of this idea in White *The Revolt Against Formalism* (note 21).
104. A similar trend is apparent in England, particularly witnessed in the major role of H. L. A. Hart.

NOTES TO CHAPTER 4

1. To stress his concern with he social order does not imply that such a concern is necessarily static. For this reason Giddens is wrong in identifying the association of Durkheim with a theory of social order as a myth; see Giddens, Anthony, 'Four myths in the history of social thought' 1 *Economy and Society* 357—85 (1972).
2. Durkheim, E., *Professional Ethics and Civic Morals* (London, 1957), p. 60. Hereafter referred to as *Professional Ethics*.
3. Durkheim, E., *The Division of Labour in Society* (Glencoe, Ill. 1964). First published in 1893. Hereafter referred to as *Division of Labour*.
4. Durkheim, E., '*The Rules of Sociological Method*' (Glencoe, Ill., 1964), p. 14, hereafter referred to as *Rules*.
5. Durkheim, E., *ibid.*, p. 3.
6. See pp. 67—8 of this chapter.
7. Durkheim, E., *Rules*, p. 123.
8. See pp. 66—74 of this chapter.
9. Durkheim, E., *Division of Labour*, p. 103.
10. There have been controversies over the translation of the expression; its meaning lies somewhere between 'collective conscience' and 'collective consciousness'. In order to avoid ambiguity the original form of 'conscience collective' will be retained.
11. Durkheim, E., *Rules*, p. 123.
12. Durkheim, E., 'The determination of moral facts' in E. *Sociology and Philosophy* (Glencoe, Ill., 1953), p. 57.
13. In Durkheim, E., *Moral Education* (Glencoe, Ill., 1961) he argues that education should be used as an agency for installing the appropriate reverential attitudes towards the state.
14. Durkheim, E., *Professional Ethics*, p. 48.
15. Durkheim, E., *Rules*, p. 104.
16. Durkheim, E., *Division of Labour*, pp. 84—5.
17. Durkheim, E., *rules*, p. xlix.
18. Durkheim, E., *ibid.*, p. li.
19. Durkheim, E., 'Individual and collective representations' in *Sociology and Philosophy*, p. 26.
20. Durkheim, E., 'Sociology and its scientific field' in Wolff (ed.), *Essays on*

Sociology and Philosophy by Emile Durkheim (New York, 1964), p. 367.

21. Durkheim, E., *The Elementary Forms of Religious Life: A Study in Religious Sociology* (London, 1915). Hereafter referred to as *Elementary Forms*. First published in French, 1912.

22. Durkheim, E., *Moral Education: A Study in the Theory and Application of the Sociology of Education* (Glencoe, III., 1961).

23. See in particular Coser, L. A., 'Durkheim's conservatism and its implications for his sociological theory' in Wolff (ed.) *Emile Durkheim 1858 – 1917* (Columbus, 1960) and Nisbet, R. A., 'Conservatism and sociology' 58 *American Journal of Sociology* 167–75 (1952), and his *Emile Durkheim* (Englewood Cliffs, N. J., 1965); albeit in a more qualified form Lukes also emphasises the conservatism of Durkheim's social and political thought; Lukes, Steven, *Emile Durkheim: His Life and Work* (London, 1973).

24. It is equally incorrect to deduce a 'radical' position from his commitment to the abolition of inheritance as do Taylor, Walton and Young *The New Criminology* (London, 1973) pp. 87–88.

25. See Therborn, G., *Science, Class and Society* (London, 1976), Chapter 5, and Hirst, Paul, *Durkheim, Bernard and Epistemology* (London, 1973).

26. Durkheim, E., *Suicide: A Study in Sociology* (Glencoe, Ill., 1951) hereafter referred to as *Suicide*.

27. Durkheim, E., 'Two laws of penal evolution'. Originally appeared in *Année Sociologique* in 1899–1900. An English translation has appeared in 2(3) *Economy and Society* 285–308 (1973). Hereafter referred to as 'Two laws'.

28. See detailed analysis of the contents of *Année Sociologique* in Alpert, H., *Emile Durkheim and his Sociology* (New York, 1961) pp. 217–24.

29. The continuing debate has at one time or another involved such writers as Malinowski, Hogbin, Hoebel, Gluckman and Bohannan and owes much to he stimulus of Durkheim's ideas.

30. Zeitling, Irving, *Ideology and the Development of Sociological Theory* (Englewood Cliffs, N.J., 1968).

31. Durkheim, E., 44 *Revue Philosophique* 200–5; quoted Lukes (1973), p. 232.

32. Durkheim, E., *Division of Labour*, p. 227.

33. Durkheim, E., *ibid.*, p. 299.

34. Durkheim, E., *ibid.*, p. 64.

35. Durkheim, E., *ibid.*, pp. 64–5.

36. Durkheim, E., *ibid.*, p. 68.

37. Reported in Lukes, *Emile Durkheim*, p. 297.

38. Durkheim, E., *ibid.*, p. 69.

39. See pages 74–85 of this chapter.

40. Durkheim, E., *op cit.*, p. 69 (Durkheim's emphasis).

41. Durkheim, E., *ibid.*, p. 127.

42. Durkheim, E., *ibid.*, p. 119.

43. Durkheim, E., *ibid.*, p. 123.

44. Durkheim, E., *ibid.*, p. 68.

45. Alpert, *op. cit.*, p. 197.

46. See in particular Malinowski, B., *Crime and Custom in Savage Society* (London, 1 1961).

47. Hogbin, H. I., *Law and order in Polynesia* (London, 1934).

48. Radcliffe-Brown, A. R., 'Primitive law', vol. 9 *Encyclopaedia of the Social Sciences*.

49. Llewellyn, K. N. and Hoebel, E. A., *The Cheyenne Way* (Norman, 1941) and Hoebel, E. A., *The Law of Primitive Man* (Cambridge, Mass., 1961).

50. Radcliffe-Brown, A. R., *op. cit.*

51. See in particular, Gluckman, Max, *The Judicial Process Amongst the Barotse* (Manchester, 1955).

52. Bohannan, P. J., *Justice and Judgement Among the Tiv* (London, 1957).
53. Pospisil, L., *Anthropology of Law: A Comparative Theory* (New York, 1971).
54. Diamond, A. S., *The Evolution of Law and Order* (London, 1951) and his more recent version *Primitive Law, Past and Present* (London, 1972).
55. Alpert, *op. cit.*
56. Diamond, *op. cit.*
57. Seagle, William, *The Quest for Law* (New York, 1941).
58. Schwartz, R. D. and Miller, J. C., 'Legal evolution and societal complexity' 70 *American Journal of Sociology* 159–69 (1964).
59. See, for example, Friedmann, Wolfgang, *Law in a Changing Society* (London, 1964) and Sayre, F., 'Public welfare offences' 33 *Columbia L. R.* 55 (1933).
60. Like Weber, Durkheim's treatment of modern society is never that of an apologist; his theory is never simply a ligitimating ideology. Indeed the persistence of the influence of both lies precisely in the fact that they do not treat capitalist society as unproblematic; had they done so their views would have soon been discarded as pure ideology.
61. Taylor, Walton and Young, *They New Criminology* (London, 1973) Chapter 3.
62. Durkheim, E., *Division of Labour*, p. 80.
63. Durkheim, E., *ibid.,.*p. 81.
64. Durkheim, E., 'The determination of moral facts' *op. cit.*, p. 43.
65. Durkheim, E., *Division of Labour*, p. 103.
66. It is this view that leads Wolin to argue that Durkheim carried forward the political theory of Rousseau into modern sociology; Wolin, S. S. *Politics and Vision: Continuity and Innovation in Western Political Thought* (London, 1971), Chapter 10. However it should be noted that Durkheim is direct and explicit in his rejection of 'social contract' theory as an explanation of the fact of human sociality; see Durkheim, E., *Division of Labour*, p. 202.
67. Giddens, Anthony, 'Durkheim's political sociology' 19(4) *Sociological Review* 509 (1971).
68. Keat, R., and Urry, J., *Social Theory as Science* (London, 1975), p. 85.
69. Durkheim, E., *Division of Labour*, p. 96.
70. Durkheim, E., *ibid.*, p. 89.
71. Durkheim, E., *ibid.*, p. 87.
72. Hart, H. L. A., 'Social solidarity and the enforcement of morals' 55 *Univ. Chicago L. R.* 1–13 (1967). It should be noted in passing that this is a persistent jurisprudential assumption that can be traced from Hobbes to modern jurists such as Dennis Lloyd, see Lloyd, D., *The Idea of Law* (Harmondsworth, 1964) Chapter 1.
73. Durkheim, E., *Rules*, p. 50.
74. Durkheim, E., *ibid.*, p. 55.
75. Durkheim, E., *ibid.*, p. 67.
76. Durkheim, E. 'Crime et santé sociale' 39 *Revue Philosophique* 518–23 (1895).
77. Durkheim, E., *Rules*, p. 96.
78. Durkheim, E., *ibid.*, p. 72.
79. Durkheim, E., *Division of Labour*, p. 93.
80. Durkheim, E., *Elementary Forms*, Book III, chapter 1.
81. 44 *Revue Philosophique* 645–651 at 650 (1897).
82. Durkheim, E., *Professional Ethics*, pp. 113–20.
83. Durkheim, E., *ibid.*, 113.
84. Durkheim, E., 'Two laws', p. 285.
85. Durkheim, E., *ibid.*, p. 294.
86. Durkheim, E., *ibid.*, p. 299.
87. Durkheim, E., *ibid.*, p. 307.
88. Seagle, William, *The Quest for Law* (New York, 1941).
89. Durkheim, E., 'Two laws', p. 300.

90. It is this feature of Durkheim's methodology that Rodney Needham suggests manifests the logical fallacy of *petitio principii* taking as a premise that which the argument purports to demonstrate; Needham, R. 'Introduction' to Durkheim and Mauss, *Primitive Classification* (London, 1970), p. xiv.
91. Durkheim, E., *ibid.*, p. 300.
92. Durkheim, E., *ibid.*, p. 303.
93. He opposes this to the utilitarian individualism which would emphasise a self-interested calculus of concern with our own safety which view he does not regard as providing an adequate causal analysis.
94. Durkheim, E., *ibid.*, p. 288.
95. Richter is being overgenerous in suggesting that the introduction of the relationship of governmental forms remains an 'unexplored insight'; Richter, M., 'Durkheim's politics and political theory' in Wolff (ed.), *Emile Durkheim 1858–1917* (Columbus, 1960), p. 193.
96. Durkheim, E., *ibid.*, p. 296.
97. Rusche, G. and Kirchheimer, O., *Punishment and Social Structure* (New York, 1968).
98. Durkheim was clearly familiar with Maine's work and refers explicitly to him in fotnotes on a number of occasions.
99. Durkheim, E., *Division of Labour*, p. 215.
100. Durkheim, E., *ibid.*, p. 114.
101. Durkheim, E., *ibid.*, p. 381.
102. Durkheim, E., *Professional Ethics*, p. 177.
103. It should be noted that the notion of ritual played a central part in his theory of the evolution of religion.
104. Durkheim, E., *ibid.*, p. 189.
105. Durkheim, E., *ibid.*, p. 191.
106. Durkheim, E., si,ibid., p. 203.
107. Durkheim, E., *ibid.*, pp. 121–70.
108. This same proposition, though from different philosophical antecedents, is to be found at the root of Locke's theory of property.
109. Durkheim, E., *Professional Ethics*, p. 215.
110. Durkheim, E., *ibid.*, p. 138.
111. Durkheim, E., *ibid.*, pp. 143–4.
112. Durkheim, E., *Professional Ethics*, p. 160.
113. Durkheim, E., *ibid.*, p. 167.
114. Stone, Julius, 'Review of *Division of Labour*' 47 *Harvard Law Review* 1451 (1934).
115. Gurvitch, G., *The Sociology of Law* (New York, 1942), p. 83.
116. This argument about the relationship between sociology and Marxism is developed by Hirst, Paul, *Social Evolution and Sociological Categories* (London, 1976) and by Therborn, Goran, *Science, Class and Society* (London, 1975).
117. Durkheim, E., *Division of Labour*, p. 37.
118. Parsons, Talcott, 'Durkheim's contribution to the theory of integration of social systems' in Wolff (ed.), *op cit.*, p. 151.
119. A recent and extreme example of this tendency is to be found in McDonáld, Lynn, *The Sociology of Law and Order* (London, 1976) which classifies every thinker from Plato to the present day around a consensus-conflict dichotomy.
120. One exception is Alpert who places much stress on Durkheim's persistent concern with law and legal phenomena; Alpert, H., *Emile Durkheim and his Sociology* (New York, 1961).

NOTES TO CHAPTER 5

1. See for example the importance accorded to Weber in Aron, Raymond, *Main Currents in Sociological Thought*, vol. II (London, 1968); Zeitlin, Irving, *Ideology and the Development of Sociological Theory* (New Jersey, 1968); Gouldner, Alvin, *The Coming Crisis of Western Sociology* (London 1971); Therborn, Göran *Science, Class and Society* (London, 1976); and Giddens, Anthony, *New Rules of Sociological Method* (London, 1976).

2. *Economy and Society: An Outline of Interpretive Sociology* Edited by Guenther Roth and Claus Wittich (New York, 1968) 3 vols. hereafter referred to as *Economy and Society*.

3. This tension differentiates my approach to Weber from that adopted by Hirst, Paul, *Social Evolution and Sociological Categories* (London, 1976) who treats Weber as a worthy opponent but one who must be conquered who mystifies the central problems not only of method but also of domination and of the state.

4. For detailed bibliographical treatment of Weber see: Benidix, Rheinhart, *Max Weber: An Intellectual Portrait* (London, 1960); Roth, Guenther, 'Introduction' to Weber, *Economy and Society* (New York, 1968); Mills, C. Wright, 'Introduction' to Gerth, H. H. and Mills, C. W., *From Max Weber* (London, 1948).

5. Weber, Freiburg Inaugural Address, quoted Therborn, *op. cit*, p. 311.

6. Weber, M., *History of Commercial Societies in the Middle Ages* (1889).

7. Weber, M., *Roman Agrarian History in its Bearing on Public and Private Law* (Stutggart, 1891).

8. Certain parts of this large work have appeared in separate English translations; the most important of these are *The Theory of Social and Economic Organization*. Trans. Henderson, A. M. and Parsons, Talcott, (Glencoe, 1947); *On Law and Economy in Society* ed. Rheinstein, Max, (Cambridge, Mass., 1966), hereafter referred to as *Law and Economy; The Sociology of Religion* ed. Parsons, Talcott, (Boston, 1963). Since some of the separate translations are more readily available I have relied on them, in particular on *Law and Economy; Economy and Society* has only been used for sections not elsewhere translated.

9. With respect to Weber's involvement in German politics, see in particular: Kohn, Hans, *The Mind of Germany* (New York, 1960); Meyer, J. P., *Max Weber and German Politics* (London, 1947); Jaspers, Karl, 'Max Weber as politician, scientist, philosopher' in his *Leonardo, Descartes, Max Weber: Three Essays* (London, 1965).

10. See pp. 105—6.

11. Salomon, Albert, 'Max Weber's political ideas' 2 *Social Research* 372 (1936).

12. Horkheimer, Max, *The Eclipse of Reason* (New York, 1947).

13. Heller, Hermann, Article in *'Die Neue Rundschau'* (1933) quoted in Niemeyer, G., *Law Without Force* (Princeton, 1941).

14. 'The pursuit of wealth, stripped of its religious and ethical meaning, tends to become associated with purely mundane passions', *The Protestant Ethic and the Spirit of Capitalism* (London 1930) 182; for a detailed, but psychologistic, study of Weber's 'pessimism' see Mitzman, Arthur, *The Iron Cage: An Historical Interpretation of Max Weber* (New York, 1970).

15. See for example Salomon, Albert, 'German sociology' in Gurvitch, G. and Moore, W. E. (eds), *Twentieth Century Sociology* (New York, 1945), p. 596. See also Bendix, R., *Max Weber: An Intellectual Portrait*; Loewith, Karl, 'Weber's interpretation of the bourgeois capitalist world in terms of the guiding principle of rationalisation' in Wrong, D., (ed.), *Max Weber* (New Jersey, 1970); Mannheim, Karl 'German sociology 1918—1933' 1 *Politica* 12—33 (1934);

Albrow, Martin, 'Legal positivism and bourgeois materialism', **2** (1) *B.J.L.S.* 14—31 (1975).

16. Weber, Marianne, *Max Weber: Ein Lebensbild* (Tübingen, 1926) 617.
17. Quoted by Baumgarten, E (ed.), *Max Weber, Werk und Person* (Tübingen, 1964) 554—5.
18. Colletti, Lucio, 'Marxism as a sociology' in *From Rousseau to Lenin* (London, 1972) 37; an essentially similar position is argued by Albrow, M., *op. cit.*, p. 15.
19. See for example Therborn, G., *op. cit.*, p. 270. Albrow goes so far as to characterise Weber's sociology as 'bourgeois materialism', but thereby commits the error of equating positivism and materialism; see Albrow, *op. cit.*, p. 14.
20. This is the same point as that made by Therborn when he insists that the distinction between Marx and Weber lies in the fact that they are discourses on quite different levels.
21. Weber, M., 'R. Stammler's "surmounting" of the materialist conception of history' 2(2) *B. J. L. S.* 129—52 (1975) and 3 (1) *ibid.* 17—43 (1976).
22. See for fuller elaboration pp. 99—101.
23. Weber, M., quoted by Kohn, H., *op. cit.*, p. 282.
24. Weber, M., *ibid.*, p. 285.
25. Weber, M., quoted in. Salomon, Albert, 'Max Weber's methodology' 1 *Social Research* 151 (1934) (no original source reference is given by Salomon).
26. Weber, M., Letter to Freidrich Crusius (24 November 1918) quoted by Kohn, H., *op. cit.*, p. 286.
27. Parsons, Talcott, (Glencoe, Ill., 1964).
28. This for example is the theme which underlies his monumental study of world religions. Weber, M., *The Religion of China* trans. and ed. Gerth, H. H., (Glencoe, 1951); Weber, M., *The Religion of India* trans. and ed. Gerth, H. H. and Martindale, Don, (Glencoe, 1958); Weber, M., *Ancient Judaism* trans. and ed. Gerth, H. H. and Martindale, Don, (Glencoe, 1952); and in addition *Protestant Ethic* and *The Sociology of Religion*.
29. Weber, M., *General Economic History* (New York, 1961); *The City* (Glencoe, Ill., 1958); *The Theory of Social and Economic Organization* (Glencoe, Ill., 1947).
30. Weber, M. *Wirtschaft und Gesellschaft* (1925), p. 6.
31. Parsons, Talcott, 'Introduction' to Weber, M., *The Methodology of the Social Sciences*, trans. Shils, E. A. and Finch, H. A., (Glencoe, 1949), p. 10.
32. See the sweeping critique in Gouldner, Alvin, 'Anti-minataur: the myth of a value-free sociology' in Gouldner, *For Sociology* (London, 1973); and for an epistemological critique see Hirst, Paul, *Social Evolution and Sociological Categories* (London, 1976).
33. Marcuse, H. 'Industrialisation and capitalism' in *Negations* (London, 1968), p. 203.
34. Jordan, H. P., 'Some philosophical implications of Max Weber's methodology', 48 *Ethics*, 230 (1938).
35. Friedrich, Carl J., 'Some observations on Weber's analysis of bureaucracy' in Merton, R., (ed.) *Reader in Bureaucracy* (New York, 1952).
36. Loewith, *op. cit.*, p. 109.
37. Marcuse, *op. cit.*, p. 207.
38. Antoni, Carlo, *From History to Sociology: The Transition in German Historical Thinking* (London, 1962), p. 146.
39. As Hirst observes 'Weber's "positivism" exists at the level of technique'; Hirst, *op. cit.*, p. 64.
40. Hirst, Paul, *ibid.*, chapters 3—6.
41. Roth, 'Introduction' to *Economy and Society*, p. lxxvi.
42. Freund, *The Sociology of Max Weber* (New York, 1965), p. 245.
43. Parsons, Talcott, 'Max Weber, 1864—1964' 30 *American Sociological Review* 174—5 (1965).

44. Parsons, Talcott, 'Value-freedom and objectivity' in Stammer, O. (ed.), *Max Weber and Sociology Today*, p. 40.
45. This is the case in Bendix, R., *Max Weber: An Intellectual Portrait*; Honigsheim, *On Max Weber*; Wrong, D., *Max Weber*; Aron, R., *Main Currents in Sociological Thought* Vol. II 'Durkheim, Pareto, Weber', Freund, *The Sociology of Max Weber*. The most extensive treatment is provided by Bendix; see Bendix, Rheinhart, *Max Weber: An Intellectual Portrait* (London, 1960), chapters 12 and 13.
46. Morris, Clarence, 'Law, reason and sociology' 107 *University of Pennsylvania Law Review* 147—65 (1952).
47. Skoljar, S. J., 'Weber's sociology of law' in Sawer, G., *Studies in the Sociology of Law* (Canberra, 1961).
48. For examples see: Pound, Roscoe, *Jurisprudence* Vol. I pp. 314—18 (St. Paul, 1959); Pound, R., 'Sociology of law' in Gurvitch and Moore (eds), *Twentieth Century Sociology* 309—10; Stone, Julius *Social Dimensions of Law and Justice* (numerous passing references); Schur, *Law and Society: A Sociological View* (New York, 1968), pp. 75—77 and 108—10; Evan, W. (ed.), *Law and Sociology* (Glencoe, 1962) (passing references).
49. Trubek, David, 'Max Weber on law and the rise of capitalism' 3 *Wisconsin L. R.* 720—53 (1972); 'Toward a social theory of law: an essay on the study of law and development' 82 (1) *Yale L. J.* 1—50 (1972); Albrow, Martin, 'Legal positivism and bourgeois materialism: Max Weber's view of the sociology of law' 2 (1) *B. J. L. S.* 14—31 (1975); and Walton, Paul, 'Max Weber's sociology of law: a critique' in Carlen, P., (ed.) *The Sociology of Law* (Keele, 1976).
50. Weber, M., *Economy and Society*, see in particular pt. I chapter 3 'The types of legitimate domination' and pt. II chapter 1 'The economy and social norms'.
51. Weber, M., *Law and Economy*, p. 5 (Weber's emphasis).
52. Skoljar, S. J., *op. cit.*, p. 33.
53. This attack on Ehrlich is parallel to his attack on the 'Germanists' of the Historical School with heir emphasis upon law as a product of a particular *Volksgeist*. See in particular *Law and Economy*, chapter 5.
54. Lasswell, H. D., Review of 'Law and economy' 7 *Journal of Legal Education* 301—3 (1954—5).
55. Albrow, Martin, 'Legal positivism and bourgeois materialism' 2 (1) *B. J. L. S.* 14—31 (1975).
56. Weber, M., *Law and economy* pp. 62—3. The latter category he subdivides into (a) logical and (b) extrinsic forms of rationality.
57, Weber, M., *ibid.*, p. 62.
58. Eldridge, J. E. T., *Max Weber: The Interpretation of Social Reality* (London, 1970); Freund, *op. cit.* A similar position is taken by Bendix.
59. Weber, M., *Law and Economy*, p. 319.
60. Weber, M., *ibid.*, p. 308.
61. Weber, M., *ibid.*, p. 511.
62. Weber, M., *ibid.*, p. 303.
63. Weber, M., *Ancient Judaism* (Glencoe, Ill., 1952), p. 84.
64. Morris, 'Law, reason and sociology' 107 *U. Penn. L. R.* 147—65 (1958—9).
65. Weber, M., *Economy and Society*, p. 976.
66. Weber, M., *The Religion of China* (Glencoe, Ill.) pp. 149—50.
67. See below pp. 122—8.
68. From the point of view of the formal quality of his paradigm this subdivision is not without significance. It may be suggested that it exposes a certain lack of clarity in his conceptual thought. His use of the term 'logic' seems to stand mid-way between the terms 'formal' and 'rational'. Thus his importation of 'logic' into a typology founded upon the dual concepts of formality and rationality obstructs the distinction which he seeks to make. From a juris-

prudential standpoint Weber may be taken as suggesting a distinction between 'formal legalism' and 'rational legalism' which are to be distinguished by reference not simply to the presence or absence of logical treatment of data, but by reference to the form of logic which is applied to that data.

69. Keat and Urry *Social Theory as Science* (London, 1975), p. 220.
70. Weber, M., *op. cit.*, p. 63.
71. Weber, M., *ibid.*, p. 226.
72. Weber, M., *Protestant Ethic*, p. 26.
73. Weber, M., *General Economic History*, trans. Knight, F. H. (Glencoe, Ill., 1927), p. 232.
74. Weber, M., *The Religion of China*, p. 149.
75. Weber, M., *Law and Economy*, pp. 266—7.
76. Weber, M., *Economy and Society*, p. 977.
77. For Weber 'bureaucracy' is a specialised concept referring to a system of administration in which the administrative tasks are carried out by persons not personally owning the means of production or administration, but who work as salaried officials following a career.
78. Weber, M., *ibid.*, p. 975.
79. Weber, M., *Law and Economy*, p. 201. This stage is frequently associated with the widespread use of legal fictions.
80. Weber, M., *ibid.*, p. 201.
81. Weber, M., *ibid.*, p. 204.
82. Weber, M., *ibid.*, p. 97.
83. Weber, M., *ibid.*, pp. 217 ff.
84. Weber, M., *ibid.*, p. 131.
85. One chapter of *Law and Economy* and important passages in *The Religion of China* are devoted to a discussion of natural law.
86. Weber, M., *op. cit.*, p. 287.
87. Weber, M., *ibid.*, pp. 287—8.
88. Weber, M., *ibid.*, p. 288.
89. Weber, M., *The Religion of China*, p. 148.
90. Weber, M., *ibid.*, pp. 147—50.
91. Weber, M., *Economy and Society*, p. 941.
92. Weber, M., *Theory of Social and Economic Organization*, p. 324.
93. Weber, M., *Economy and Society*, p. 943.
94. It is however important to stress that in his substantive discussion of the forms of legitimate domination, particularly with respect to traditional and charismatic domination, he devotes considerable attention to their historical forms and to their development.
95. Weber, M., *Economy and Society*, p. 945.
96. See for the most systematic discussion Bendix, R., *Max Weber: An Intellectual Portrait* (London, 1960) chapter X—XII; Hirst, Paul, *op. cit.*, chapter 5.
97. Weber, M., *Economy and Society*, p. 215.
98. Weber, M., *ibid.*, p. 215.
99. See below, p. 105.
100. See below, p. 107
101. Weber, M., *General Economy History*, p. 232.
102. Yet Weber also recognises that this impersonal order operates to the advantage of dominant economic groups; see further pp. 120—1 but he sees this as an incidental function that arises from a congruence of concern for predictability on the part both of bureaucratic and capitalistic interest.
103. Bendix, R., 'Max Weber's interpretation of conduct and history' 51 *A. J. S.* 525—6 (1946).
104. Weber, M., *Theory of Social and Economic Organization*, p. 324.
105. For fuller elaboration see Hunt, Alan, 'Perspectives in the sociology of law' in

Carlen, P. (ed.), *The Sociology of Law* (Keele, 1976) pp. 22–43.
106. Except that it should be noted that it has connections with the tendency in modern American sociology to treat the court as an organisation, for example in the work of Blumberg and the judicial behaviouralists.
107. Weber, M., *Law and Economy*, p. 131.
108. Weber, M., *ibid.*, p. 176.
109. Weber, M., *Economy and Society*, p. 1394.
110. Weber, M., *Protestant Ethic*, p. 25.
111. Weber, M., *Economy and Society*, pp. 155–88.
112. Weber, M., *ibid.*, p. 37.
113. Weber, M., *Law and Economy*, p. 189.
114. Weber, M., *ibid.*, pp. 228–9.
115. Weber, M., *Economy and Society*, pp. 812–13.
116. Weber, M., *Law and Economy*, p. 230.
117. Weber, M., *ibid.*, p. 38.
118. Weber, M., *ibid.*, p. 61.
119. Weber, M., *Economy and Society*, p. 83.
120. This silence concerning the relation between law and the economy has persisted in modern sociology of law. The exceptions have occurred in what has emerged as a separate strand 'of 'emergence studies'; see for example Chambliss, William, 'A sociological analysis of the law of vagrancy' 12 (1) *Social Problems* 67–77 (1964); Carsons, W. G., 'Symbolic and instrumental dimensions of early factory legislation' in Hood, R. (ed.), *Criminology and Public Policy* (London, 1974).
121. The fact that he recognised the general importance of English economic development is given full testimony.
122. He gave the subject no systematic treatment but it could never have been far from his mind because he returns to it time and again. The most important source outside Weber's own discussion are Trubek, David, 'Max Weber on law and the rise of capitalism' 3 *Wisconsin L. R.* 720–53 (1972) and Little, David, *Religion, Order and Law* (New York, 1969).
123. Weber, M., *Law and Economy*, p. 202.
124. Weber, M., *Law and Economy*, p. 317.
125. Weber, M., *Economy and Society*, p. 976.
126. Weber, M., *ibid.*, p. 976.
127. Rheinstein, 'Introduction' to Weber, *Law and Economy*, p. lvi.
128. It is precisely this openness to pressure from new social and economic needs and its consequent flexibility that leads Talcott Parsons to insist upon the direct relationship between the common law and the rise of capitalism in Britain.
129. Weber, M., *Law and Economy*, p. 178.
130. Weber, M., *Law and Economy*, p. 231 (my emphasis added); it is interesting to note the parallel between this position of Weber's and that developed in much more detail by Karl Renner who in his treatment of English property law focuses upon the 'functional transformation' of law through which process rules whose content remains relatively unchanged come to serve totally new economic functions.
131. Trubek's discussion of the 'England problem' largely fails to grasp this dimension of Weber's treatment; he proceeds as if it were an insuperable obstacle for Weberian analysis. This deficiency arises from attempting to treat Weber's sociology of law in isolation from his wider theoretical and ideological concerns.
132. Weber, M., *ibid.*, pp. 178 ff.
133. Weber, M., *ibid.*, p. 131.
134. See pp. 110–11 above.
135. Weber, M., *Economy and Society*, p. 976.
136. Weber, M., *ibid.*, p. 1395.

137. Weber, M., *Law and Economy*, p. 278.
138. Weber, M., *Religion in China*, p. 102.
139. Weber, M., *Law and Economy*, p. 268.
140. Weber, M., *ibid.*, p. 179.
141. Little, David, *Religion, Order and Law* (New York, 1969).
142. This alliance has also been stressed by Hill, Christopher, *Puritanism and Revolution* (London, 1958).
143. A number of valuable individual pieces of work appeared in an earlier period of the sociological movement; perhaps the most significant being: Hall, Jerome, *Theft, Law and Society* (Boston, 1935); Commons, John, *Legal Foundations of Capitalism* (New York, 1924); Berle and Means, *The Modern Corporation and Private Property* (New York, 1932). In modern sociology of law the growth of 'emergence studies' (see note 120) has gone some way to remedy this defect, as has the even more recent demand for a 'political economy of law and crime' within radical sociology of law; see for example Chambliss, W. and Mankoff, M., *Whose Law? What Order?* (New York, 1976).
144. Weber, M., *Law and Economy*, chapter VI 'Forms of creation of rights'.
145. Weber, M., *ibid.*, p. 100.
146. Weber, M., *ibid.*, p. 100.
147. Weber, M., *ibid.*, p. 105.
148. Weber, M., *ibid.*, p. 189.
149. Weber, M., *ibid.*, p. 189.
150. Weber, M., *ibid.*, pp. 188—9.
151. For fuller elaboration of this characterisation of modern sociology of law see Hunt, Alan, 'Perspectives in the sociology of law' in Carlen, P. (ed.), *Sociology of Law* (Keele, 1976).
152. See in particular Parsons, Talcott, *Politics and Social Structure* (New York, 1969) and *Structure and Process in Modern Societies* (New York, 1960) in which law is treated as an 'integrative mechanism'; Parsonian influence finds its direct expression in modern sociology of law through the work of Harry Bredemeier, 'Law as an Integrative mechanism' in Aubert, V. (ed.), *Sociology of Law* (Harmondsworth, 1969) and of Black, Donald, 'The boundaries of legal sociology' 81 *Yale L. J.* 1086—1100 (1972).
153. See the articles by Trubek, Albrow and Walton referred to in note 49 above.

N OTES TO CHAPTER 6

1. This anxiety is explicitly reflected in Rostow, Eugene (ed.), *Is Law Dead?* (New York, 1970); Wolff, Robert (ed.), *The Rule of Law* (New York, 1971); and Mazor, Lester, 'The crisis of liberal legalism' 81 *Yale L. J.* 1032—53 (1972). It can also be seen as an underlying theme of the liberal democratic jurisprudence of Morris Cohen, Lon Fuller and H. L. A. Hart.
2. This has been characteristic of the sociology of law of Selznick, Skolnick and Parsons and, at a lower level of generality, by Kalven Zeisel and from a more overtly radical stance in Blumberg.
3. Aubert, V., 'Researches in the sociology of law' 7 *Am. Behav. Sci.* 16—20 (1963); Schur, Edwin, *Law and Society: A Sociological View* (New York, 1968); and Sawer, Geoffrey, *Law in Society* (Oxford, 1965).
4. For example Schur, E., *op. cit.*, p. 5 argues that the normative realm is 'a realm in which sociologists find themselves very uncomfortable.'
5. Adopted is Gouldner's view that no social theory presents itself in a pure form but always carries with it, constituting the 'silent partners in the theoretical enterprise', certain 'domain assumptions'; Gouldner, Alvin, *The Coming Crisis of Western Sociology*, p. 29 (London, 1971).

6. Thompson, E. P. *The Making of the English Working Class*, p. 431 (London, 1968).
7. Stone, Julius, *Law and the Social Sciences: The Second Half-Century*, p. 5 (Minneapolis, 1966).
8. Campbell, Colin, 'The expansion of the sociology of law' (mimeographed paper 1972).
9. See in particular the work of Schubert, Glendon, *Judicial Decision-Making* (New York, 1963) and *The Judicial Mind* (Evanston, 1965); Nagel, Stuart, *The Legal Process From a Behavioral Perspective* (Homewood, Ill., 1969).
10. While Giddens is correct in criticising the conception of sociology as being concerned with a narrowly static and conservative conception of social order, he is incorrect in dismissing the importance of the general problematic of social order in the history of sociology; Giddens, Anthony, 'Four myths in the history of social thought' 1 *Economy and Society* 357–85 (1972).
11. For example the definition of law as the most specialised form of social control is explicit in Pound.
12. Gusfield, J. R., *Symbolic Crusade: Status Politics and the American Temperance Movement* (Urbana, Ill., 1966).
13. As a further extension of this line of thought it may be tentatively suggested that this process receives further momentum from another consideration. Where the existing social order comes under increasing tensions, especially where these manifest themselves in a declining legitimacy then, because the legal system is generally enveloped in a higher level of legitimacy than other constituents of the social order, it comes to be invoked more frequently in the maintenance of that social order. Thus it comes to play a more direct and explicit role in the maintenance of the existing order. The development of statutory incomes policy in Britain lends support to such an analysis which may have much wider applicability.
14. Expressions of this radical trend include amongst their more important expressions Balbus, Isaac, *The Dialectics of Legal Repression* (New York, 1973); Chambliss, W. and Seidman, R., *Law, Order and Power* (Reading, Mass., 1971); Lefcourt, R., (ed.) *Law Against the People* (New York, 1971); and Quinney, Richard, *Critique of the Legal Order* (Boston, 1974).

Bibliography: References and Principal Sources

CHAPTER 1

Ehrlich, Eugen, *Fundamental Principles of the Sociology of Law*, Russell and Russell (New York, 1962).
Gurvitch, Georges, *Sociology of Law*, Routledge and Kegan Paul (London, 1973).
Hunt, Alan, 'Law, state and class struggle' 20 (6) *Marxism Today* 178–87 (June 1976).
Hunt, Alan, 'Perspectives in the sociology of law' in Carien, P. (ed.), *The Sociology of Law*, Sociological Review (Keele, 1976).
Mills, C. W., *Sociology and Pragmatism: The Higher Learning in America*, Oxford U. P. (New York, 1966).
Stone, Julius, *Social Dimensions of Law and Justice*, Stevens (London, 1966).
Timasheff, N. S., *An Introduction to the Sociology of Law*, Harvard U. P. (Cambridge, Mass., 1939).
Treves, R. and Van Loon, G., *Norms and Actions: National Reports on Sociology of Law*, Nijhoff (Hague, 1968).

CHAPTER 2

Aronson, M., 'Roscoe Pound and the resurgence of juristic idealism' 6 *Journal of Social Philosophy* 47–83 (1940).
Braybrooke, E. K., 'The sociological jurisprudence of Roscoe Pound' in Sawer, G. (ed.), *Studies in the Sociology of Law*, Australian National University (Canberra, 1961).
Cohen, Felix, *Ethical Systems and Legal Ideals*, Cornell U. P. (New York, 1959).
Cohen, Felix, 'Field theory and judicial logic' 59 *Yale L. J.* 238 (1950).
Cohen, Morris, *Law and the Social Order*, Harcourt Brace (New York, 1933).
Cooley, C. H., *Human Nature and Legal Order*, Charles Scribner (New York, 1912).
Cooley, C. H., *Social Organization*, Charles Scribner (New York, 1912).
Friedmann, W., Review, 4 *J. L. E.* 506 (1952).
Gluek, S. (ed.), *Roscoe Pound and Criminal Justice*, Oceana (Dobbs Ferry, N.Y., 1965).
Goodhart, A., 'Roscoe Pound' 78 *Harvard L. R.* 23–37 (1964).

Bibliography 173

Grossman, W., 'The legal philosophy of Roscoe Pound' 44 *Yale L. J.* 605—18 (1935.

Gurvitch, G., *Sociology of Law*, Kegan Paul (London, 1942), pp. 124—30.

Hart, H. L. A., *The Concept of Law*, Clarendon Press (London 1961).

James, W., *The Will To Believe*, Longmans (London, 1897).

Kohler, J., *The Philosophy of Law*, Macmillan (New York, 1921).

Lepaulle, P., 'The function of comparative law' 35 *Harvard L. R.* 838—58 (1922).

Llewellyn, K. 'Roscoe Pound' 28 *U. Chicago L. R.* 174 (1960).

Llewellyn, K., 'A realistic jurisprudence — the next step' 30 *Columbia L. R.* 431 (1930).

Maine, H., *Ancient Law*, Routledge (London, 1905).

Morris, H., 'Dean Pound's Jurisprudence', 13 *Stanford L. R.* 185—210 (1960).

Paton, G. W., 'Pound and contemporary juristic theory 22 *Canadian Bar Review* 479—91 (1944).

Patterson, E., 'Roscoe Pound on jurisprudence' 60 *Columbia L. R.* 1124—32 (1960).

Patterson, E., 'Pound's theory of social interests' in Sayre, P. (ed.), *Interpretations of Modern Legal Philosophies*, Oxford U. P. (London, 1947).

Patterson, E., *Jurisprudence: Men and Ideas of the Law*, Foundation Press (Brooklyn, 1953).

Pound Roscoe (books by)
  Outlines of Lectures on Jurisprudence (1st ed. 1903) 5th ed. Harvard U. P. (Cambridge, Mass, 1943).
  An Introduction to the Philosophy of Law (1st ed. 1922) Yale U. P. (New Haven, 1954).
  The Spirit of the Common Law, Marshall Jones (Boston, 1921).
  Interpretations of Legal History, Macmillan (New York, 1923).
  Law nd Morals, University of North Carolina Press (Chapel Hill, 1924).
  Contemporary Juristic Theory, Claremont Colleges (Claremont, 1940).
  Social Control Through Law, Yale U. P. (New Haven, 1942).
  Jurisprudence (5 volumes), West Publishing (St. Paul, Minn., 1959).
  Criminal Justice in Cleveland, (edited with Frankfurter, Felix) Patterson Smith (Montilian, N. J., 1968).

Pound, Roscoe (articles by)
  'Sociology of law' in Gurvitch, G. and Moore, W. E., *Twentieth Century Sociology*, Philosophical Library (New York, 1945), chapter 11.
  'Causes of popular dissatisfaction with the administration of justice' 40 *American L. R.* 729 (1906).
  'Law in books and law in action' 44 *American L. R.* 12—36 (1910).
  'Mechanical jurisprudence' 8 *Columbia L. R.* 605—23 (1908).
  'The need of a sociological jurisprudence' 19 *Green Bag* 607—15 (1907).
  'The scope and purpose of sociological jurisprudence' 24 *Harvard L. R.* 591—619 (1911) and 25 *ibid.* 140—68, 409—516 (1911—12).
  'The end of law as developed in legal rules and doctrines' 27 *Harvard L. R.* 195—234 (1914).
  'The end of law as developed in juristic thought' 27 *Harvard L. R.* 605—28 (1914) and 30 *ibid.* 201—25 (1917).
  'The call for a Realist jurisprudence' 44 *Harvard L. R.* 697 (1931).
  'Fifty years of jurisprudence' 50 *Harvard L. R.* 557—82 (1937) and 51 *ibid.* 777—812 (1938).
  'A survey of social interests' 57 *Harvard L. R.* 1—39 (1943).
  'A survey of public interests' 58 *Harvard L. R.* 909—29 (1945).
  'The role of will in law' 68 *Harvard L. R.* 1—19 (1954).
  'Sociology of law and sociological jurisprudence' 5 *U. Toronto L. J.* 1—20 (1943).

Reuschlin, H., *Jurisprudence — It's American Prophets*, Bobbs-Merrill (Indianapolis, 1951).

Ross, E. A., *Social Control: A Survey of the Foundations of Order*, Macmillan (New York, 1910).

Rumble, W. E., *American Legal Realism: Scepticism, Reform and Judicial Process*, Cornell U. P. (Ithaca, 1968).

Sayre, Paul, *Life of Roscoe Pound*, Iowa State University (Iowa City, 1948).

Schiff, D., 'Socio-legal theory: social structure and law' 36 *M. L. R.* 287—310 (1976).

Setaro, F. C. *Bibliography of the Writings of Roscoe Pound* Harvard U. P. (Cambridge, Mass., 1942).

Simpson, S. P., 'Roscoe Pound and the interpretation of modern legal philosophies' 23 *New York Univ. L. Q. R.* 393—411 (1948).

Stammler, R., *The Theory of Justice*, Macmillan (New York, 1925).

Stone, Julius, *The Province and Function of Law*, Stevens (London 1947).

Stone, Julius, *Human Law and Human Justice*, Stevens (London, 1965).

Stone, Julius, *Social Dimensions of Law and Justice*, Stevens (London, 1966).

Stone, Julius, 'The golden age of Pound' 4 *Sydney L. R.* 1—27 (1962).

Stone, Julius, 'Roscoe Pound and sociological jurisprudence' 78 *Harvard L. R.* 1578—94 (1965).

CHAPTER 3

Works by Karl Llewellyn and other Realists:

Arnold, T., *The Symbols of Government*, Yale U. P. (New Haven, 1935).

Arnold, T., *The Folklore of Capitalism*, Yale U. P. (New Haven, 1968).

Bingham, J. W., 'What is the law?' 7 *Fordham L. R.* 203 (1938).

Clark, C. E. *et al.*, *A Study of Law Administration in Connecticut* Yale U. P. (New Haven, 1937).

Cook, W. W., 'The logical and legal basis of the conclict of law' 33 *Yale L. J.* 457 (1924).

Douglas, W. and Thomas 'The business failure project — a study in methodology', 39 *Yale L. J.* 1013 (1930).

Frank, Jerome, *Law and the Modern Mind*, Coward-McCann (New York, 1930).

Frank, Jerome, *Courts On Trial — Myth and Reality in American Justice*, Princeton U. P. (Princeton, N.J., 1950).

Frank, Jerome, 'Are judges human?', 80 *U. Penn. L. R.* 17—53, 233—67 (1931).

Gehlke, C., *Criminal Actions in the Common Pleas of Ohio*, Johns Hopkins (Baltimore, 1936).

Holmes, O. W., *The Common Law*, Macmillan (London 1968).

Holmes, O. W., 'The path of law', 10 *Harvard L. R.* 457—78 (1897).

Holmes, O. W., 'Law in science and science in law', 12 *Harvard L. R.* 443—63 (1899).

Llewellyn, Karl, *The Bramble Bush: On our Law and Its Society*, Oceana (New York, 1960).

The Common Law Tradition: Deciding Appeals, Little, Brown (Boston, 1960).

Jurisprudence: Realism in Theory and Practice, University Chicago P. (Chicago, 1962).

Cases and Materials on the Law of Sales, Callahan (Chicago, 1930).

Llewellyn and Hoebel, E. A., *The Cheyenne Way: Conflict and Case Law in Primitive Jurisprudence*, University of Oklahoma P. (Norman, 1941).

Llewellyn, K., 'Effect of Legal Institutions upon Economics', 15 *American Economic Review* 665—83 (1925).

Llewellyn, K., 'The conditions for and the aims and methods of legal research', 6 *Am. Law School R.* 670—8 (1929).

Llewellyn, K., 'Law and the social sciences — especially sociology', 14 *A. S. R.* 451—62 (1949) and, with different introductory paragraph, in 62 *Harvard L. R.* 1286 (1949).

Llewellyn, K., 'A realistic jurisprudence — the next step' 30 *Columbia L. R.* 431

(1930).

Llewellyn, K., 'Frank's "Law and the Modern Mind": legal illusion', 31 *Columbia L. R.* 82 (1931).

Llewellyn, K., 'Behind the law of divorce', 32 *Columbia L. R.* 1281–1308 (1932) and 33 *ibid.* 249–94 (1933).

Llewellyn, K., 'Some realism about realism', 44 *Harvard L. R.* 1222 (1931).

Llewellyn, K., 'A united front on the court', 144 *Nation* 289 (1937).

Llewellyn, K., 'On the good, the true, the beautiful in law' 9 *U. Chicago L. R.* 224–65 (1942).

Llewellyn, K., 'On philosophy in American law', 82 *U. Penn. L. R.* 205–12 (1934).

Llewellyn, K., 'The normative, the legal and the law-jobs: the problem of juristic method', 49 *Yale L. J.* 1355–1400 (1940).

Moore, U., 'Rational basis of legal institutions', 23 *Columbia L. R.* 609–17 (1923).

Moore, U. and Callahan, C., 'Law and learning theory: a study in legal control', 53 *Yale L. J.* 1–143 (1943).

Oliphant, H., 'Parallels in the development of legal and medical education', 167 *Annals of the American Academy of Political and Social Sciences* 162 (1933).

Oliphant, H., 'A return to stare decisis', 14 *American B. A. J.* 71 (1928).

Radin, M., *Law as Logic and Experience*, Yale U. P. (New Haven, 1940).

OTHER REFERENCES

Allen, C. K., *Law in the Making* (7th ed.), Oxford U. P. (London, 1964).

Becker, T. L., *Political Behavioralism and Modern Jurisprudence*, Rand-McNally (Chicago, 1964).

Bodenheimer, E., *Jurisprudence*, Harvard U. P. (Cambridge, Mass. 1968).

Bohannan, P., *Justice and Judgement Among the Tiv*, Oxford U. P. (London, 1957).

Cahill, F. V., *Judicial Legislation: A Study in American Legal Theory*, Ronald Press (New York, 1952).

Cohen, M. R., *Law and the Social Order*, Archon (Hamden, Conn, 1967).

Cowan, T., 'Legal pragmatism and beyond' in Sayre, P. (ed.), *Interpretations of Modern Legal Philosophies*, Oxford U. P. (New York, 1947).

Friedmann, W., *Legal Theory*, Stevens (London, 1967).

Fuller, Lon, 'American legal realism', 82 *U. Penn. L. R.* 429–62 (1934).

Garlan, E., *Legal Realism and Justice*, Columbia U. P. (New York, 1941).

Gilmore, G., 'Legal realism: its cause and cure', 70 *Yale L. J.* 1037–48 (1961).

Gluckmann, M., *The Judicial Process Among the Barotse in Northern Rhodesia*, Manchester U. P. (Manchester, 1955).

Hofstadter, R., *The Age of Reform: From Byran to F. D. R.*, Knopf (New York, 1956).

Hofstadter, R., *Social Darwinism in American Thought*, Beacon Press (New York, 1955).

Hofstadter, R., *The American Political Tradition*, Cape (London, 1962).

Ingersoll, D., 'Karl Llewellyn, American legal realism and contemporary legal behavioralism', 76 *Ethics* 253 (1966).

Jones, H. W., 'Law and morality in the perspective of legal realism', 61 *Columbia L. R.* 799–809 (1961).

Leuchtenburg, W., *Franklin D. Roosevelt and the New Deal*, Harper (New York, 1963).

McDougall, M., 'Fuller v. the American legal Realists: an intervention', 50 *Yale L. J.* 827–40 (1941).

Malinowski, B., *Crime and Custom in Savage Society*, Routledge and Kegan Paul (London, 1961).

Mills, C. W., *Sociology and Pragmatism*, Oxford U. P. (New York, 1966).

Mulkay, M. J., *Functionalism, Exchange Theory and Theoretical Strategy*, Routledge and Kegan Paul (London, 1971).

Paton, G. W., *A Textbook of Jurisprudence*, Oxford U. P. (London, 1964).

Patterson, E., *Jurisprudence: Men and Ideas of the Law*, Foundation Press (Brooklyn, 1953).

Pound, R., 'The case for a Realist jurisprudence', 44 *Harvard L. R.* 697 (1931).

Pound, R. *et al. Criminal Justice in Cleveland*, Patterson Smith (Montilain, N. J. 1968).

Rehbinder, M., 'The development and present state of fact research in the United States', 24 *J. L. E.* 567–89 (1972).

Rumble, W. E., *American Legal Realism*, Cornell U. P. (Ithaca, 1968).

Schlesinger, A., *The Age of Roosevelt: The Coming of the New Deal*, Oxford U. P. (New York, 1959).

Shuman, S., *Legal Positivism: Its Scope and Limitations*, Wayne State U. P. (Detroit, 1963).

Twining, W., *Karl Llewellyn and the Realist Movement*, Weidenfeld and Nicholson (London, 1973).

Twining, W., 'Two works of Karl Llewellyn', 30 and 31 *M. L. R.* 514 and 165 (1967–8).

White, Morton, *Social Thought in America: The Revolt Against Formalism*, Beacon Press (New York, 1957).

Yntema, H., 'Legal science and reform', 34 *Columbia L. R.* 207 (1934).

Yntema, H., 'American legal realism in retrospect', 9 *Vanderbilt L. R.* 317 (1960).

CHAPTER 4

Alpert, H., *Emile Durkheim and his Sociology*, Russell and Russell (New York, 1961).

Aron, R., *Main Currents in Sociological Thought*, vol. II, Weidenfeld and Nicholson (London, 1968).

Barnes, J. A., 'Durkheim's division of labour in society', 1/2 *Man* 158–75 (1966).

Baxi, U., 'Durkheim and legal evolution', 8 *L. & S. R.* 645–51 (1974).

Bellah, R. N., 'Durkheim and history' 24 *A. S. R.* 447–61 (1959).

Beniot-Smullyan, E., 'The sociology of Emile Durkheim and his school' in Barnes, H. E. (ed.), *An Introduction to the Histroy of Sociology*, University of Chicago Press (Chicago, 1948).

Bohannan, P., *Justice and Judgement Among the Tiv*, Oxford U. P. (London, 1957).

Cartwright and Schwartz, 'The invocation of legal norms: an empirical investigation of Durkheim and Weber' 38 *A. S. R.* 340–54 (1973).

Coser, L. A., 'Durkheim's conservatism and its implications for his sociological theory' in Wolff, K. H. (ed.), *Emile Durkheim 1858–1917*, Ohio State U. P. (Columbus, 1960).

Diamond, A. S., *The Evolution of Law and Order*, Watts (London, 1951).

Diamond, A. S., *Primitive Law Past and Present*, Methuen (London, 1972).

Durkheim, Emile (works by)

 The Division of Labour in Society, (1st edition 1893) Free Press (New York, 1964).

 Professional Ethics and Civic Morals, Routledge and Kegan Paul (London, 1957).

 The Elementary Forms of Religious Life, Allen and Unwin (London 1964).

 The Rules of Sociological Method, (1st edition 1895) Free Press (New York, 1964).

 Sociology and Philosophy, Free Press (New York, 1953).

 Suicide: A Study in Sociology, Routledge and Kegan Paul (London, 1970).

 Moral Education, Free Press (New York, 1961).

 'Deux lois de l'evolution pénale', 4 *L'Année Sociologique* 65–95 (1900). Translated as 'Two laws of penal evolution', 2 *Economy and Society* 285–308 (1973).

'Crime et santé sociale', 39 *Revue Philosophique* 518–23 (1895).

Selected Writings, ed. Giddens, A., Cambridge U. P. (London, 1972).

Essays on Sociology and Philosophy, ed. Wolff, K., Harper, (New York, 1964).

Friedmann, W., *Law in a Changing Society*, Penguin (Harmondsworth, 1964).

Giddens, A., 'Durkheim's political sociology', 19 *Sociological Review* 477–519 (1971).

Giddens, A., 'Four myths in the history of social thought', 1 *Economy and Society* 357–85 (1972).

Gluckmann, M., *The Judicial Process Among the Barotse*, Manchester U. P. (Manchester, 1955).

Gouldner, A., 'Emile Durkheim and the critique of socialism' in *For Sociology*, Penguin (Harmondsworth, 1975).

Gurvitch, G., *The Sociology of Law*, Kegan Paul (London, 1947).

Hart, H. L. A., 'Social solidarity and the enforcement of morals', 55 *U. Chicago L. R.* 1–13 (1967).

Hirst, P. Q., *Durkheim, Bernard and Epistemology*, Routledge and Kegan Paul (London, 1975).

Hoebel, E. A., *The Law of Primitive Man*, Harvard U. P. (Cambridge, Mass., 1961).

Hogbin, H. I., *Law and Order in Polynesia*, Christophers (London, 1934).

Keat, R. and Urry, J., *Social Theory as Science*, Routledge and Kegan Paul (London, 1975).

Llewellyn, K. and Hoebel, E. A., *The Cheyenne Way*, University of Oklahoma Press (Norman, 1941).

Lloyd, D., *The Idea of Law*, Penguin (Harmondsworth, 1964).

Lukes, Steven, *Emile Durkheim — His Life and Work*, Allen Lane (London, 1973).

McDonald, L., *The Sociology of Law and Order*, Faber (London, 1976).

Malinowski, B., *Crime and Custom in Savage Society*, Routledge and Kegan Paul (London, 1961).

Merton, K. N., 'Durkheim's *Division of Labour in Society*', 40 *A. J. S.* 319–28 (1934).

Needham, R., Introduction to Durkheim and Mauss *Primitive Classification*, Routledge and Kegan Paul (London, 1970).

Nisbet, R. A., *Emile Durkheim*, Prentice Hall (Englewood Cliffs, N. J., 1965).

Nisbet, R. A., 'Conservatism and sociology', 58 *A. J. S.* 167–75 (1952).

Parsons, T., *The Structure of Social Action*, McGraw-Hill (New York, 1937).

Pospisil, L., *Anthropology of Law*, Harper and Row (New York, 1971).

Radcliffe-Brown, A. R., 'Primitive law', 9 *Encylopaedia of the Social Sciences*.

Rusche, G. and Kirchheimer, O., *Punishment and Social Structure*, Russell and Russell (New York, 1968).

Sayre, P., 'Public welfare offences', 33 *Columbia L. R.* 55 (1933).

Schiff, D., 'Socio-legal theory: social structure and law', 39 *M. L. R.* 287–310 (1976).

Schwartz, R., 'Legal evolution and the Durkheim hypothesis' 8 *L. & S. R.* 653–67 (1974).

Schwartz, R. and Miller, J. C., 'Legal evolution and societal complexity', 70 *A. J. S.* 159–69 (1964).

Seagle, W., *The Quest for Law*, Knopf (New York, 1941).

Stoetzel, J., 'Sociology in France: an empiricist view' in Becker and Boskoff (eds), *Contemporary Sociological Theory* (New York, 1957).

Stone, J., Review of 'The Division of Labour', 47 *Harvard L. R.* 1448–51 (1934).

Taylor, Walton and Young, *The New Criminology*, Routledge and Kegan Paul (London, 1973).

Therborn, G., *Science, Class and Society*, New Left Books (London, 1975).

Webb, S., 'Crime and the division of labour: testing a Durkheimian model', 78 *A. J. S.* 643–56 (1972).

Wolff, K. (ed.), *Emile Durkheim 1858—1917*, Ohio State U. P. (Columbus, 1960).

Wolin, S. S., *Politics and Vision*, Allen and Unwin (London, 1961).

Zeitlin, I. M., *Ideology and the Development of Sociological Theory*, Prentice-Hall (Englewood Cliffs, N. J., 1968).

CHAPTER 5

Albrow, M., 'Legal positivism and bourgeois materialism: Max Weber's view of the sociology of law', 2 *B. J. L. S.* 14—31 (1975).

Antoni, C., *From History to Sociology: The Transition in German Historical Thinking*, Merlin (London, 1962).

Aron, Raymond, *Main Currents in Sociological Thought*, vol. II, Weidenfeld and Nicolson (London, 1968).

Baumgarten, E. (ed.), *Max Weber, Werk und Person*, Mohr (Tübingen, 1964).

Beetham, D., *Max Weber and the Theory of Modern Politics*, George Allen and Unwin (London, 1974).

Bendix, R., *Max Weber: An Intellectual Portrait*, Heinemann (London, 1960).

Bendix, R., 'Max Weber's interpretation of conduct and history', 51 *A. J. S.* 518—26 (1946).

Berle, A. and Means, G., *The Modern Corporation and Private Property*, Macmillan (New York, 1932).

Black, D., 'The boundaries of legal sociology', 81 *Yale L. J.* 1086—1100 (1972).

Blau, P., 'Critical remarks on Weber's theory of authority', 57 *Am. Pol. Sci. R.* 305—16 (1963).

Bredemeier, H., 'Law as an integrative mechanism' in Aubert, V. (ed.), *Sociology of Law*, Penguin (Harmondsworth, 1968).

Carlen, P. (ed.), *The Sociology of Law*, Keele University (Keele, 1976).

Carson, W. G., 'Symbolic and instrumental dimensions of early factory legislation' in Hood, R. (ed.), *Criminology and Public Policy*, Heinemann (London, 1974).

Chambliss, W., 'A sociological analysis of vagrancy', 12 *Social Problems* 67—77 (1964).

Chambliss, W. and Mankoff, M. (eds), *Whose Law? What Order?*, John Wiley (New York, 1976).

Colletti, L., *From Rousseau to Lenin*, New Left Books (London, 1972).

Commons, J. *Legal Foundations of Capitalism*, Macmillan (New York, 1924).

Eldridge, J., *Max Weber: The Interpretation of Social Reality*, Micheal Joseph (London, 1970).

Evan, W. (ed.), *Law and Sociology*, Free Press (Glencoe, Ill., 1962).

Falk, W., 'Democracy and capitalism in Max Weber's sociology', 27 *Sociological Review* 373—93 (1935).

Freund, J., *The Sociology of Max Weber*, Random House (New York, 1965).

Friedrich, C., 'Some observations on Weber's analysis of bureaucracy' in Merton, R. (ed.), *Reader in Bureaucracy* Free Press (Glencoe, Ill., 1952).

Giddens, A., *New Rules of Sociological Method*, Hutchinson (London, 1976).

Gouldner, A., *For Sociology*, Allen Lane (London, 1973).

Hall, J., *Theft, Law and Society*, Little Brown (Boston, 1935).

Hill, C., *Puritanism and Revolution*, Secker and Warburg (London, 1958).

Hirst, P. Q., *Social Evolution and Sociological Categories*, George Allen and Unwin (London, 1976).

Honigsheim, P., *On Max Weber*, Free Press (New York, 1967).

Horkheimer, M., *The Eclipse of Reason*, Oxford U. P. (New York, 1947).

Hunt, A., 'Perspectives in the sociology of law' in Carlen, P. (ed.), *The Sociology of Law* (Keele, 1976).

Jaspers, K., *Leonardo, Descartes and Max Weber*, Routledge and Kegan Paul

(London, 1965).

Jordan, H. P., 'Some philosophical implications of Max Weber's methodology', 48 *Ethics* 221–31 (1938).

Keat, R. and Urry, J., *Social Theory as Science*, Routledge and Kegan Paul (London, 1975).

Kohn, Hans, *The Mind of Germany*, Macmillan (London, 1961).

Lasswell, H. D., Review of *Law and Economy*, 7 *J. L. E.* 301–3 (1954–5).

Lewis, John, *Max Weber and Value-Free Sociology*, Lawrence and Wishart (London, 1975).

Little, D., *Religion, Order and Law*, Harper (New York, 1969).

Loewith, K., 'Weber's interpretation of the Bourgeois capitalistic world in terms of the guiding principle of rationalization' in Wrong, D. (ed.), *Max Weber*, Prentice-Hall (Englewood Cliffs, N.J. 1970).

Mannheim, K., 'German sociology 1918–1933', 1 *Politica* 12–33 (1934).

Marcuse, H., 'Industrialization and capitalism' in *Negations*, Allen Lane (London, 1968).

Meyer, L. P., *Max Weber and German Politics*, Faber and Faber (London, 1956).

Mitzman, K., *The Iron Cage: An Historical Interpretation of Max Weber*, Knopf (New York, 1970).

Mommsen, W., *The Age of Bureaucracy: Perspectives on the Political Sociology of Max Weber*, Blackwell (Oxford, 1974).

Morris, C., 'Law, reason and sociology', 107 *U. Penn. L. R.* 147–65 (1958–9).

Niemeyer, G., *Law Without Force*, Princeton U. P. (Princeton, 1941).

Parsons, T., *The Structure of Social Action*, McGraw-Hill (New York, 1937).

Parsons, T., *Structure and Process in Modern Societies*, Free Press (New York, 1960).

Parsons, T., *Politics and Social Structure*, Free Press (New York, 1969).

Parsons, T., 'Max Weber 1864–1964', 30 *A. S. R.* 171–5 (1965).

Pound, R., *Jurisprudence*, West Publishing (St. Paul, Minn. 1959).

Pound, R., 'Sociology of law' in Gurvitch and Moore (eds), *Twentieth Century Sociology*, Philosophical Library (New York, 1945).

Rheinstein, M., Introduction to Rheinstein, M. (ed.), *Max Weber on Law in Economy and Society*, Harvard U. P. (Cambridge, Mass., 1966).

Roth, G., 'Political critiques of Max Weber', 30 *A. S. R.* 213–22 (1965).

Runciman, W. G., *A Critique of Max Weber's Philosophy of Social Science*, Cambridge U. P. (Cambridge, 1972).

Salomon, A., 'Max Weber's methodology', 1 *Social Research* 147–68 (1934).

Salomon, A., 'Max Weber's political ideas', 2 *Social Research* 368–84 (1935).

Schur, Edwin, *Law and Society*, Random House (New York, 1968).

Skoljar, S. J., 'Weber's sociology of law' in Sawer, G. (ed.), *Studies in the Sociology of Law*, Australian National University (Canberra, 1961).

Spencer, M., 'Weber on legitimate norms and authority', 21 *B. J. S.* 123–34 (1970).

Stammer, O. (ed.), *Max Weber and Sociology Today*, Blackwell (Oxford, 1971).

Therborn, G., *Science, Class and Society*, New Left Books (London, 1976).

Trubek, D., 'Max Weber on law and the rise of capitalism', 3 *Wisconsin L. R.* 720–53 (1972).

Trubek, D., 'Toward a social theory of law', 82 *Yale L. J.* 1–50 (1972).

Walton, Paul, 'Max Weber's sociology of law' in Carlen, P. (ed.), *The Sociology of Law* (Keele, 1976).

Weber, Marianne, *Marianne, Max Weber: Ein Lebensbild*, Mohr (Tübingen, 1926).

Weber, Max (works by)

    Max Weber on Law in Economy and Society, edited Max Rheinstein, Harvard U. P. (Cambridge, Mass., 1966).

    Economy and Society: An Outline of Interpretive Sociology, edited by G. Roth and C. Wittich, Bedminster Press (Totowa, N.J., 1968).

    The Methodology of the Social Sciences, Free Press (New York, 1949).

The Theory of Social and Economic Organization, Free Press (Glencoe, Ill., 1949).
The Sociology of Religion, Beacon Press (Boston, 1963).
The City, Free Press (Glencoe, Ill., 1958).
The Religion of China, Free Press (Glencoe, Ill., 1951).
The Religion of India, Free Press (Glencoe, Ill, 1958).
Ancient Judaism, Free Press (Glencoe, Ill., 1952).
General Economic History, Collier Books (New York, 1961).
The Protestant Ethic and the Spirit of Capitalism Allen and Unwin (London, 1930).
From Max Weber: Essays in Sociology, ed. Gerth and Mills, Oxford U. P. (New York, 1958).
'R. Stammler's "surmounting" of the materialist conception of history', 2 and 3 *B. J. L. S.* 129−52 and 17−43 (1975−6).
Wright, E. O., 'To control or to smash bureaucracy: Weber and Lenin on politics, state and bureaucracy', 14 *Berkeley J. S.* 69−108 (1974−5).
Zeitlin, I. M., *Ideology and the Development of Sociological Theory*, Prentice-Hall (Englewood Cliffs, N.J., 1968).

CHAPTER 6

Aubert, V., 'Researches in the sociology of law', 7 *A. B. S.* 16−20 (1963).
Balbus, Isaac, *The Dialectics of Legal Repression*, Russell Sage (New York, 1973).
Campbell, C., 'The expansion of sociology of law: some conjectures, doubts and misgivings', mimeographed paper, 1972.
Chambliss, W. and Seidman, R., *Law, Order and Power*, Addison-Wesley (Reading, Mass., 1971).
Giddens, A., 'Four myths in the history of social thought', 1 *Economy and Society* 357−85 (1972).
Gouldner, A., *The Coming Crisis in Western Sociology*, Heinemann (London, 1971).
Gusfield, J. R., *Symbolic Crusade: Status Politics and the Temperance Movement*, University of Illinois Press (Urbana, Ill., 1966).
Lefcourt, R. (ed.), *Law Against the People*, Random House (New York, 1971).
Mazor, L., 'The crisis of liberal legalism', 81 *Yale L. J.* 1032−53 (1972).
Nagel, S. S., *The Legal Process From a Behavioral Perspective*, Dorsey Press (Homewood, Ill., 1969).
Quinney, R., *Critique of Legal Order*, Little, Brown (Boston, 1974).
Rostow, E. (ed.), *Is Law Dead?*, Simon and Schuster (New York, 1971).
Sawer, G., *Law in Society*, Oxford U. P. (London, 1965).
Schubert, G., *Judicial Decision-Making*, Free Press (New York, 1963).
Schubert, G., *The Judicial Mind*, Northwestern U. P. (Evanston, 1965).
Schur, Edwin, *Law and Society: A Sociological View*, Random House (New York, 1968).
Stone, J., *Law and the Social Sciences*, University of Minnesota Press (Minneapolis, 1966).
Thompson, E. P., *The Making of the English Working Class*, Penguin (Harmondsworth, 1968).
Wolff, R. (ed.), *The Rule of Law*, Simon and Schuster (New York, 1971).

Index

Albrow, M., 104, 166, 167, 170
Allen, C. K., 159
Alpert, H., 70, 162, 163, 164
American Legal Realism, *see* Realism
Amos, M. S., 154
Anthropology of law
    Realism, and, 49–50, 57–8
    Durkheim, and, 66, 70
Antoni, C., 166
Arnold, Thurman, 48, 157, 158
Aron, Raymond, 165, 166
Aubert, V., 139, 170
Austin, John, 104

Balbus, I., 171
Baumgarten, E., 166
Becker, Theodore, 160
Behaviouralism, 46, 53–4, 55, 59, 145
Bendix, R., 117, 165, 167, 168
Bentham, Jeremy, 36
Berle, A., 170
Bingham, J. W., 45, 159
Black, Donald, 170
Blumberg, A., 169
Bodenheimer, H., 157
Bohannan, P., 49, 70, 159, 162, 163
Brandeis, L. D. 45, 158
Braybrooke, E. K., 156
Bredemeier, H., 170

Cahill, F. V., 37, 157
Cain, Maureen, 154

Callahan, C. C., 54, 158, 160
Campbell, C., 145, 171
Cardozo, B., 14
Carlen, Pat, 167, 169, 170
Carson, W. G., 169
Chambliss, W., 169, 170, 171
Clark, C. E., 160
Cleaver, E., 37
Cohen, Felix, 23, 48, 154, 155, 157
Cohen, Morris, 59, 154, 158, 170
Coke, Sir E., 127
Colletti, Lucio, 96, 166
Common law, 13, 14, 31, 33, 121,
          122–8
Commons, J., 170
Comte, A., 15, 20, 97, 99
Cook, W. W., 159
Cooley, C. H., 19, 155
Coser, L. A., 162
Criminology, 66, 75, 138, 143

Davy, G., 66
Deviancy theory, 81, 138, 143
Dewey, J., 42
Diamond, A. S., 70, 163
Dilthey, 99
Douglas, W., 54, 157, 160
Durkheim, Emile, 3, 6, 7, 9, 20,
          46, 60–92, 93, 99, 107,
          128–9, 130–2, 139, 146–7,
          150–1, 161, 162, 163, 164

Durkheim, Emile, *Cont.*
  anomie, 78, 91
  collective representations, 63, 67, 79
  'conscience collective', 63, 73, 74, 75
    76, 78
  contract, on, 69, 85–8, 89
  crime, 70–1, 74–9
  criminality
    human 78, 80–2
    religious, 78, 80–2
  homicide, 77–8
  methodology, 61–5, 66–8, 74–5,
    79–81
  and positivism, 62, 63
  property, 88–90
  punishment, 75, 78, 79–85
  repressive law, 68–72, 81
  restitutive law, 68–72, 81
  and sociological theory, 61–5, 90–2

Ehrlich, Eugen, 8, 21, 33, 104, 153, 167
Eldridge, J. E. T., 106, 167
Empiricism, 43, 54, 55–6, 58, 141, 144
Evan, W., 167

Fischoff, E., 103
Frank, Jerome, 41, 42, 43–4, 48, 53, 54,
    157, 158, 159
Frankfurter, F., 148, 155
Freud, S., 43
Freund, J., 102, 106, 166, 167
Friedmann, W., 16, 154, 160, 163
Friedrich, C. J., 166
Fuller, Lon, 59, 157, 158, 170
Functionalism
  and Durkheim, 62, 64–5, 90–1
  and Realism, 47, 48–53, 58–9

Garlan, E., 157
Gerth, Hans, 165, 166
Gehlke, C. E., 160
Giddens, Anthony, 91, 161, 163, 165,
    171
Gierke, O., 94
Gilmore, G., 157
Gluckman, Max, 49, 70, 159, 162
Goodhart, A. L., 154
Gouldner, A., 165, 166, 170
Gray, Chipman, 45
Grossman, W. L., 12, 16, 154, 155
Gurvitch, G., 90, 153, 155, 164, 165
Gusfield, J. R., 149, 171

Hall, Jerome, 170
Hart, H. L. A., 20, 76, 155, 161, 163,
    170

Hauriou, M., 66
Hegel, 16, 29, 31–2, 33, 96, 116
Heller, H., 165
Henderson, A. M., 103, 165
Hill, C., 170
Hirst, Paul Q., 102, 162, 164, 165, 166,
    168
Hobbes, T., 60, 142, 163
Hoebel, Adamson, 49, 70, 159, 160, 161,
    162
Hofstadter, R., 157, 159
Hogbin, H. I., 70, 162
Holmes, O. W., 14, 41–2, 43, 45, 55,
    158
Honigsheim, P., 167
Hood, R., 169
Horkheimer, M., 95, 165
Hunt, Alan, 153, 154, 168, 170

Idealism, 13, 16, 28, 33, 64, 96–7, 98,
    101
Individualism, 14, 21, 31, 32–3, 36, 39,
    43, 61, 63–4, 66, 77–8, 81,
    85, 88, 99, 135, 140
Ingersoll, D., 160

James, William, 23, 26, 28, 42, 155
Jaspers, K., 165
Johns Hopkins Institute, 56, 160
Jordan, H. P., 166
Judicial process, 34, 44, 50–1, 55, 59,
    136–7
Jurisprudence
  analytical, 3, 13, 14, 35, 59, 105–6,
    115, 135, 153
  Anglo-American, 9, 14
  free law school, 106
  functional, 21, 48
  historical school, 3, 16, 94, 96, 110,
    167
  natural law, *see* Natural law
  sociological, *see* Sociological
    jurisprudence

Kalven, H., 170
Kant, E., 14, 81, 88, 99, 101
Keat, J., 75, 109, 163, 168
Kelsen, Hans, 109
Kirchheimer, O., 84, 164
Kohler, J., 16, 27, 28, 31, 155
Kohn, Hans, 165, 166

Laski, Harold, 157
Lasswell, H. D., 104, 167

Law, definitions, 21, 48
  in Llewellyn, 57
  in Durkheim, 69
  in Weber, 103–4, 111
Law reform, 36, 39
Lefcourt, R., 171
Legal academics, 1, 5, 15
Legal education, 39–40, 56, 59, 110–11
Legal ideology, 51–2, 141–3
Legal profession, 1, 13, 33, 40, 48, 56,
    110–13
  English, 111–12, 125–6
Legal Realism, *see* Realism
Legal traditionalism, 5, 13, 32, 33, 41,
    45, 48, 52, 55, 59
Lepaulle, P., 22, 23, 155
Leuchtenburg, W. E., 157
Little, D., 127, 169, 170
Llewellyn, K. N., 6, 7, 9, 18, 20, 27,
    38–59, 153, 155, 156, 157,
    158, 159, 160, 161
  grand style, 50–1
  law-jobs theory, 49–53, 56
  trouble case method, 44, 49, 50,
    57–8
Lloyd, D., 163
Locke, John, 60, 88, 164
Loewith, K., 165, 166
Lukes, S., 162

McDonald, Lynn, 164
Maine, Sir H., 3, 32, 72, 85, 128, 156,
    164
Malinowski, B., 49, 70, 159, 162
Mankoff, M., 170
Mannheim, K., 165
Marcuse, H., 100–1, 166
Martindale, D., 166
Marx, K., 66, 73, 95–6, 98, 113, 114
  Marxism, 9–10, 90, 96, 118, 121
Mauss, M., 66, 164
Mazor, L., 170
Means, G., 170
Merton, R., 78, 166
Mayer, J. P., 165
Miller, J. C., 71, 163
Mills, C. Wright, 1, 153, 158, 160, 165
Mitzman, A., 165
Montesquieu, 20, 60
Moore, Underhill, 43, 54, 55, 158, 160
Moore, W. E., 155, 165
Morris, Clarence, 103, 108, 167
Morris, H., 154
Mulkay, M. J., 159

Nagel, S. S., 171
Natural law, 16, 17, 27, 29, 59, 112
Naumann, F., 94
Needham, R., 164
New Deal, 41, 48
Niemeyer, G., 165
Nietzsche, 96
Nisbet, R. A., 162

Oliphant, H., 41, 43, 54, 157, 158, 160

Parsons, Talcott, 21, 51, 78, 80, 98, 102,
    103, 106, 108, 130, 164, 165,
    166, 167, 169, 170
Paton, G., 157
Patterson, E. W., 24–5, 33, 155, 156
Piaget, J., 43
Pierce, C. S., 42
Pluralism, 18, 39, 43, 47–8, 112, 136,
    143, 145
Political economy, 22, 46, 64, 90
Positivism, 15, 31, 33, 138, 144, 151
  and Durkheim, 62–3
  and realism, 43, 46–8
  and Weber, 102, 104, 113
Pospisil, L., 70, 163
Pound, Roscoe, 3, 6, 8, 9, 11–36, 38–9,
    41, 45, 46, 47, 59, 68, 92,
    124, 133, 145, 146, 150, 153,
    154, 155, 156, 157, 158, 167,
    171
  and conservatism, 33
  definition of law, 34
  ends of law, 27–8, 29, 31
  ethical theory, 25–9
  intellectual origins, 12–17
  methodology, 11, 17–18
  social engineering, 15, 21–2, 26, 34
  social interests, 16, 24–9, 39
  stages of development, 29–33
  theory of interests, 22–9
    individual interests, 24–9, 39
    public interests, 24–6
Pragmatism, 15, 16, 21, 23, 25, 26, 28,
    29, 33, 41–3, 47, 136, 150
Psychiatry, 43
Psychology
  and Durkheim, 72
  impact on Realism, 43, 54

Quinney, R., 171

Radcliffe-Brown, A. R., 70, 162
Realism, 3, 6, 7, 14, 25, 35, 37–59, 92,
    124, 133, 136–7, 138, 142,
    150, 153, 158, 159

Realism, *Cont.*
  functionalism, 48–53
  intellectual roots, 40–4
  methodology, 55–8
  prediction, 43–4, 46, 55
  social origins, 38–40
  theoretical framework, 45–55
Rehbinder, M., 160
Reisman, David, 57
Renner, Karl, 169
Reuschlin, H. G., 16, 155
Rheinstein, Max, 103, 124, 165, 169
Richter, M., 164
Rodell, F., 159
Roosevelt, Theodore, 39, 158
Ross, Edward, 19, 155
Rostow, Eugene, 170
Roth, G., 102, 165, 166
Rousseau, J. J., 60, 163
Rumble, W. E., 154, 160
Rusche, G., 84, 164

Salomon, A., 165, 166
Savigny, F. K. von, 3
Sawer, G., 139, 156, 170
Sayre, P., 155, 163
Schiff, D., 156
Schlesinger, A., 157
Schubert, Glendon, 171
Schur, E., 139, 167, 170
Schwartz, R. D., 71, 163
Seagle, W., 70, 80, 163
Seidman, R., 171
Selznick, P., 170
Setaro, F. C., 154
Shils, Edward, 103, 166
Shuman, S. I., 43, 158
Simpson, S. P., 12, 154
Skoljar, S. J., 103–4, 167
Skolnick, Jerome, 170
Small, Albion, 19, 155
Social control, 15, 19–20, 21, 73, 92,
    131–2, 145–7, 150–1
Social Darwinism
  and Durkheim, 79
  and Realism, 47
Social engineering, 15, 21–2, 26, 34,
    41; *see also* Pound, R., social
    engineering
Social legislation, 13, 33, 39
Sociological jurisprudence, 7, 12, 15, 19,
    20, 21, 92, 130, 135–8, 141,
    144–5
  and Pound, 33–6, 37, 38–9
  and Realism, 38–9, 40–1, 52–3, 55,
    58–9

Sociological jurisprudence, *Cont.*
  and Weber, 130–1
Sociological movement in law, 1–10,
    33–4, 36, 37, 58–9, 61, 92,
    121, 130–3, 134–51
Sociology of law, 1–3, 9–10, 37–8,
    98–9, 114–15, 117, 134–51
  and Durkheim, 60–1, 65–6, 81–2,
    83, 90–2
  and Realism, 45, 46, 53, 59
  and Weber, 93–4, 102–33
Spencer, Herbert, 20, 61, 85, 97, 99
Stammer, O., 167
Stammler, R., 16, 97, 155, 166
State, the, 5, 33, 47, 63, 70–1, 74–5,
    78, 79, 82–3, 91, 99, 126–7,
    132, 135, 142–3
Stone, Julius, 8, 13, 24–5, 28, 33, 89,
    144, 153, 155–6, 164, 167,
    171
Subjectivism, 94, 97, 99
Sumner, W. G., 19, 47, 49, 57, 155

Taylor, Ian, 73, 162, 163
Therborn, G., 162, 164, 165, 166
Thomas, D., 160
Thompson, E. P., 141, 171
Timasheff, N. S., 8, 153
Treves, R., 153
Trubek, D., 167, 169
Twining, William, 51, 157, 159, 160, 161

Utilitarianism, 21, 25, 28, 36, 46–7, 54,
    66, 135–6, 138, 143
Urry, John, 75, 109, 163, 168

Value neutrality, 46, 99–100, 115, 140
Van Loon, G., 153
Von Jhering, R., 14, 22, 28, 32, 104

Walton, Paul, 71, 162, 163, 167, 170
Weber, Marianne, 166
Weber, Max, 3, 6, 7, 9, 20, 21, 29, 49,
    57, 73, 83, 93–133, 139,
    142–3, 148, 150–1, 153,
    161, 163, 165, 166, 167, 168,
    170
  bureaucracy, 110–12, 116–17
  and capitalism, 118–28
  domination, 98, 112–18, 131–2, 148
  on English law, 120, 121, 122–8
  methodology of, 99–100, 112
  and politics, 94–5, 97–8
  rationalisation of law, 107–12
  rationality, 95, 100, 102, 103,
    104–5, 118–19

Weber, Max, *Cont.*
  typologies of law, 104—12
  uniqueness of the West, 94—5, 98—9,
      102, 103, 109, 113
White, Morton, 158, 161
Wittich, C., 165
Wolff, K., 161, 162, 164
Wolff, R., 170

Wolin, S. S., 163
Wrong, D., 165, 166

Yntema, H., 54, 55, 160
Young, Jock, 71, 162, 163

Zeisel, Hans, 170
Zeitlin, I., 66, 165